The de Brailes Hours

The de Brailes Hours

*Shaping the Book of
Hours in Thirteenth-Century
Oxford*

Claire Donovan

THE BRITISH LIBRARY

1991

Lovingly dedicated to the men of
my household:
my sons, Giles and Dunstan,
and Colin, the father of my book.

Frontispiece: detail of fig. 37.

First published 1991 by
The British Library, Great Russell Street,
London WC1B 3DG

British Library Cataloguing in Publication Data

Donovan, Claire
    The De Brailes hours: shaping the book of hours
    in 13th-century Oxford.
    1. Illuminated manuscripts. Books of hours
    I. Title
    091

ISBN 0-7123-0193-3

Designed by James Shurmer

Typeset in Monophoto Baskerville with Octavian
by August Filmsetting, Haydock, St Helens

Printed in England by BAS Printers, Over Wallop,
Hampshire

Contents

Author's note

Biblical quotations throughout are taken from:
The Holy Bible (Douay Version), translated
from the Latin Vulgate (Douay AD 1607:
Rheims AD 1582), London, 1955.

The captions in the manuscript are quoted
from S. C. Cockerell, 'Description of Brailes
Horae: MS 4', pp.11–25, in G. Warner,
*Descriptive Catalogue of Illuminated Manuscripts in
the Library of C. W. Dyson Perrins*, Oxford, 1920.

Preface and Acknowledgements

The home of the de Brailes Hours is now The British Library. Often on display, it is recognised, even in the company of so rich a collection, as a rather special book. When C. W. Dyson Perrins bought it from J. Rosenthal in Munich in 1906, with the advice of Sydney Cockerell, he certainly recognised this special quality. He asked Cockerell, once William Morris's librarian but by then Director of the Fitzwilliam Museum in Cambridge, to examine the book in detail and write a full description of it. Cockerell began his description: 'This book is remarkable in four important particulars, which, taken together, place it in the first rank of English manuscripts of the thirteenth century.' Our understanding of thirteenth-century manuscript illumination has developed immensely since that notice was written in 1906. Yet none of those four features seems any less remarkable as a result. The manuscript's early date as a book of hours has not been challenged. The character and subjects of the illuminations, have become better understood in relation to the book's purpose, and it is now seen as more remarkable, not less. The importance of the descriptions of the subjects in contemporary French remains, and the recognition of their role in both imagery and devotion has been particularly significant in understanding its purpose. And the named illuminator has, since 1906, become something of a personality in his own right. Years later, in 1930, Cockerell himself wrote *The Work of W. de Brailes*, by that time recognising a considerable group of manuscripts by this illuminator. Cockerell was clearly fascinated by de Brailes, and was himself the owner of one of those manuscripts. When in 1955 Graham Pollard published his 'William de Brailles', establishing the identity of de Brailes in Oxford archives, he demonstrated the high importance of the professional illuminators of Oxford in the story of thirteenth-century manuscript illumination. The wanderings of the de Brailes Hours, unrecorded for some 650 years, ended when the British Museum acquired it in 1959.

In my case, it was the first of Cockerell's observations about the de Brailes Hours that began my interest in this manuscript. Working on English books of hours, it was the early date of the de Brailes Hours that determined the starting point of my study. The formulation of a new type of book, the creation of a new design – especially one which was to be so spectacularly successful – inevitably holds special interest. Where that artist is as well represented in other surviving manuscripts as William de Brailes, there is much additional evidence to help unravel the design process.

The form of this manuscript is lavish and entirely new. Yet this first book of hours was clearly designed for daily use. It was designed by a professional, but its shape was determined by its purpose as a devotional book to be used by its first lady owner. Every part of the book's design reflects that purpose. And, as my own study took shape, it was the shaping of William's book for its original owner that took over as the focus for my text. My text has increasingly centred on that process of design, and the re-creation of its origins has become my purpose.

Inevitably I have many people to thank. A most memorable dinner with Graham Pollard at New College, Oxford, brought William de Brailes to life for me. For that I thank Christopher de Hamel, whose invitation it was, and who followed it up with many inspiring William de Brailes conversations. But that was all long ago.

Graham Pollard's insistence that the manuscript was in its original binding, just as it had been left in the thirteenth century, brought me to consider it as a whole. The confirmation of this by Mirjam Foot, of The British Library, was most valuable. The solution of the problem of the added leaves that was offered by Michelle Brown, also of The British Library, cleared up my worries that William's book had been tampered with in later centuries, as Cockerell had certainly believed. For these two expert opinions I am most grateful.

The encouragement offered by Janet Backhouse has been constant, and her sense of these far-off owners and makers of books as our contemporaries is one which I share. I hope that my book, with such a wonderful little manuscript as its focus, will help to convey that sense of the thirteenth-century present to a wider audience than has yet been acquainted with it.

Without the generosity of my publishers, the sense of the manuscript could not have been conveyed at all. It is the whole book – text, pictures, binding, and all – which becomes real through the many plates that they have provided. Sadly, to convey the smell of the parchment proved beyond them. My thanks for the enthusiasm for this project, both that of David Way, my editor, and of Jane Carr, cannot be adequate. My experience of working with them as publishers has been most happy.

I have received much help and encouragement from many colleagues. Linda Brownrigg, Michael Michael, Nigel Morgan, Sylvia Wright, Albinia de la Mare, John Higgitt, Eric Fernie and, as always, John Gage, have in different ways kept me at it. Many friends and students have also made their contribution, chief among them Walter Greenway, and Elizabeth Skeet – an unfailing support. With Colin Platt's wise criticisms this book has taken its shape. To him I owe my greatest debt.

1. William de Brailes, illuminator of Oxford

The designer and painter of the very first book of hours is his own best advocate. With the caption: *w. de brail' qui me depeint*, William de Brailes introduces his self-portrait, enclosed in the historiated initial which opens the prayer at the end of Terce of the Virgin. Without doubt he was the painter of all the historiated initials which stand at the beginning of each new section of text. Moreover, it is surely with his own hand that this caption or signature was written. Almost all the historiated initials in the manuscript are accompanied by such captions in French, which were written in red ink in a tiny script by the same non-scribal hand, and informally tucked in the margins next to the illustration they describe. In this first book of hours the particular selection of semi-liturgical and devotional texts which was to become so popular with the laity is drawn together for the first time, and fully illustrated with over a hundred historiated initials.

fig. 1

plate 1

In three of these historiated initials William de Brailes paints his self-portrait. In the first, he shows himself kneeling in prayer with the hand of God reaching down to touch him under the chin. He wears a pink and white cloak, with a hood that is thrown back and hangs neatly around his neck. It is the garb of a cleric, the sign of a literate and learned man, and with it he wears the tonsure. The second signed self-portrait is similar, and accompanies a prayer at the end of Sext of the Virgin. At the final prayer of the Litany of Saints he painted himself for a third time, although here there is no signature. By this point in the manuscript he needed no introduction.

1. f.43, Terce of the Virgin.
Prayer.
w. de brail' qui me depeint.
The illuminator prays, blessed by God, at the final prayer of Terce of the Virgin.

William de Brailes is the best-recorded professional illuminator of thirteenth-century England. It is in this book of hours that he introduced himself most readily. But he painted his self-portrait again in the Last Judgement miniature of a series of pictorial pages of biblical scenes, designed to accompany a bible or a psalter.[1] This time his name is recorded with a Latin inscription: W DE BRAIL' ME FECIT written in a formal Gothic script on a scroll. In the book of hours he shows himself personally blessed by God. In the Last Judgement miniature he also depicts himself among the saved, but not among the Blessed on God's right hand. Instead he shows himself rescued from damnation by the skin of his teeth. While the rest of the group of naked souls are consigned to hell by the sword of the avenging angel, William de Brailes has been plucked from their number, and is shown held firmly, clutched beneath the angel's left arm. His formal Latin scroll provides the explanation for his salvation: saved by virtue of his art.

fig.2

Around these signed self-portraits a group of finely illuminated manuscripts can be assembled, in which the very distinctive style of William de Brailes can be found, both as an artist and as a designer. This group of manuscripts includes his one book of hours, bibles, psalters and two sets of pictorial pages detached now from any text.[2] His distinctive style is there to be recognised in all these manuscripts. But only the book of hours is the work of William alone, his unmistakable touch there in the decoration as well as in all the illustration.

Elsewhere William's touch can be identified in company with the work of a number of other illuminators. Trained in similar style, the artists worked together to design, decorate and illustrate, each artist to a different degree contributing miniatures, historiated initials, line endings and decoration. Together with the parchment makers, scribes and binders, they each contributed to the completed volume. Plainly, it was a professional group of craftsmen that made such high quality luxury volumes.

This much can be discovered from the manuscripts themselves. Yet analysis of the texts of these manuscripts, in particular their calendars and litanies, yields little information that would locate the place where William de Brailes and his assistants worked. Indeed the usual indicators of the liturgical origins of these books conflict within the group: an indication in itself of an origin in a centre making manuscripts for sale and to order.[3]

Professional manuscript-making was in its infancy in the first half of the thirteenth century. While the production of manuscripts was dominated by the work of the monastic scriptoria at least until the end of the twelfth century, the continuity of style of production persisted, despite the occasional employment of individual lay artists to work on the illumination.[4] This continuity was based on the clearly defined function of the scriptorium, which was to satisfy the needs of the community, whether for liturgical,

2. Cambridge, Fitzwilliam Museum, MS 330, leaf 3, W DE BRAIL' ME FECIT. The illuminator saved from Hell, in the Last Judgement of the Fitzwilliam Museum pages.

theological or scholarly books. Professionals worked differently, responding to a much more varied market. Evidently the de Brailes group was produced by specialists in highly illuminated liturgical manuscripts, tailor-made for their patrons. Yet these manuscripts too have a 'house-style', just as do those from the monastic scriptoria. It is this house-style that ties these manuscripts in a group, through all aspects of their design and style, from the layout of the page to the detail of the figure style. Characteristic is the distinctive accomplished and tightly controlled decorative style, which makes use of rich pigments and plenty of gold leaf, like highly wrought metalwork laid on the page.

These characteristics, this house-style, are evident even earlier than the de Brailes manuscripts. Just this same type of rich decoration is the hallmark of a number of lavish illuminated manuscripts which can be dated to the first thirty years of the century.[5] Moreover the small, active, expressive people who inhabit the miniatures and historiated initials of the de Brailes manuscripts are clearly descended from the rather more stately figures of this earlier group. The illuminators of these earlier manuscripts also specialised in psalters and bibles, and it was a well-established tradition that William de Brailes followed. The continuity of style plainly indicates a single centre of production. But, unlike the quiet concentration of the monastic scriptorium, the setting in which these craftsmen worked was that of a commercial book trade. Here any text could be adapted to suit a variety of liturgical destinations and the decoration and illustration would be designed in response to the needs of customers.[6]

The location of this centre of production was evidently Oxford. Constantly invoked in the calendars and litanies of a number of these psalters is the name of St Frideswide, Oxford's patron saint. She intrudes even where the manuscript was destined to be used elsewhere, and thus her invocation becomes a sign that locates the origin of these professionally made manuscripts.[7] It was at just this time that the university was beginning to take shape. By the mid-thirteenth century the streets of Oxford were already full of university men, churchmen and friars. These incomers depended upon the services provided by the long-established town community, with its good communications and its regional market. No university could develop where the town was not ready to receive it; to house, feed and supply its scholars with books and teaching accommodation. Oxford had developed into a sizable town, particularly in the years since the Conquest. Charters of the early part of the thirteenth century reveal that its status and independence as a borough were confirmed.[8] It was well equipped to host the influx of scholars who were to make up the university, and to provide them with its full range of specialist trades.

Among the most important of these specialist needs was the provision of books. Plentiful evidence of the profession of writing survives, and the wealth of documents from the late twelfth century onwards confirms that there must have been many professional scribes making a good living in Oxford. Even by the end of the twelfth century they show that the written record was an essential part of everyday business in Oxford. Furthermore the discovery of the tools of the trade – pens, knives, pins for pricking, together with an oyster-shell palette for an illuminator – has established that a scribe and an illuminator had a workshop in St Aldates in the thirteenth century.[9]

The documents which survive in such numbers chiefly relate to property, and they reveal the shape of Oxford. They disclose the existence of the embryonic university together with the already thriving town. The accounts kept by the landholders, which included the large monastic estate of the Abbey of Oseney, enable the pattern of the tenements and the names of their occupants to be reconstructed.[10] Through a collation of these and other records, H. E. Salter compiled his pioneering *Map of Medieval Oxford* in 1934, setting out the streets and tenements. Further study of these records enabled him to compile a comprehensive *Survey of Oxford*, which was published posthumously by William Pantin. Names and sometimes the occupation of tenants may be identified, and this Survey makes it possible to follow individuals from place to place during the thirteenth and fourteenth centuries.[11] Where it has been possible to excavate in Oxford, archaeology has revealed plans of buildings and streets that were similar to those laid out in Salter's maps, creating a pattern of tenement-holding that was familiar in the development of many thriving towns at this time.[12] North of the High Street the streets around St Mary's Church – Catte Street and School Street – were mapped through analysis of the documents. And it is through these maps, related to the names of the tenement holders in this area of Oxford, that a centre of craftsmen making books is revealed. In these streets lived

fig.3 parchment-makers, scribes, illuminators and book binders, both living and working in close contact with one another.[13] Each individual craftsman needed the services of the others; book production is inevitably a cooperative enterprise. Living in close proximity like this, producing texts of many kinds to satisfy the growing market for the written word, the writing of documents and the making of books must have determined the character of this area of the city, which plainly hummed with commerce.[14]

Even in the thirteenth century this corner of the town was the heart of the new university. It is here that William de Brailes is recorded, living among the illuminators and the scribes between 1230 and 1260.[15] His house is buried now beneath the quiet of All Souls College in Catte Street, close to the spot where the Chapel now stands. Flanked by other small properties, Catte Street then was busy with burgesses, living their lives and making their

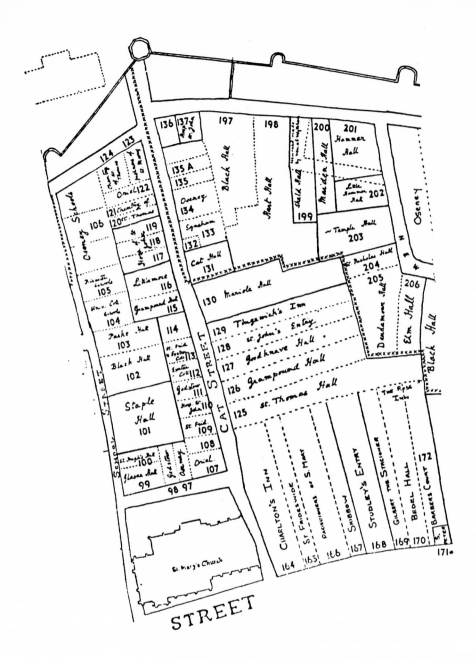

3. H. E. Salter, *Survey of Oxford*, Map NE III.
Map of Catte Street and School Street, around St Mary's Church drawn by Salter. The site of William de Brailes's tenement is described as next to the tenement granted to William Russel, which itself was next to that of John Curci. These plots were all within the area set out on the map as 'Charlton's Inn', which was given this name in 1376. See Appendix 5, Item 5, p.207.

livings chiefly through the book trade. While the records in which he appears are solely to do with property, and his profession is not revealed, William was evidently a neighbour to be trusted among the manuscript-makers of Oxford, to be called upon as a witness, even to solve a property dispute; undoubtedly one of their number. It is these records that supply his Christian name, William, reveal the existence of his wife, Celena, and identify the location of his house.[16]

William's first appearance is as a witness among others, to the transfer of a plot of land just north of the church of St Mary the Virgin. Walter, the grantee, son of Paulinus of Eynsham, was an illuminator. William was one of twelve witnesses, and seven of those were also engaged in the making of books. In 1238 Walter moved on and, in granting the site to Martinus de Wintonia, he again summoned his neighbours to stand for him as witnesses, and again these included manuscript makers: an illuminator, a scribe, and William de Brailes. In 1246 William again acted as witness to a deed, though this time the property concerned was in the western part of Oxford, in the parish of St Peter le Bailey, and no member of the community of makers of books can be defined among the list of witnesses. In 1252, and even further afield, William is engaged in a property dispute about a piece of land in the suburb of Oxford. He and his wife, Celena, urge mutual agreement among a group of neighbours to give possession of certain adjoining portions of land to Henry Perle, and on its agreement they are awarded $4\frac{1}{2}$ marks in compensation. He was evidently a man of substance by this date. This impression of the well-established property-holding burgess is reinforced by a document of about 1260 identifying him as the holder of a tenement in the area around the church of St Mary the Virgin. It is on the basis of this document that his house can be located in Catte Street, next to Berford's Hall, which stood on the corner of Catte Street and High Street. All of the tenements around this corner, to the east of St Mary's, were bought up by Archbishop Chichele in the fifteenth century and demolished to make space for his elaborate new college, dedicated to All Souls.[17] Any archaeological remnants from William's thirteenth-century occupation lie buried now beneath Chichele's fine chapel.

Behind the documentary sources for William's life there is a clear image of a commercial book-making enterprise. The most obvious clients for such a book trade were the university men, and there is no doubt that the professional scribe was an essential part of the developing university.[18] Texts for study were wide-ranging, and while there were some common and much-produced texts, forming the foundation of thirteenth-century university education, new works were proliferating too.[19] The speedy production of texts was vital to the Oxford student, as was comparative cheapness and accuracy. There is some evidence that, to meet these needs, the organization of scribal practice based on the *pecia* system was adopted, developed on the pattern established in the highly organised book trade which served the needs of the university in late twelfth-century Paris. In this system, sections of the texts required were hired out for copying, directly to the student who would commission a copy from a scribe, or to the scribes themselves who would pay for the exemplar and organise their own market among the students. *Pecia* marks in manuscripts written in thirteenth-century Oxford indicate the lively workings of this system, each mark recording the extent of the *pecia* from which it was copied.[20] No doubt many of these copies were never properly bound, and would have been scraped down and used again, or even cut up to be reused in the formation of a binding for some more luxurious volume. In just this way some scraps of parchment of the early fourteenth century have been found re-used as binding stiffening. Evidently fragments of a sample sheet, they contain sections of different types of liturgical text, written in a variety of different scripts. Advertising the scribe's versatility, they may even have been hung outside the scribe's shop in Oxford, providing a glimpse of the commercial enterprise which governed the making of books by that time.[21] It was clearly a trade that demanded commercial instincts, and an eye for what would bring in the customer.

The lavishly illuminated manuscript would also have been an item to attract custom. The documents reveal that in the Catte Street area the members of the book-making community included a remarkably high proportion of illuminators. Judging from the records chiefly of property transactions, these illuminators were successful men, widely-known to their neighbours and elsewhere in Oxford. In addition to the production of university texts, this community was evidently making finely decorated and illuminated manuscripts, which can be identified with books such as the de Brailes group and their ancestors. The evidence of their origin in Oxford is reinforced by the existence of these men – Walter of Eynsham, Job the Illuminator, Radulfo and Roberto, and many others.[22]

Indications of the professional manuscript-maker are plentiful in these books. They were designed with common decorative and illustrative schemes, and their illuminators can be seen to be sharing both the iconography and design of miniatures and historiated initials – clear signs of a cooperative group of craftsmen. Yet, while evidently these manuscripts were made in Oxford, they could be adapted to suit the needs of their patrons, with texts modified to be used elsewhere. Included among their number is a psalter with an Augustinian flavour and with a prominence given to saints important in Gloucester; a glossed psalter with illustration at the liturgical divisions suitable for both scholarly and devotional use; and another psalter that, despite the prominence given to St Frideswide, was clearly destined for the far-flung nunnery of Iona.[23] These varied destinations are to be expected from a centre where custom would have come from a wandering population of students and scholars, buying their books in Oxford together with their education. Oxford must already have gained a high reputation for quality books by the end of the first two decades of the thirteenth century. And it is evidently a reputation that was sustained by de Brailes and his assistants.[24] The quality of the production was assured, although the quantity of illustration and decoration could be determined according to their patrons' specific requirements, as could the detail of their texts and of their calendars and litanies.

The purchasers of these very early products of the professional book trade were mostly laypeople.[25] This in itself was new. Although literacy was on the increase, the laity rarely owned books before the mid-thirteenth century.[26] Furthermore, while the increase in the ownership of books by the laity reflected the development of literacy, it also reflected a different attitude to books. The large-scale ceremonial objects that had been characteristic of the twelfth century had been designed for reading aloud and were owned, and at least partially produced, by a community. The community would have acted as patron, in its fullest sense, to the illuminators who contributed their specialist skills to the project. Such grand books continued to be produced but, in the early thirteenth century, a new compact format for the illuminated book was introduced. These manuscripts were designed to be used by individuals, for personal and silent reading and for study. Such books were cheaper and more speedily made, and satisfied the desire of increasing numbers of readers to possess their own bible or psalter. Designed partly in response to the developing lay market, they would belong to a single individual, whether clerical or lay, or would become the treasured possession of a family.[27]

The change in format of the bible is particularly dramatic. From being the giants of the twelfth century written on huge sheets of parchment in a large and stately script and usually bound in two or more volumes, the thirteenth-century bible is frequently pocket-sized and written on very thin parchment in a compressed script. Many tiny decorative or historiated initials divide up the text and, bound into a single volume, these bibles would have been easy to handle and carry about, to satisfy the needs of both the laity and the mendicant friars for personal books.[28] By the time of William de Brailes and his fellows in the second quarter of the century, this had become the characteristic format for bibles.[29] And while psalters could still be larger, these also tended to be on a more modest scale than their twelfth-century predecessors. A new style of book had been created to meet the requirements of a new market.

As Catte Street bustled with well-to-do and literate burgesses, so also it bustled with students and teachers, all potential customers for William de

Brailes's wares. While many of the tenements in the closely packed streets beneath the shadow of St Mary's were held by members of the book trade, it was also an area packed with students: many student 'halls' and 'schools' are shown on Salter's map of this area, in School Street, and in Catte Street.[30] It was therefore a largely literate community that surrounded the workshop of William de Brailes: a community eager for books. It was an increasingly wealthy community, and this, together with the growth of literacy and respect for the written word, fuelled the market for luxury volumes. In these early days the familiar biblical texts, the bible itself and the psalter, were the most in demand. Used both for prayer through the recitation of the psalms and for the study of the bible, the popularity of these manuscripts reflects the increasing involvement of the laity in the life of the Church.

The participation of these newly wealthy and literate laypeople in the life of the Church was essential to its welfare and, in recent years, the Church had realised the need to educate its clergy in the essentials of the faith, to ensure that they could perform their prescribed liturgical routines, and that they were able to guide and teach their congregations. The Fourth Lateran Council of 1215 reflected these reforms. The resolutions spelt out the duties of the Church and its people, and emphasised the role of the bishops in ensuring that these precepts were properly fulfilled.[31] The laity of Oxford – both university men and burgesses – were evidently taking an interest in the exercise of spiritual and devotional routines modelled on those of the clergy. And in this they were encouraged by the many clerks, monks, and canons, joined in the later 1220s by the friars, who had flooded into Oxford in the wake of the university. These clerics had arrived to take advantage of the teaching that was offered, and to provide teaching themselves, some of it suited to the instruction of the laity. It was a community rich in teaching, of every kind.

Among the community of scholars, such men as Edmund of Abingdon and his protege Richard Wych, who were both canonised as saints later in the century, were particularly concerned to develop the interest of their lay followers towards new religious observances. Both men, in their roles as bishops and teachers, saw it as an essential part of their task to encourage the laity in regular habits of worship. Both St Edmund and St Richard are known for their devotion to the Virgin, and stories of their special favour with the Virgin are an essential part of their hagiography. It was Edmund who wrote a sequence of meditations on the Passion and the Life of Christ for contemplation at the canonical Hours, together with other contemplative writings. St Richard's devotion to the Virgin was widely known, and encouraged in others through the prayers and hymns he composed, and through the importance he attached to his own recitation of the Hours of the Virgin.[32] There is good evidence that St Edmund was responsible for the building of a Lady Chapel onto the north side of the church of St Peter in the East, which stands next to the site long associated with his house. This, already called by its present title St Edmund Hall in the early fourteenth century, persists as the oldest surviving Oxford hall. In the university corner of Oxford, surrounded in the thirteenth century by other such student halls, it is just five minutes' walk from Catte Street and the house of William de Brailes.[33]

This concern for the spiritual welfare of the ordinary people was not confined to Oxford. Spreading from Italy in the early thirteenth century the new orders of mendicant friars, both Franciscans and Dominicans, saw this as their primary mission: to reach the ordinary people with effective preaching that was accessible and readily understood. For both, it was a preaching mission dependent on charity. And both orders of friars concentrated their energies on places full of people. Both orders, however, developed a scholarly role too, and the new university towns, particularly Paris and Oxford, were among their earliest targets. They arrived in England during the 1220s, and the friaries in Oxford were among the first to be set up in England; the Franciscans in 1224–5, the Dominicans by 1226.[34] Over the following century their intellectual and spiritual influence in Oxford was immense, and their power was expressed through the building of vast and complex friaries, in both cases within the bounds of the town, in close contact with the townspeople.[35]

Laypeople and their souls were being courted on all sides. They were being urged to take care of their salvation with prayers, with penances and with charitable gifts. The welfare of the Church increasingly depended upon the ordinary laity. And the rapid development of the communities of friars was built upon their success in attracting funds from the townspeople among whom they settled.[36] The contact between the friars and the laity and the importance of their mutual support is demonstrated not only through the buildings that they raised but through references to the friars which can be seen in the illuminated manuscripts made in Oxford, chiefly for the laity. Added to the de Brailes book of hours is a series of prayers in French, which begins with a reminder to pray for the Dominicans, the friars preacher, and then singles out three by name for special attention.[37] The friars were part of the community, and these prayers suggest that they would have been personally known to the owner of this manuscript, and to its illuminator.[38]

Earlier than the book of hours, and among the first manuscripts illuminated by William de Brailes, is a bible with strong Dominican connections. In the 1230s, perhaps even before 1232, it is the first manuscript that can be securely ascribed to his hand, and illuminated almost entirely by him alone. Now in the Bodleian Library in Oxford, just across the road from the spot where it was made, it is a small but lavishly illustrated bible. It also includes

some elements of the text of the mass, and specifically masses for the feast of St
Dominic, with the addition of the text for the feast of his translation written
in a contemporary hand in the margin. With an exceptionally large number
of small historiated initials, opening virtually every one of the books of the
bible, it was written in the most up-to-date format, in a compressed script in
two columns. It is compact and portable, and its Dominican origins, in these
first years of their presence in Oxford, are made plain. It would have been a
fine book indeed for a Dominican of the Oxford friary, or for a layperson
caught up in the enthusiasm for St Dominic, just at the time that he was
being officially canonised as a saint.[39] Similar bibles, ideal for private study,
were made by William, with less or more assistance, between about 1235 and
1250. They all followed this format of a highly compressed script written on
fine parchment. And it was this small format that William adapted for the
book of hours which was designed from the first with the laity in mind.

In contrast, although these too were for the use of laypeople, a rather
grander style continued to govern the format of the psalters that were made
by William de Brailes and his associates. The largest of these is the New
College Psalter, which clearly demonstrates the cooperative organisation of
these manuscript makers. Thirteen large scale historiated initials are the
work of William himself but, with the exception of one complete bifolium
which is both illustrated and decorated entirely by his hand, the small historiated initials and all the decoration are the work of a number of identifiable individual artists.[40] Like the workings of the *pecia* system, the cooperation
between craftsmen must have been highly organised to produce these
quality books. Through the evidence provided by the structure of the manuscripts themselves, this collaborative operation can be surmised, at least in
outline. Sections of parchment would be moved from individual to individual. The designer would lay out the pages and supervise the ruling of lines,
and these would be handed to the scribe, who would write the text, leaving
spaces for decoration and any illumination. An illuminator would provide
all the decorative initials, the line fillers, and any marginal decoration, and it
may be that this same artist would also complete the historiated initials and
provide any miniatures. However, as can be seen in the New College Psalter,
it may be that the major illustration would be undertaken by another artist.
Finally the completed quires would be assembled for the binder. In laying
out the task for his associates, the designer might well have taken a section of
the text to demonstrate the 'house-style' to be followed. It may be that this

fig.4

fig.5

(*Opposite*) 4. Oxford, Bodleian Library MS lat. bibl.e.7, ff.4ᵛ–5. *c*.1235.
Miniature of Moses seated before a lectern blessed by God at the end of the prologue to the
pentateuch. Facing is the opening of Genesis with the Creation in medallions up the stem of
the 'I' of In principio. The Crucifixion is in a miniature at its foot.

5. Oxford, New College MS 322, f.99, detail. David's temptation and penance before the Lord. Historiated initial at the opening of Psalm 101, the fifth Penitential Psalm (compare figures 12, 69, 70).

was the purpose of William's one completed bifolium in the New College Psalter, to provide the exemplar for the other decorators and illuminators contributing to the completion of the manuscript. Some of the large historiated initials in this manuscript are stuck onto the text page into an initial frame, both initial and frame painted by William himself. This procedure, as well as providing a firm base to be painted, would have freed the illumination, the most time-consuming operation, from the progress of the quires of text.[41]

Also freeing the illuminator from the progress of the decoration, full-page miniatures may be produced independently of the text quires. In the fully completed manuscripts of the William de Brailes group there are none that contain sections of full-page miniatures, though single ones occur within the collation of his book of hours. Yet there survive two sets of miniatures without texts, painted by William and his assistants. The pages of complex imagery fig.2 that comprise the group now in the Fitzwilliam Museum in Cambridge relate closely to the multi-medallioned designs of the miniatures in the book of hours. The opening of Psalm 1, the **Beatus vir**, survives, although small in scale for a psalter. Now only single framed sheets, these pages might have been designed for a bible or an unusually lavish but small-format psalter. Also the work of William and his assistants are a number of gatherings of small-scale full-page miniatures of biblical scenes with brief captions, but no indication of a text to accompany them.[42] Both the multi-medallioned pages and these small full-page miniatures would have been appropriate to prefix a variety of texts – even books of hours. Their existence clearly contributes to the evidence of a commercial enterprise for which de Brailes and his fellow artists produced a wide range of arrangements of text and illustration. The various combinations of miniatures, historiated initials and decoration, designed to embellish books and contribute to the meaning of texts through the use of imagery, were evidently at the command of these skilled and imaginative craftsmen.

In about 1240, in the midst of all this productivity, developing new formats within an established tradition, William designed and illuminated the first book of hours. For this he had no established tradition, although the Hours of the Virgin text was not unknown, and had been included in some psalters made in Oxford earlier in the century.[43] William's book of hours followed the new format of the portable book, although it was modified to accommodate a large and easily read script, structured by historiated initials and laid out with but few lines to a page. Its text was straightforward and supplemented by a scheme of illustration based on narrative, carrying the reader along. Together, text and illustration presented a devotional routine that was direct and easy to follow. This new combination of text and imagery provided a layperson with a manuscript designed to guide his or her necessary daily devotions, through the close linking of words and pictures.

The book of hours, with its small format, large script and many images, and with its concentration on the Virgin, was the perfect devotional manual for a laywoman. In his book of hours, William painted not only his own self-portrait but also the portrait of his patron, the book's first owner. She appears four times in historiated initials to the prayers.[44] She wears a pink robe. Gathered at the waist, it falls in loose folds, its tight sleeves neatly covering her wrists. Her red cloak is pushed up over her shoulders, and from underneath her white hat her dark auburn hair cascades down her back. She gazes up, her arms raised above her head. She kneels in prayer, and the features of her face are quietly composed. In this image, as in each of her portraits, she appears alone. Each time she is in prayer, though her posture varies. Each time she wears a similar robe and her hair flows loosely.

No caption now accompanies her first appearance. Even so, without spec- fig.6
ific confirmation, her name is revealed. This same woman, wearing the same
pink robe, with the same dark cascade of hair, kneels in prayer at the opening plate 2
of the Gradual Psalms.[45] The caption describes her: *ele clama deu en sa tribu-*
laciun. The next historiated initial reveals that this is Susanna, from the bible plate 16a
story of Susanna and the Elders. This story, taken from the Book of Daniel,
was only very rarely depicted in the thirteenth century.[46] To find it depicted
in such detail, in a narrative series of eight historiated initials, is unique,
seeming to show that it was selected for a very special reason. Probably the
Susanna depicted here is not just the biblical Susanna but the book's first
owner, a young and fashionable lay woman who shared Susanna's name.[47]

This first book of hours, then, has a clearly defined origin. It was made in
Oxford in about 1240, designed and illustrated by William de Brailes, and
made for a lady whose name was Susanna. From her portrait it appears that
she was no aristocrat. But when this book was produced she was evidently
young, unmarried, fashionable and devout. And the manuscript is designed
in every way to suit her needs. William de Brailes pictured Susanna in prayer
just as he depicted himself. They are in it together: the lettered lady in
possession of her devotional book and the professional illuminator, skilled
and imaginative, who developed his idea for a new sort of devotional prayer-
book and shaped it just for her. Her book is her only record and her name is
no more than supposition. Yet it is an eloquent record for all that: witness to
at least some of the daily routine of a thirteenth-century life, both hers and
that of William de Brailes.

6. f.64^v. Compline of the Virgin.
The patron in prayer, in the initial
to the final prayer of Compline of
the Virgin.

2. Shaping the Book

No long ancestry determined the shape of the de Brailes Book of Hours. There is no earlier surviving exemplar. Nor had the devotional routine set out in this manuscript for Susanna in about 1240 ever been written into a single volume before. Indeed, no more than eight other English hours manuscripts datable to the thirteenth century survive, and the first of these can hardly be earlier than 1250. Not until the fourteenth century were books of hours made with any regularity but, during the next two centuries, thousands were made.[1]

Yet the shape of Susanna's book of hours, its size, page layout, design and textual contents, became the shape of the characteristic book of hours of the future. Designed for a new and special purpose, here was an illustrated devotional handbook with a simple text, ideally suited to a devout laywoman. Its purpose shaped the selection and arrangement of the texts and the way that these texts were illustrated. From these beginnings, the popularity of the book of hours grew, and in the following two centuries the book of hours gradually became a necessity of life for the prosperous and devout layperson.[2]

The book of hours which William de Brailes shaped for Susanna provides a repertoire of illustrated texts which, as we will see, fulfilled her devotional needs. Its main text, the Hours of the Virgin, was supplemented pictorially by a meditative devotion to the Passion of Christ. This was followed by the Penitential Psalms, the Litany and the Gradual Psalms, each written as separate easy-to-read sequences. The de Brailes Hours expected no complex liturgical knowledge of its reader, but provided a series of unchanging texts that could be simply read through and absorbed.

None of these texts was newly composed. This textual compilation was carefully selected, and drawn chiefly from two well known devotional and liturgical types of manuscript, the psalter and the breviary – the psalter already often owned by laypeople in the early thirteenth century, but the breviary very much a cleric's book.[3] By the late twelfth century, the breviary contained the essential liturgy that was followed by the clergy. Together with the Divine Office itself, it regularly included services with a specific devotional focus. The Offices of All Saints, of the Holy Cross and of the Dead had become widely celebrated. Very early in the development of the liturgy, a short Office of the Virgin was known to have been celebrated. This Office had become an occasional addition to the monastic routine by the eleventh century, witness to the long-established cult of the Virgin and, by the beginning of the thirteenth century, the Hours of the Virgin was sometimes included in the breviary too.[4] The breviary had become a compact and portable book of offices, but its contents varied widely. Often compiled in sections, the breviary could be expanded at will, to include whatever special liturgical texts were needed by their clerical owners.

Essential for the daily routine of all clerics was the text of the psalms, and often the breviary included a complete psalter section, although most of the psalms were included in any case as they provided the basis for all the offices. By the early thirteenth century some of these offices were to be found as a part of the psalter. The Litany of the Saints and the Office of the Dead had become all but essential to the manuscript psalter, together with a calendar of the feasts of the liturgical year. Increasingly, devout laypeople owned manuscript psalters and, through the addition of such devotional material, they could use their psalters not just to recite the psalms, but also to invoke and petition the saints, to commemorate and pray for the souls of the dead. By this time too the Hours of the Virgin was an occasional interloper in the psalter, and this provided the means devoutly to celebrate and supplicate to the Blessed Virgin Mary. Such a psalter was no substitute for a breviary, but with these additions, had become a more flexible liturgical and devotional volume, for both clerical and lay use.[5]

The text of the Hours of the Virgin was divided into a sequence of short services, each unchanging and prescribed for the canonical hours. The routine of the eight canonical 'hours' for prayer was long-established, and the passage of the day was thought about in canonical terms not just by the clergy but by laypeople also. The day began with Matins which, under the 'rule' of the clergy, was usually said shortly after midnight as the 'morning' service. This would be followed immediately by Lauds. Prime was said at first light, followed by Terce, Sext and None, at three-hourly intervals. Vespers was the evening prayer service and finally, to end the liturgical day, there was Compline.[6] The regular recitation of the Hours of the Virgin created a devotional routine that structured the day on the pattern of the monastic *Opus Dei*, though lay practice would certainly have been less rigorous about the timing of the canonical hours.[7] Moreover, unlike the Divine Office, this regular routine, from Matins to Compline, would have been dedicated primarily to praising and honouring the Blessed Virgin Mary.

In William de Brailes's design for Susanna, the Hours of the Virgin is marked out as the most important section of the manuscript, and it is this text that is of central importance to the independent book of hours. For the first owners of these books, the Hours of the Virgin would have provided only a supplementary form of devotion to their regular routine which would have been based on the recitation of the psalms. This first book of hours was, therefore, a psalter-supplement. Through the complex interweaving of William's design, the structure of Susanna's devotional day was set out in full, from Matins to Compline. She would have turned to a psalter for the calendar, which she needed to set out the details of her liturgical year. And she would have gone to the psalter too for the Office of the Dead. The devotional routine that was set out for her was based on the recognition of the new devotional priorities for the laity, and the future of the book of hours depended upon the acceptance of these priorities and of this new routine. That it did so is clearly shown through the developing popularity of the independent volume. Over the next thirty years, with the addition of the calendar and the Office of the Dead from the psalter, the book of hours gradually became a familiar devotional volume and, during the course of the fourteenth century, it gradually outstripped the psalter's lay popularity. Based on William's design, but with any number of additional texts, the book of hours became an echo of the clerical breviary: a portable book of prayer routines and simple offices which could expand at will to satisfy the devotional needs of laypeople.[8]

plate 3 Susanna's book of hours was evidently designed to be carried about. It was made to be used: to be handled and leafed through. Its text, pictures and captions were there to be read. And, most of all of course, it was a book to be prayed with. Although small, and grubby now from centuries of use, its script is large, clear, and easy to read. Complemented by lavish illustration, with historiated initials on almost every page, the layout of its decoration makes it easy to find each of the various texts. As well as providing a valuable book-marking system, the illustration is essential to its purpose as a book of devotions. The devotional themes of its text are made visible in these historiated initials, and new themes are introduced through the imagery. Carefully selected and arranged, these little images enrich the formal recitation of the text, they encourage meditation on the life of the Virgin and the life of Christ, and display the benefits of prayer for ordinary people. It is a rich and colourful little volume with a tightly organised design, and its devotional purpose for its thirteenth-century owner was quite evidently achieved. No manuscript could be more clearly designed to ease and to brighten the daily spiritual routine of a devout lady.

The manuscript measures only 150 × 123 mm (almost 7 inches by 6), just slightly smaller than a modern paperback and, with its full complement of texts written on only 101 folios (including one added at the same time as the original work), it is a reasonably slim and pocketable book. Though its binding is battered now, the original skin-covered wooden boards readily recall the feel of the book in the hands of its thirteenth-century owner. Written on fairly thick parchment, dark cream or yellow in colour, the difference

between the hair side and the flesh side of the parchment is easily felt: one side smooth, the other soft to touch, with a surface like suede. The rich parchment smell lingers as the manuscript is opened, and fragments of the dirt of long use cling to the edges of the pages and in the gutter. Around the text area of each page there is only a narrow marginal border, figs.7, 10 showing that the pages were considerably – brutally – trimmed by the binder.

The page layout, with a text area which measures 115 × 80 mm, is straightforward. The folios are laid out using a simple ruling pattern, of two full-width horizontals almost 5 mm and 15 mm from the top, and two more to define the last two lines at about 32 mm and 42 mm from the bottom. Vertical rulings run on either side of the text space, 22 mm and 100 mm from the gutter. There are no traces of the preparation of the folios by pricking. The prick holes must have been only on the outer edges of each bifolium, and have now been trimmed away.[9] The text area is ruled with 13 lines in a soft chalky substance, each ruling almost 10 mm apart to provide twelve lines of text, in a single column, the text written below the top line.[10] These wide spaced lines provide for a large and very clear square formal book hand which is extremely easy to read.[11] The only exception to this format is the added, but contemporary, folio 28. While superficially identical, the ruling begins one line-width lower, providing therefore only eleven text lines. The scribe remedied this by writing above the top line, retaining the appearance fig.9 of the page.[12]

The final three folios of the manuscript are written in French on pages unused in the formal layout of the text. These pages are ruled informally to provide between 28 and 31 lines of text. The script is quite different too, smaller and less formal, but it dates to much the same time as the main text.[13] These prayers were added very shortly after the manuscript was made, very probably at Susanna's own direction, and for her personal use.

With the manuscript's easy-to-read script and simple page layout comes a decorative design which defines the structure of the manuscript and makes the different texts easy to find. The form of the text of the book of hours is dominated by the short verse structure of the psalms, which constitute a considerable part of the Hours of the Virgin text and the whole of the psalm sequences. In William de Brailes's design each of these verses is written on a new line, each verse opening with a small decorated initial, of penwork designs in blue and gold, or red and blue, which are written to the left of the text area in a vertical column not defined in the ruling scheme.[14] The unused

(*Opposite*) 7. ff.14ᵛ–15. Lauds of the Virgin. Psalms 99 and 62. *La nativite nr seinur*. The nativity is told in three scenes formed from the extended 'I', to begin Jubilate half-way down the page at Lauds. Facing is the three-line initial of the Presentation, *la purification*.

end of each text line is completed with line endings also of penwork designs. Some of these contain animal designs, but most are simple scrollwork, or herring-bone patterns.

Each initial of three lines in height or more is historiated, and may be accompanied by decorative bands or sprays into the border. These three-line historiated initials open each of the psalms, each hymn, each capitulum of the Hours of the Virgin, and each of the prayers at the conclusion of the hours. Often, therefore, a single opening will contain two or even three initials. Sometimes these form a complex combined 'initial' with medallions containing a series of scenes. Or an initial 'I' may be elongated to contain more than one scene, as is the case on f.14v, where William makes good use of Iubilate to tell the Nativity story in three episodes. But even where there is only fig.7 a single picture, the historiated initials may be accompanied by marginal decoration: vertical or horizontal bars of decoration that may widen into a block of foliage, turn into a dragon's tail or develop into large foliate knots on a cusped background. Characteristic of the page design of the manuscript, these decorative bands or squares are usually attached to the more important psalm initials. On f.13v, at the opening psalm of Lauds of the Virgin, a fig.22 scroll in a square is topped by a triangular spike, which provides a convenient perch for a grimacing bird. On f.34 the 'Q' on the lowest three lines of the page lent itself easily to a border extension, via a dragon's body. A fig.39 similarly low-placed initial on f.23 has an initial extension of a pair of scrolls plate 6 with no intervening animal. These border extensions form an important part of the organisation of the page and the text – once again acting as a pointer to an important section.

It is a tightly regulated design, with each decorative element used to clarify the text structure, from the breaks between verses to major new text beginnings. These new texts are readily identifiable and easily found. The page layout and decoration of William's design, just as much as its size and format, reinforces the purpose of Susanna's manuscript.

The completed leaves were gathered and sewn into quaternions, each of eight leaves.[15] Thirteen quires in all were sewn together with three bands, and were bound in heavy wooden boards, only slightly thicker in the centre than at the edges. They were covered with pink, kermes-stained skin, and fig.8 this survives, though now faded and worn.[16] The spine has long-since fallen off, and the tail band is also missing, though presumably it matched the head band, which remains and is made of hemp tightly wound around a thong of pink skin. Studded with five decorative metal bosses, it was held neatly together with a pin and strap fastening. Only the pin on the front cover remains, a shiny metal stud encircled by six radiating leaves, but fragments of the strap survive showing that it was made of pink silk. Susanna's book, when new, was robustly clad in a well-constructed binding. With the gilded

8. The orignal binding is well-worn now. Covered in pink skin, traces of the metal bosses remain, and the stud for the strap has survived. The loss of the spine shows the three sewn bands and fragments of the head band remain.

edges to the pages in sparkling new condition, it must have made a very pretty book: a book of which to be proud.

Recent interpretations have accepted that it was bound like this for its original owner.[17] Graham Pollard concluded that the book has never been rebound, asserted that this binding is 'strictly contemporary English work', and ruled out the possibility that any other texts could ever have been a part of the manuscript.[18] However there is no doubt that alterations to William's original design were made. He himself made one change, adding a single folio, f.28, to the structure of quire 4. But, showing no traces of William's own intervention, in quires 7 and 8 folios were cut out from the original gathering structure to be replaced by pages of a modified text.[19] These were written in a quite different hand, although decorated in imitation of William's design. While this has always been identified as a later and Italianate hand, dating to as late as the fifteenth century, it is now recognised that this Italianate script was found in English manuscripts of the thirteenth century, and that these leaves were probably the contribution of an Italian scribe, working in thirteenth-century England.[20] No substitution was attempted to replace the two full-page miniatures that were cut out, nor to replace the historiated initials, one or two of which might have contained portraits of the patron, Susanna.[21] These substitute pages, rather crudely done, are clear evidence of a change from the original design, as they do not fit into the original collation. Despite that, it is also clear that they were sewn into place before the manuscript was bound and, therefore, they represent a textual change made very soon after the script, illustration and gathering were completed to William's satisfaction.

Why these mysterious events took place cannot be explained so readily. The book which William de Brailes so carefully designed was undoubtedly mutilated. And, it seems, it was mutilated even before it was so prettily bound. There is no doubt that it was de Brailes and his favourite scribe who together added the single page on f.28 (though incorrectly ruled) containing a prayer to St Laurence, complete with its fine historiated initial. The stub of fig.9 this added folio must surely have been cut before the binding was under- plate 3 taken. But then, still before the book was bound, could it have been William who allowed two illuminations and a number of small historiated initials to be cut out, so that they could be replaced with rather clumsy imitations of the original scribe's text, layout, and pen flourishing? Finally, what could have motivated the binder, while trimming the margins of the book to size, to cut fig.10 off the edges – so savagely that the decorative terminals were consistently thrown away, and chopping William de Brailes's neatly written French captions into pieces?

For all the book's appearance of completeness, these changes can only have happened within a very few years of its production. While it is as

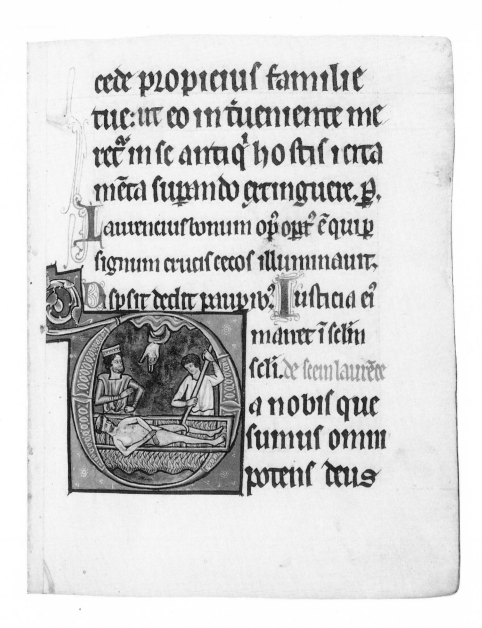

cede propicius familie
tue:ut eo interuemente me
rere in se antiq̄ hostis i erra
meta supando extinguere. ꝑ
Laurencius bonum op opr̄ ē quip
signum crucis cecos illuminauit.
dispsit dedit pauib⁊ Iusticia ei
manet i selm
seli. de scein laurēte
a nobis que
sumus omni
potens deus

9. f.28 Following Lauds of the Virgin, this suffrage to St Laurence was added by William
de Brailes. The cut stub of the folio and a fragment of the string from the binding can be
seen – this folio was added to the centre of the quire. The scribe wrote above the top line,
to correct the error in the ruling. The large scale historiated initial is accompanied by a
'formal' rubric, *de scein laurence*.

difficult to imagine the original owner permitting such mutilation as to conceive William himself overseeing it, it may be that these changes reflected the special requirements of Susanna, in response to changes in her particular devotional needs.[22] Despite its mutilation, the book retains a special character which speaks eloquently of its thirteenth-century owner. It is a personal book, an intimate possession. Passed down, from hand to hand, its grubbiness is witness to centuries of loving use.

That the book was loved by its first owner would be hardly surprising. The easing of her daily devotional routine is achieved through every part of the design – text, decoration, illustration. Each aspect – the selection and layout of the formal Latin texts, the role of the informal French captions, and the integration of the sequence of illustration with the text – is just as highly controlled as is the decoration. The four main texts of the manuscript, together with the integrated illustration, perfectly reflect the devotional range of the thirteenth century. The Hours of the Virgin (ff.1–66); the seven Penitential Psalms (ff.66–80); the Litany of the Saints (ff.81–89); the Gradual Psalms (ff.90–102v) – all are copiously illustrated by narrative sequences, together with occasional devotional images. These formal texts were followed by prayers written in French on the last three folios of the final quire (ff.102v–105).

The use of illustration in the de Brailes Hours shows the designer working with all the elements of his manuscript in mind – ensuring that the text layout, the decorative scheme and the subject matter of the illustration, each contributed to its devotional purpose. Yet, as we have seen, William de Brailes had no exemplar for such a book. Without the legacy of a programme of illustration for a book of hours, but having devised so rich a decorative scheme demanding so many historiated initials, the selection and arrangement of the imagery required an imaginative structure. The organisation is indeed complex. The illustration – as many as 111 separate scenes – comprises a number of narrative series, together with a few single scenes. Reading the text and the illustration together, imagery combining with prayers, the manuscript's devotional quality is created. Religious themes which are not expounded in the text are developed through the imagery, while the subject of the image may emphasize the meaning of the prayer. A change in devotional focus may be marked by a change in the imagery when, for example, the focus on meditation on the Passion of Christ is replaced by a

(*Opposite*) 10. ff.3–4ᵛ Savagely cropped pages, as here, indicate that the original scale of the manuscript would have been more stately. This opening, from Matins of the Virgin, shows first Joachim and then Anna receiving word from the angel forewarning of the birth of the Virgin. Reconstructing the captions, *[le ange]l dit a [ioachim] returne*, and *le angle dit a anna quele voist encuntre sun barun.* See p.46.

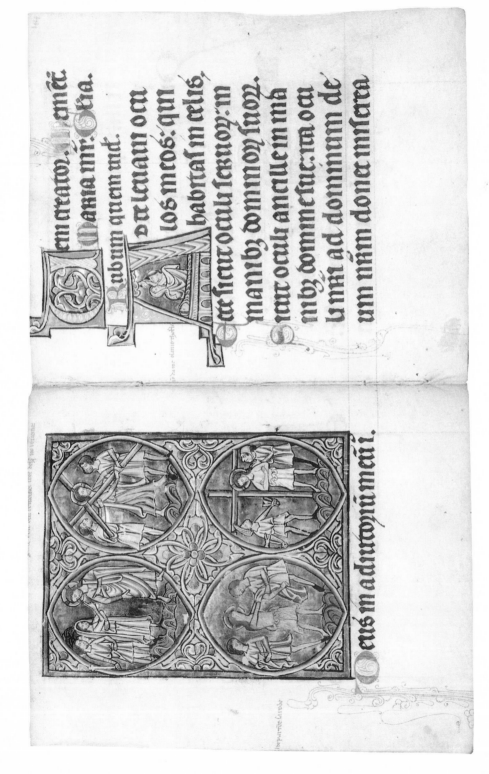

narrative of his Nativity.[23] Moments of personal prayer are reflected in the design too, marked by the interruption of the narrative scheme with an iconic image, or by an image of the designer or his patron in prayer. Through reading William's design, the manuscript's first impact can be rediscovered as it unfolds the spiritual routine for its first owner.

Emphatically stated in William's design is the primary importance of devotion to the Virgin. The Hours of the Virgin is the first text in the manuscript, and there can be no doubt that the double-bodied biting creature who supports the almost full-page historiation on f.1 opens the manuscript's key text. Each of the Hours of the Virgin is prefaced by nearly full-page illustration, apart from Lauds which is written immediately following on from Matins.[24] Only for Matins is this prefatory historiation in the form of an initial, which encloses four medallions, and leaves space for two lines of text below. All the other main divisions of the Hours of the Virgin are marked by a miniature, but these too are divided up into separate medallions. These medallions, mostly oval (though circular in the Matins initial), are enclosed within tightly designed decorative foliage frames, similar to the scrollwork of the border extensions. Only the prefatory page for None is different, with a rectangular full-width scene above a pair of oval medallions. These prefatory pages, marking the main divisions of the Hours of the Virgin, set the devotional scene with a sequence of images of the Passion story, told in great detail. They ensure that, although there is no Passion text as such in the de Brailes Hours, the significance of the Passion of Christ is never in doubt. Each of the medallions contains an episode of the narrative, a sequence of imagery that continues from prefatory page to prefatory page. But the story remains unfinished. The two full-page miniatures that would have preceded Vespers and Compline have been cut out, cutting off the narrative that de Brailes would undoubtedly have designed to fill four medallions on each prefatory page – a further eight images.

Paradoxically, the devotional importance of the illustration is most obviously true of this narrative sequence of the Passion, all but detached from the text as it is. Only the almost full-page historiated initial at Matins is actually a part of the text, and the frontispiece miniatures have otherwise only a line of text at most to accompany them. Moreover, the Passion narrative is not in any way illustrative of the text in honour of the Virgin Mary that it prefaces. Yet it forms a devotional sequence for all that: a devotion without a text. The artist's narrative goes beyond simple story-telling into the creation of a

plate 4

fig.11

fig.52
plate 10

(*Opposite*) 11. ff.43ᵛ–44 The opening of Sext of the Virgin with the full-page miniature facing the start of the text. The four vesica-shaped medallions enclosed in highly wrought decorative foliage face the decorative and historiated initial. The medallions continue the passion story, the historiated initial concludes the narrative of Theophilus. See pp.79–81.

mystical and human drama, linking Christ's Passion with the human emotions of betrayal, false judgement and isolation. It is through evoking this human emotion that the imagery connects its historical narrative in relation to the Life of Christ with the thirteenth-century present: the time of William de Brailes and his patron.

But this narrative, in truth, has even greater meaning. The little red captions, which accompany these images, serve to transform the scenes into a meditation on the Passion. These captions explain and amplify the meaning of the scenes. Furthermore, they introduce the link between the canonical hours set aside for prayer and the hours that passed on the day of Christ's Passion; the historical time of each step of the Passion story. In this way, these captions created a devotional exercise which was structured around the passage of the canonical hours, based chiefly on meditation inspired by the pictorial sequence itself: a devotion without a text maybe, but not without words.

Such captions occur throughout the manuscript, accompanying almost all the historiated initials as well. They are written in French, in a tiny red script completely unlike the book-hand of the text itself. It seems certain that they were written by William de Brailes himself, in the same hand as the two instances of his 'signature' accompanying his self-portraits; on f.43 the very plate 1 explicit *w. de brail' qui me depeint*, followed on f.47 by the simple giving of his name.

The captions have a variety of functions in the manuscript, and the interpretation of their purpose reveals much about both the making and the use of the manuscript. Clearly they are not simply instructions to an illuminator, as they do not always include the information needed for the design of a picture. Nor are they prepared texts, designed to tell the stories depicted, akin to a *Bible historiale*, as there is little descriptive narrative in the captions.[25] In point of fact, they are more like marginal notes than captions, their function varying from one part of the manuscript to another, sometimes noting the subject of the picture and identifying the scenes and characters in the stories, sometimes introducing the theme of a new narrative series.

Useful for a reader, these captions were also part of the designing process, written in by William de Brailes himself as he set out the pages for the scribe. This aspect of their role is evident in the opening caption to the Penitential fig.12 Psalms. The top ruled line of this page is entirely occupied by the caption, delaying the start of the text. Obviously the caption was already there before the scribe got to work, which confirms that these marginal notes did have a role in setting out the design of the manuscript and the organisation of the illustration.[26] The caption here does not confine itself to describing the image depicted in the historiated initial. Its main purpose is to set the scene for the following series of images, and to achieve this it is full of explanation

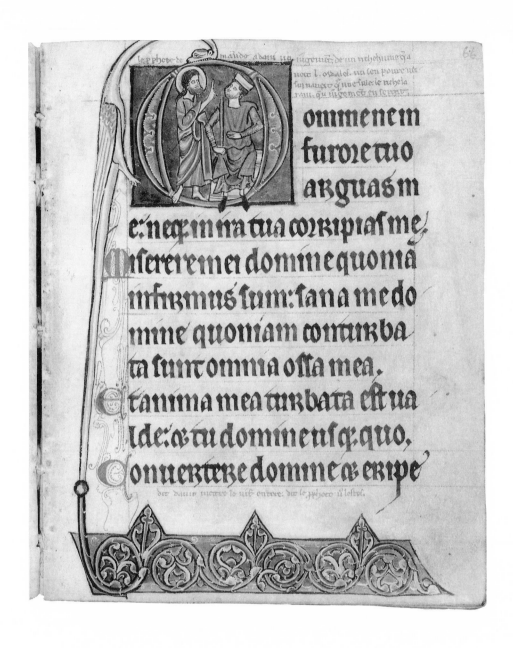

12. f.66 Marking the opening of a new section, the Penitential Psalms starts a new quire – see sewing onto thong at the left edge of the page. Without full-page illustration, the importance of the new text is emphatically stated in the rich design of the page. The dragon terminates in a heavy band of decoration, and anchors the initial in place with its mouth. The top line of text is fully occupied by the caption, which sets the scene both for the text of the new section and its illustration, the penance of David. See pp.104–10.

about the narrative background to the scene depicted. Here, as elsewhere in the manuscript, it is evident that, as well as identifying the scene, this caption suggests an interpretation and creates the devotional context for the text. While they plainly had a role for William in setting out the design, these captions are of central importance to the reader, both to act as a guide to the illustration itself, and to aid the interpretation of the scene in relation to the text.

Indeed, this little book of hours is full of illustration in need of interpretation. Quite apart from the prefatory miniatures, the text is copiously illustrated by historiated initials, and each one is closely integrated with the text. Chiefly narrative, the series of historiated initials accompanying the Hours of the Virgin creates a visual chronicle of the life of the Virgin. It is told complete with miraculous events drawn from the apocrypha and from legend, as well as from the gospels. Linked as they are to the text, their themes enlarged by the captions, these initials create their own pictorial narrative of devotion to the life of the Virgin in all its miraculous detail.

Pointing to the importance of the next text, the Penitential Psalms, William designed a dragon to mark out its first page. The dragon's mouth grasps the opening initial and, with a body which curves down the margin of the text, ends in an elaborate tail of decorative scrollwork which runs the width fig. 12 of the base of the page. It is a large-scale initial and as the text block starts one line down to make space for its extra-long caption, this too emphasises the plate 12 size of the initial. Illustrating the seven psalms is a sequence of historiated initials, which link the penance of David, reflected in the text of the psalms themselves, with the penitential needs of the thirteenth-century owner.

After penance the Litany of the Saints opens the way to mercy with a large-scale initial to mark its importance. Although equal in size to the plate 14 Penitential Psalms initial, there is no added decoration to the page and no extension to the initial frame. Small historiated initials to the petitions at the end of the litany show both William de Brailes and Susanna at prayer.

The first of the Gradual Psalms, Ad dominum, opens with less of an emphatic fanfare than either the Penitential Psalms or the Litany. Simply plate 16a illustrated by a three-line historiated initial, this is the first episode of the two moralising tales which, like sermon parables of the time, accompany the sequence of the Gradual Psalms. Both specifically refer to the original owner of the manuscript and her everyday life, and mix warnings against sin with encouragement to sincere prayer and almsgiving.

The role of these illustrations is clear. They develop the devotional context which is set out in both the Hours of the Virgin and the psalm sequences. They refer to Susanna through the portraits, showing her constantly at prayer. And they illustrate Susanna's life, though less directly, through the parables that William de Brailes has chosen. This is Susanna's devotional day, structured and prescribed by both the texts and the illustrations of William's design.

There is little grandeur in the figure style that William de Brailes uses to illustrate the texts; the emphasis is all on story-telling, on the depiction of emotion, and on the evocation of empathy with his characters. Every part of each small image contributes to this. The initial frame is always important, defining the relationships of William's figures and emphasising their movement in and out of the frame of dramatic action. Gesture, movements of the body, indeed the very size and scale of the figures in relation to one another, are important in defining the dominant figure in the episode, and in showing the sense of self-confidence of a character.[27] Long arms and pointing fingers create the dialogue; firmly focused eyes and expressions define the emotions. Crisply drawn and boldly coloured, each element of William's style contributes to his dramatic purpose, creating the devotional backdrop to the text.

These interwoven threads – decoration, text, imagery, style, captions – continue throughout the whole of William's book of hours, and create the complex texture of the whole design. Together they ease the devotional rites of the day. Followed truly, it is a passage of rites that starts on waking with Matins and ends at bedtime with Compline. Probably that is just how the owner of this first book of hours lived her days. Over the course of the century, such devotional routines did indeed develop into a veritable rite followed by the leisured and the literate. Shaping this book created a model and exemplar for the books of hours of the future.

3. The Devotional Day

However much the passage of the daily rite was eased by William de Brailes's design, it was still a demanding routine. There was a constant and unremitting pattern to the devotional day of this Oxford lady in the mid-thirteenth century, as she kept to the Hours, recited the Psalms, and invoked the intercession of the Saints. Yet, with the aid of her carefully structured manuscript, such an arduous routine was not difficult to follow. Every element of the book's design contributed to this ease. It is easy to read, its decoration ensures that it is easy to follow the pattern of the hours, and the illustration enriches every part of the solemn Latin text. Its organisation is clear and neat and it begins directly. There are no preliminaries here; no calendar to consult to determine the saint's day; no pictorial preface. Matins of the Virgin – morning prayer – opens on the very first page.

Matins

The devotional day begins with a meditation on the dawn of Christ's Passion, a meditation on the theme of betrayal. Entirely visual, it is read in the pictures contained in the four circular medallions of the historiated initial to the first request of Matins: Domine labia mea aperies, 'Lord open thou my lips..', which occupies all but two lines of text on the opening page. The devotion is conducted through the pictures – a sequence of scenes to be read plate 4 like a text from left to right – with the words of the captions contributing the background to the imagery. They describe, but they also point to the complexity of the visual narrative here: a main plot with a sub-plot interposed to expound the theme of betrayal. The captions are extensive, neatly set to either side of the initial, a caption relating to each medallion. The first scene shows the betrayal of Christ by Judas, the embrace itself taking place centrally. Christ is the larger figure and his head is bowed down towards Judas, seemingly in a gesture of trust. The crush of soldiers presses about them and, to the left, Peter stands over the cowering figure of Malchus whose ear is struck off by Peter's massive sword. Peter here aligns himself publicly with Christ, unlike the other apostles who turn and rush away, deserting and betraying their Master.

Yet, in the following three roundels, Peter also rejects and betrays Christ – instantly signalled by the loss of his halo. While the main plot of these scenes shows Christ subjected to scourging and mockery, the sub-plot, inserted to

13. f.1 Matins of the Virgin, (detail)
In the third of the medallions of the
Matins of the Virgin opening
historiated initial, Peter rejects Christ
vehemently, contradicting the tall
figure of the maid who gestures her
question. Perched on Peter's denial NON
SUM is the cock, herald of his betrayal.
Meanwhile Christ's eyes are bound and
he is struck by evil-faced tormentors, as
is explained in the caption, *cum il
benderent les oeus a dunerent bufes diseint quil
devinast. peres le renia.*

the right of each medallion, develops the theme of betrayal. Three times
Peter is asked, by a woman whose gesture is clearly legible, if he is one of
Christ's followers. Directing her fierce gaze at Peter, her body twists and she
crosses her arms to ask her question. The pointing forefinger aimed at Peter
interrogates, while the other indicates Christ as the subject of debate. Peter's
rejecting answers are written on scrolls, not informally in French, the language of the captions, but formally in a liturgical script and in Latin: NESCIO
QUID DICIS, NON SUM, and NON NOVI HOMINEM. On the second and third of
these scrolls, perched on the word itself, the cock crows, fulfilling the proph-
etic warning given at the Last Supper that Peter would betray Christ also.[1]
Casually Peter turns away, warming his hand at the fire as he goes. But,
outside the comfort of the frame of the initial, clearly isolated by his act of
betrayal, Peter then sits and weeps.

fig.13

fig.14

He makes no Latin statement, but his
feelings are described in the caption:
after the Betrayal comes the bitterness
of remorse.

For Susanna, as she turned to her
Matins, the message of the meditation
would have been clear. This first part

(*Right*) 14. f.1 Matins of the Virgin, (detail)
Stricken with remorse, Peter weeps, outside the
narrative frame, *peres plu[re avec] amertu[me].*

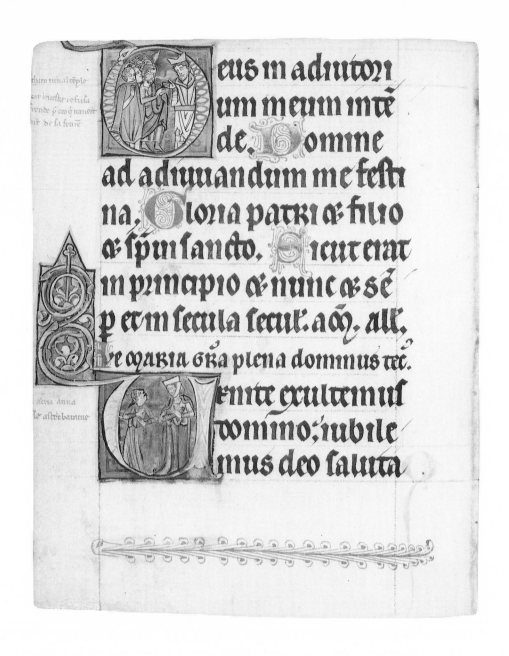

15. f.1ᵛ Matins of the Virgin, versicle and Psalm 94. The story of the life of the Virgin begins with the opening phrase of Matins. The caption sets the scene, *[ioa]chim vin al temple ... car l'eveske refusa [sa of]frende pur ceo que n'aveit [enfa]unt de sa femme.* Dressed as a bishop, the high priest rejects Joachim's offering. With the invitatory psalm, Anna too is rejected, cursed by her handmaiden, *escria anna [pur ceo que] le asteit baraine.*

44

of the drama of the Passion is shot through with betrayal by those most close to Christ – Judas, the apostles, and finally Peter. With this example before her, to be close to Christ, to be a good Christian woman, evidently provided no covenant of immunity from temptation. To see these events unfolding, to relate to Peter's remorse, to share in his sense of isolation outside the initial frame (a visual equivalent to being outside the state of grace), would have needed no words to complete the effect of a whole visual sermon at dawn.

The day turns to sunnier things with the beginning of the text, where the Virgin is honoured both in the Latin text of the hours and in the narratives told in the multitude of little historiated initials, accompanied by their French captions. As the model of love and compassion, particularly for women, the devotion to the Virgin was a joyful one and, with the turning of the page, the sorrows of the Passion meditation must have given way to a more optimistic note to the dawn.

Deus in adiutorium meum intende opens Matins and each of the subsequent hours. And with this cry for help, the story of the Virgin begins. Her birth and childhood are known only from the apocrypha, from the *Book of James*, but were already well known and illustrated by the thirteenth century.[2] Told in nine episodes, the pictorial narrative links the texts together – the hymn, the psalms, the lessons and the prayer of Matins – into a single devotion. The initial to that cry, 'God help me', introduces Joachim, expelled fig.15 from the temple for his childlessness, the obvious mark of his disfavour with God. His sacrifice is refused by the high priest (called a bishop, *eveske*, in the caption), and he is shunned by his neighbours. The invitatory psalm, Venite exultemus, shows his wife Anna suffering similar abuse from her handmaiden Judith, who gestures angrily and shouts, her mouth shaped only to curse. The caption gives the reason: *le asteit baraine*.

16. f.5ᵛ Matins of the Virgin, Psalm 18.
Filling the initial with their embrace, Joachim and Anna meet after Joachim's return from exile, *[il r]acuntrent*. The truth of the Immaculate Conception of Mary is established in this initial.

45

But with the hymn, Quem terra ponthus, and the first of the psalms, the illustration shows the reward for the cry for help, as first Joachim, discovered fig.10 among the shepherds and the sheep, and then Anna receive good news from angels: news of the conception of the child. It was the answer to their cry for help, for reinstatement in the eyes of their neighbours. And because of their old age, it was a miracle. Their embrace, as Joachim returns from exile, fig.16 illustrates Psalm 18, Celi ennarant, 'The heavens show forth the glory of God: and the firmament declares the work of his hands'. They meet alone and entirely without setting, without the Golden Gate where, as the apocrypha tells, this meeting took place. The whole pictorial emphasis is on the two figures locked together in one space.

This embrace is the key to the debate on the Immaculate Conception, a burning issue already in the thirteenth century. Only if she was conceived without sin, as a result of this miraculous but public embrace, could Mary be declared free of original sin, and worthy to be the mother of God.[3] To William this must have been clear, as it would also have been to Susanna. Despite the bland description in the caption as: [il r]acuntrent, Susanna would have seen more than a simple narrative. The embrace's depiction is testament to its truth. Helped along by plenty of clearly visible divine interven-

17. f.7ᵛ Matins of the Virgin, Psalm 23. The Virgin Mary is born, [cum nr dame g]loriuse fu nez, and is held in the arms of the midwife as Anna lies in bed.

tion, a miraculous interpretation is easy. In this context, nothing could seem more natural than an immaculate conception.

fig.17   The birth of the Virgin, illustrating the third of the psalms, Psalm 23, **Domine est terra**, 'The earth is the Lord's', is simply shown including only the mother Anna, and the child Mary in the arms of the midwife.[4]

    The destiny for this special child begins to unfold in illustration to the three lessons of Matins. The first lesson, **Sancta Maria virgo**, tells of her special nature, and her eternal virginity. The illustration shows her parents' recognition of her specialness, taking her as a young girl to the temple, and presen-

fig.18 ting her to the high priest there. William uses the form of the initial 'S' to create the space in which these figures move, and thereby to confirm the human and emotional reality of this scene. The structure of the initial isolates the young Mary from her parents, as they are thrust into the background by the horizontal bar of the 'S' cutting sharply across their bodies. Alone, Mary ascends the steps that reach up to the temple, represented by an altar here, where the high priest waits for her. Her hands are held up in prayer. Behind, Anna and Joachim turn to each other, Joachim's head inclined towards Anna and just touching hers. The doting parents watch with both pride and sorrow as their child climbs towards a higher spiritual goal.

    This event had a double significance. There were, according to the *Book of James*, fifteen steps up to the temple entrance. These steps signified the psalms of degrees, known also as the Gradual Psalms.[5] Those fifteen psalms were part of the journey to grace, the route for the spiritually ambitious, the upward climb of the human soul towards God. But this image also shows how important were these events of the Virgin's early life, becoming adopted as church feasts and recognised in the calendar of the liturgical year. The

18. f.9 Matins of the Virgin, Lesson 1. The young Mary is presented by her parents to the temple, to be received by the high priest. Separated from each other by the bar of the initial, Mary's parents watch, *cum fu porte au temple*. Again the high priest is dressed as a bishop.

19. f.9^v Matins of the Virgin, Lesson 2.
The suitors for the hand of Mary assemble and gaze up, as the grey-bearded Joseph does, to the flower flourishing on Josephs' rod, which he holds out in front of the horizontal bar of the initial 'S'. *[la] verge ioseph [flu]rist*

Presentation of the Virgin was not yet, in mid-thirteenth century England, accepted as a feast worth celebrating. But by the end of the century it was accorded some formal recognition and was recorded in certain calendars to be celebrated on 21 November.[6]

In the next two initials, to the second and third lessons of Matins, the marriage of the Virgin is arranged. The aged Joseph holds his incredible flowering rod on high, above a palisade of unpromising twigs and the disappointed heads of the rejected suitors. It bears an extravagant, formal flower, borrowed from the botany of William's repertoire of floral decoration. The marriage is celebrated without solemnity. Joseph extends his hands to the Virgin while he turns back anxiously to look for the blessing of the high priest, who is fully garbed as a bishop, wearing a mitre and carrying a pastoral staff.[7] It is narrative history, but told in a contemporary language and in modern dress.

fig. 19

fig. 20

The final part of the text of Matins is the Canticle Te Deum, a hymn of praise and thanksgiving ascribed to St Ambrose. Among the many reasons called upon for thanksgiving in the Te Deum is the role of the Virgin in the salvation of Man; that Christ: non horruisti Virginis uterum, 'did not abhor

(*Opposite*) 20. ff.10^v–11 Matins of the Virgin, Lesson 3, Canticle.
A highly decorative opening completes Matins, with a strap of border decoration growing from the initial to the third lesson, perch for a pair of back-to-back birds. The high priest marries Mary to Joseph, who twists away, in echo of the birds, for blessing, *[ioseph espo]use [nre dam]e*. The facing initial is supported on a triangle of scrollwork, from which a lion's mask supports the central column of the 'T'.

48

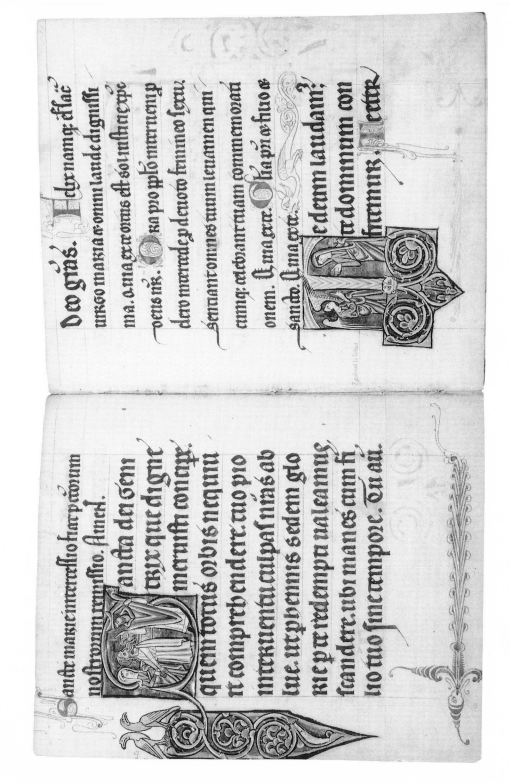

the Virgin's womb'.[8] And it is this role of the Virgin that is echoed in the illustration. The Annunciation is the very first part of the story of the Nativity of Christ, the moment at which the destiny is fulfilled. The scene is simply depicted, with no elaboration of setting. The vertical bar of the 'T' acts as an architectural column, creating a double-celled 'room', separating the Virgin from Gabriel. Despite this barrier, they salute each other with raised hands –   fig.21 his, a gesture of command; hers, one of acceptance. Gabriel bears no symbolic lilies, but the Virgin, as a literate and learned lady, carries a book.[9]

It is only with the Annunciation that the Virgin enters the New Testament accounts of the infancy of Christ, and her importance there is vested entirely in her role as the mother of God.[10] Already by the thirteenth century, the Annunciation was universally celebrated as one of the most important feasts of the liturgical year.[11] Its importance to the devotion to the Virgin was clearly expressed in the illustrative programmes of the later book of hours where the Annunciation was to become the first and most important scene: the opening of Matins.[12] As it appears here the Annunciation is the culmination of the Virgin's childhood and a key moment in her life. Her role as mother of Christ is shown in this sequence to depend upon her miraculous conception, childhood and marriage, which were the essential preliminaries to the fulfilment of the prophecies of the coming of the Messiah.[13] For Susanna, and for William de Brailes, this scene marked the final part of the devotional preliminary to the day: the end of Matins.

21. f.11 Matins of the Virgin, Canticle.
The canticle Te Deum concludes Matins, and opens the infancy cycle of Christ, with the Annunciation. Separated from each other by the central column of the 'T', the angel's finger is raised in greeting and command. Her gesture is acquiescence, her book tucked in the folds of her robe. The announcement is made, *cum gabriel la salua*.

Lauds

Lauds followed on quickly, often immediately; and William de Brailes has designed an all but continuous text and illustration to carry the prayer through from Matins into Lauds with barely a break. Indeed the final words of the Te Deum spill over onto the top line of the page on which the Lauds text begins. This opens with a three-line historiated initial, no larger than the normal, though a decorative terminal has been trimmed away.[14] No full-page prefatory illustration begins this text, and there is therefore no continuation of the Passion story to interrupt the narrative of the small initials. With Matins ending at the Annunciation, the initial to the opening Deus in adiutorium of Lauds shows the second important embrace of the story, echoing the meeting of Joachim and Anna. This, the Visitation of Mary to her cousin Elizabeth, who was shortly to be the mother of John the Baptist, comes immediately after the Annunciation in the New Testament account. The description of this meeting, as told in the gospel of St Luke, gives it immense significance not just to the two women but to their infant sons. Locked in a firm embrace, it is Elizabeth who is the larger figure, as emphasised in the
fig.22   caption, *elizabet la beisa*, and she wears a thirteenth-century type of pill-box hat in contrast to Mary's traditional veil. Crowning the event in St Luke's gospel are the ecstatic words of Mary, Magnificat anima mea, 'My soul does magnify the Lord', one of the key Marian prayers, which is included in the Hours of the Virgin as the canticle of Vespers.[15]

In the later book of hours this scene becomes as closely linked with the opening of Lauds as does the Annunciation with Matins. In this manuscript, where the narrative illustration is so much more complex, the arrangement of the sequence to create this link is intriguing, providing further evidence of the very careful construction of the iconographic design. The iconographic continuity from the Annunciation to the Visitation reinforces the textual continuity, skilfully moulding the break.[16]

St Luke tells no more of Joseph than the simple fact that he was 'espoused to Mary'. But Matthew tells of the dilemma of this just man, a dilemma resolved by an angel who, appearing to him in a dream, satisfied him that Mary's Child was 'of the Holy Ghost'. The angel, pointing finger held high,
fig.22   swoops down to touch reassuringly the sleeping Joseph, who lies with his head on his hand, troubled even in sleep. This episode illustrates the first of the six psalms of Lauds, Psalm 92, Dominus regnavit. Rising from the frame of the initial, almost reaching the top of the page, is an elaborate foliate terminal, perch for a bird, troubled like Joseph. This bird, together with the two small initials, just two lines apart, creates a richly decorated page to mark the beginning of Lauds.

An even richer page follows on f.14v. In the illustration to Jubilate Deo,

22. f.13ᵛ Lauds of the Virgin, versicle and Psalm 92. At the opening of Lauds there are no Passion scenes, but the Visitation illustrates the opening versicle. The embrace of Elizabeth and Mary fills the initial space, *[cum] elizabet la beisa*. Below, beginning the first psalm of Lauds, Joseph receives angelic reassurance in his dream, *[le a]ngle dit a ioseph [quil la] gardast*.

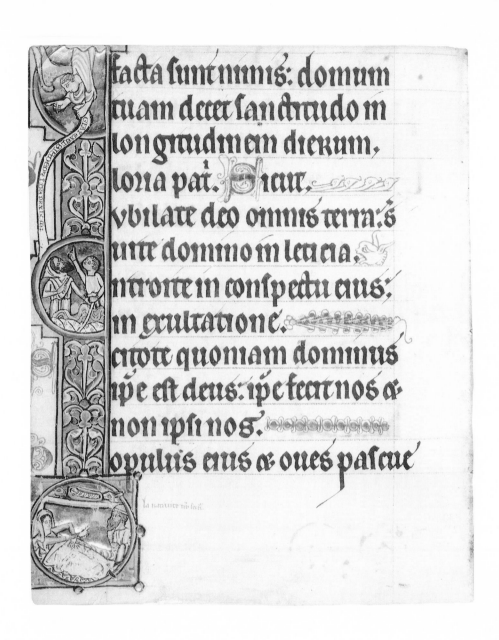

23. f.14ᵛ Lauds of the Virgin, Psalm 99. Heralded by the angel from above, the message of the birth of Christ is passed down to the shepherds. Mary conveys this message to Joseph as she lies in her bed, with the swaddled child above attended by both ox and ass. The abbreviated Latin GLA I EXCELSIS DEO E I TRA PAX HOMI of the scroll links heaven with earth, while the French caption simply describes, *la nativite nr seinur*.

Psalm 99, de Brailes exploits the design possibilities of the elongated shape of the 'I', which he transforms into a wide decorative band that runs from top to bottom of the outer margin of the text. It carries with it three linked images celebrating the Nativity and the Annunciation to the Shepherds. Richly decorative and enlivened by gestures it has a festive air. Gesture is William de Brailes's vehicle for conveying the message of the drama, and for passing the narrative from one episode to the next. The Virgin in her bed looks firmly at a rather pensive Joseph sitting at her feet, and she gestures vigorously towards the child, who is tightly wrapped in the manger, flanked by a minute ox and ass. An angel in the uppermost space, speedily descending to earth, gestures too. An enormous pointing finger indicates the message of a scroll which he bears, GLORIA IN EXCELSIS, a formal Latin announcement in Gothic liturgical script. The shepherds in the centre medallion gesture in response, both looking upwards and pointing, the younger, beardless one gesturing enthusiastically while, his crook in his other hand, he carefully restrains his flock.

fig.23

In this instance the theme of the psalm – 'Sing joyfully to God, all the earth: serve ye the Lord with gladness. Come in before his presence with exceeding great joy' is entirely reflected in the imagery. 'We are his people and the sheep of his pasture: go ye into his gates with praise, into his courts with hymns: and give glory to him' evokes the carefully folded flock of the shepherd, representing the faithful of the Church.[17]

Christ's presentation in the temple, illustrating Psalm 62, **Deus deus meus**, is a very different affair from the presentation of Mary, but with no less signifi-

fig.7

24. f.15 Lauds of the Virgin, Psalm 62.
The blessing infant Christ, his cruciform halo centrally placed in the initial space, is gathered up by the high priest, while Mary and Joseph urge him forward. With Joseph's offering of doves the sacrifice of Christ is begun. The significance of this moment to the Virgin, her purification, is the focus of the caption, *la purification*.

54

25. f.16ᵛ Lauds of the Virgin, Psalm 66.
The three kings, in search of Christ, consult Herod. Seated regally, he holds the sword in a pose of power, already suspicious. The leading king temporises with gesture. *[le iii] reis a herodes.*

cance.[18] Passed from the arms of Mary, he is received by Simeon the high priest from the other side of an altar, an unmistakably sacrificial allusion, added to by Joseph's basket of doves: 'And to offer a sacrifice according as it is written in the law of the Lord, a pair of turtledoves or two young pigeons'.[19] He is an active and well-grown child, with a cruciform halo, and fig.24 his hand and eyes raised towards heaven. It was on the reception of the child that Simeon composed the canticle Nunc dimittis. Rejoicing that he had now 'seen thy salvation', he begs to be released: 'let thy servant depart in peace'.[20]

The following five historiated initials form a continuous narrative sequence, telling the story of the Magi, closely following the text of the gospel of St Matthew.[21] Opening the fourth psalm, Deus misereatur, the fig.25 three kings confront Herod, enthroned with a sword in his hand, to ask for directions to the birthplace of the new king: 'Where is he that is born king of the Jews?'.[22]

In the next initial, illustrating the canticle Benedicite, Herod has sum- fig.26 moned four Jews, identified by their round caps. Their reply, written on a scroll, is the declaration IN BETHLEEM IUDE, the answer given in St Matthew's account, but quoting the prophecy of Micheas.[23] The Benedicite, canticle of the three companions from the Book of Daniel, is a canticle of praise, spoken by the three from the midst of the fiery furnace, blessing God and all his

26. f.17ᵛ Lauds of the Virgin, Canticle. The Canticle **Benedicite** is illustrated by Herod challenging the Jews to reveal the place of Christ's birth. Two hatless bearded Jews kneel at the feet of Herod, revealing the prophesied place on their scroll, IN BETHLEEM IUDE. The caption explains, *[her]odes demande as giues [si le cri]st nescret en beleem*.

27. f.19ᵛ Lauds of the Virgin, Psalm 148.
As described in the caption, *le iii reis aurent e offrent*, the kings offer gifts to the enthroned Virgin with Christ on her lap. Accepting the offering of the kneeling king, Christ blesses them all with his right hand.

28. f.21 Lauds of the
Virgin, Psalm 149.
Visited by an angel
bearing a scroll, NE
REDEATIS, the caption
explains, *le angle lur defend
le chemin par Herodes.* The
three kings receive their
warning in unbroken
sleep.

29. f.23 Lauds of the
Virgin, Capitulum.
Following the advice of
the angel, the three kings
go home by their various
routes, *il repeirent par autre
voie en lure regions,*
mounted on elegantly
caparisoned horses.

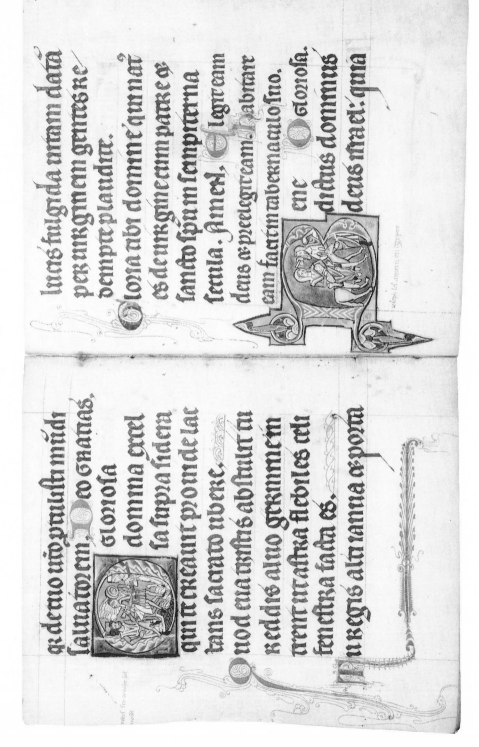

works. Like the Jews depicted here, they challenge the authority of their king.

With the knowledge that Bethlehem is their destination, the three Magi fig.27 travel on. The climax of their journey is depicted in illustration to Psalm 148, **Laudate dominum**, which shows them in adoration of Christ and presenting their gifts. The kings approach from the east, and the eldest, a grey-beard, kneels before the Virgin who wears a crown over her veil. The child, enthroned on his mother's knee, reaches out in blessing to receive the golden gift offered.

fig.28 After this long journey the kings sleep, each under his own individually coloured bed cover. But their sleep is disturbed, and they 'receive an answer in sleep that they should not return to Herod', the answer personified as usual by an angel carrying a scroll: NE REDEATIS.[24] This accompanies the last psalm of Lauds, Psalm 149, **Cantate domino**.

The final episode of the story of the Magi illustrates the capitulum in fig.29 praise of the Virgin, **Maria virgo**. This initial, as it is explained in the caption *il repeirent par autre voie en lure regions*, is one of the liveliest of de Brailes's inven-plate 6 tions. The vertical stem of the initial 'M' provides the separation into foreground and background, with the foreground king riding eagerly ahead, mounted on a splendidly spotted blue horse. His body leans forward and he points the way. His feet are set firmly in the stirrups and his whole attention is on the way ahead. Though tucked behind the initial stem, the old king is taking that path also and, equally vigorously, he points out his way. The third hangs back and, twisting in his saddle, he has obviously reached the turning-point. Pointing back, he is about to wheel away and part from his companions. These three kings carry their reader with them, looking back, forging ahead. It is the perfect 'narrative' composition.

The story moves on swiftly to the consequences of the kings' approach to fig.30 Herod, with the Massacre of the Innocents. Herod himself is seated, his sword in his hand gesturing the command to slay the children, who are shown pitilessly murdered in their mothers' arms.[25] Christ had been saved, once again through the intervention of an angel who had urged Joseph in a dream to 'take the child and his mother and fly into Egypt'.[26]

It is the Flight that illustrates the final text of Lauds. This last text is the Canticle **Benedictus dominus**, taken from the Gospel of St Luke.[27] It is Zachary's song of wondering praise as he regained his voice after naming his

(*Opposite*) 30. ff.23ᵛ–24 Lauds of the Virgin, Hymn, Canticle. The hymn of praise to the Virgin is illustrated by Herod's compassionless massacre of the innocent children of Bethlehem, and he is shown personally urging on his soldiers, despite the cry of a mother *[he]rodes fet decoler les [in] nocens*. In contrast, and facing this brutal image, the peaceful Flight into Egypt shows the Virgin seated on the ass as Joseph walks ahead, *ioseph les amein en egypt*.

son John. It is both praise and prophecy, and foretells the role of John the Baptist: 'thou shalt go before the face of the Lord to prepare his ways'. fig.30 William de Brailes portrays a peaceful Flight. Joseph leads the donkey carrying Mary and the Christ Child out of danger from Herod, the swaddled child fast asleep. The three move onward, as Joseph steps out of the initial space: the end of the story of the Infancy.[28]

Here, after nearly an hour of continuous prayer – of serious Latin prayer – Susanna can pause a while. She has had little chance yet of supplicatory prayer, prayer for herself. The images have told their tale and provoked involvement and meditation. They have been an essential part of the devotion. The consequences of the birth of Christ were faced at the very start of the devotional rite in the story of the Betrayal. The establishment of his Mother's sinlessness and purity were shown through the images at Matins. And Lauds had given the gospel account of Christ's infancy, dodging from St Luke to St Matthew and back again, threading the narrative together.

But now there is time for prayer that is a little more personal. It is at this point that William de Brailes inserts the prayers to individual special saints, called the suffrages or *memoriae*. They are almost invariably placed here at the end of Lauds in English books of hours embedded in the Hours of the Virgin, in contrast to their placement in their French equivalents, where they are found in a separate section, either at the beginning or end of the whole book.[29]

Only eight special suffrage prayers are given and illustrated, though a short section of text indicates a ninth. First in importance, of course, is the

31. f.26 Lauds of the Virgin, Suffrage to Blessed Virgin Mary. The prayers after Lauds begin with the prayer to the Virgin. This truly devotional image of the enthroned Virgin and Child shows the Virgin crowned, yet looking to her Son for blessing; a blessing shared with the devout reader of this prayer.

Virgin herself, and the prayer flows naturally out of the Lauds text. The suffrage to her begins: Concede nos, 'Grant us'; a moment when the potency of supplication to the Virgin can be evoked. Enthroned with the child on her lap, this is the first of the truly devotional or iconic images in the programme of illustration. Here for the first time is a pause in the hectic story, where the significance of the illustration is fully contained within the frame of the opening letter 'C' – an image of the Virgin and Child to embody the prayer's echo.

fig.31

The devotional significance of each suffrage prayer is illustrated in its initial. The suffrage to the Holy Spirit evokes the Pentecost, and the illustration shows the massed haloes of the apostles, with Saints Peter, Paul and John identifiable in the front, illuminated by the red beams of light cast by the Dove. The Holy Cross is venerated through a devotional representation of the crucified Christ, hung on a green cross, suggestive of the Tree of Life.[30] Flanked by the Virgin and St John, the image is like a rood, instantly recognisable – a visual Sign of the Cross.

fig.32

fig.33
plate 3

The sequence of saints in a suffrage series is usually in accordance with their order in the litany: the apostles and evangelists, the confessors, the martyrs, and finally the virgins. Following the suffrage to the Holy Cross, the first of the saints to be invoked is St Laurence, though a small section of a prayer precedes it. It is here that the inserted folio 28 disturbs the text, introducing the added suffrage to St Laurence.

This insertion is original, however, made by William de Brailes himself and using the same scribe to write the text. His own unmistakable style is

32. f.27 Lauds of the Virgin, Suffrage to the Holy Spirit.
The characteristic blessing from the Holy Spirit is the light of his inspiration and, illustrating the Pentecost, this power is revealed to encourage the devout, *de le seinte esprit*.

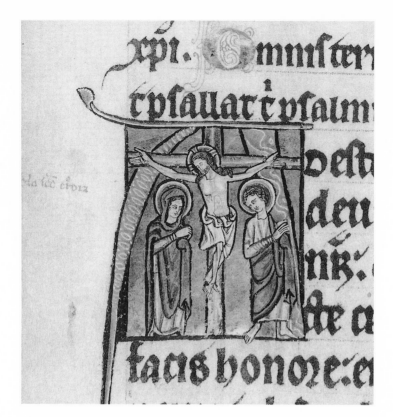

33. f.27ᵛ Lauds of the Virgin, Suffrage to the Holy Cross. Similarly captioned, like a rubric, *de la sce croiz*, the devotional image of the crucifixion emphasizes the form of the cross, with the mourning Virgin and St John beneath its arms.

there in the historiated initial of the martyrdom of St Laurence, eye-catching both for its exceptional size (the only 5-line high text initial in the manuscript), and for its French rubric, *de scein laurene*. Like the captions, it is written in red by de Brailes, but unlike his usual tiny and informal script, he copies a formal liturgical script here, and the form of words he uses follows that of a rubric, not a caption.[31]

While it is easy to understand changes and additions to a book in later years to satisfy a new owner's needs or up-to-date modifications, it is more difficult to account for this addition. It must have been achieved before the quires were bound, and certainly before it left the hands of William de Brailes. The importance of St Laurence is made quite clear. The insertion of this suffrage, at a stage after the planning of the book, would have required the preparation of a new piece of parchment and further work by both the scribe and the illuminator. Nothing less than the intervention of the patron can account for it. Further on in Susanna's book, St Laurence appears again, taking part in a pictorial narrative which strongly suggests that she belonged to a parish where its church was dedicated to him.[32] Whatever the reason for this addition, it provides clear evidence of a bespoke manuscript, and the imposition of the patron's wishes on the artist's design.

fig.9
plate 3

34. f.29 Lauds of the Virgin, Suffrage to St Katherine. The image of St Katherine needs to be explained by its caption, *de seinte katarine cum les angles la encevelirent el munt sinai*, as it depicts the carrying of her body by angels, after her eventual martyrdom, to Mount Sinai. This directly illustrates the text of the prayer.

The image chosen to represent St Laurence in this initial shows him at his most instantly recognisable moment as, condemned by the Emperor Valerian, he suffers martyrdom. He lies naked and tonsured on the gridiron, and is roasted by a cheery executioner who prods at him with a pitchfork. The hand of God descends from the top of the initial as reassurance to the martyr. But it is the emperor who responds. Enthroned to watch, he looks up to heaven and gestures in self-justification.

fig.34   The image accompanying the suffrage to St Katherine is not the familiar imagery of her torture on the wheel. Instead, William depicts the event after her death when her body was carried by angels to Mount Sinai.[33] The long descriptive caption tells the story, which also forms the focus of the prayer. Once again the close relationship between the imagery and the text is an essential part of William's design.

fig.35   St Margaret of Antioch is invoked in the next suffrage, and she is readily recognisable in the historiated initial as she bursts out of the body of the dragon who swallowed her. She is raised up in prayer by the hand of God in William's image, an image to echo her role as patroness of childbirth. This image explains her popularity with women, reinforcing her promise to all those who invoke her help to be released from the perils of birth – both mother and child.[34]

The supplication to All Saints in the last of this short sequence of prayers categorises them as the apostles, the martyrs, the confessors, and the virgins.

fig.35   Echoing this, de Brailes depicts a numerous but well ordered company. A
plate 7   slender gold stem runs the whole height of the page, doing duty for the 'I' of In firmitatem, the opening of the prayer. Attached are a series of five semi-roundels, each dedicated to one of the groups of saints. They are organised as

63

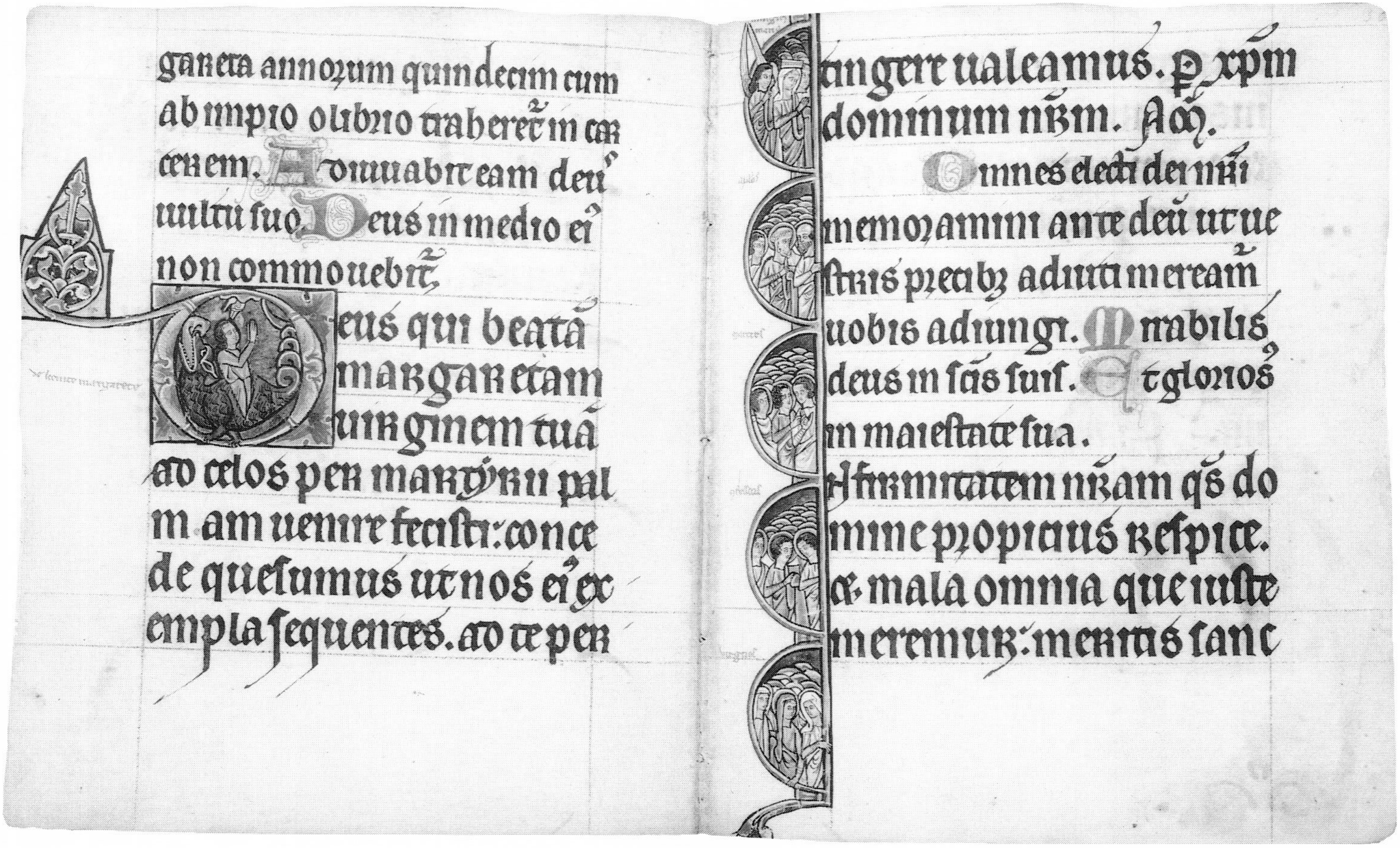

...ngere ualeamus. p xpm
dominum nrm. Amen.

Omnes electi dei nri
memoramini ante dei ultuc
et pris precib3 adiuua meream
uobis adiungi. Mobilis
deus in scis sanc. et glorios
in maiestate sua.

Sufferua tacem nram qs do
mine propicius respice.
et mala omnia que iuste
meremur; mentis sanc...

...garita annorum quindecim cum
ab impio oubrio traheret in car
cerem. Orauit ad deum dei
uultui suo deus in medio ei
non commouebit

...eus qui beatam
margaretam
uirginem tuam
ad celos per martyrii pal
mam uenire fecisti; conce
de quesumus ut nos eius
empla sequentes. ad te per xpm

in the litany: the angels and Mary at the top, with the apostles, the martyrs, the confessors and the virgins descending the stem in steps. Each contains a veritable press of saints, only the front few identifiable as individuals, with the existence of the endless company indicated only by the domes of their haloes, receding forever into the distance.

The personal prayer of the suffrages ends with a prayer for peace. The enthroned figure of Christ raises his right hand in blessing, a book in his left. fig.36 From this pictured blessing the devout owner of the manuscript might receive comfort. Like the blessing offered by the priest as he dismisses his congregation, Christ's blessing offers peace. Gathering in this blessing at the end of Lauds, Susanna may rise from her knees and start the new day.

(*Opposite*) 35. f.29ᵛ–30 Lauds of the Virgin, Suffrages to St Margaret and All Saints. St Margaret drawn by the hand of God from a rent in the belly of the dragon creates a clear reminder of her efficacy as the patron of child-birth. As on display, *omnes electi*, All Saints are there, each grouping gathered into a semi-roundel. At the top the crowned Virgin leads *aungles, marie*. St Peter and St Paul are identifiable at the front of the *apostles*, St Paul holding firmly to the stem. *martirs, confessurs*, and, at the base of the stem, *virgines*, make up the sequence, following the order in which the saints are invoked in the Litany. This elaborate elongated 'initial' derives from the 'I' of in firmitatem.

Prime

But not for long. Despite the passage of an hour or more on her knees, the Hour of Prime can hardly have been very long delayed, and it would certainly have preceded the real events of the day. This new text begins afresh, however, with a full-page prefatory miniature dividing it firmly from the end of Lauds.[35]

The four vesica-shaped medallions of the full-page miniature take up the story of the Passion once again. In contrast to the betrayal of Christ by his closest followers, Judas and then Peter, now Christ is subjected to the due process of the law. No single judge condemns him. In the grip of his accuser he is turned from judge to judge – four times he is called to account. First he is judged by Annas, father-in-law to Caiaphas; then by Caiaphas himself, the high priest; then by the governor Pontius Pilate; and finally by Herod who held jurisdiction over the Galileans. In this order, conflating the gospel accounts, the process of the condemnation of Christ is shown by William de Brailes to have been far from simple.[36] In each image, Christ is shown standing before the seated judge, accompanied by a single accuser. Annas wears a white robe which is drawn up to cover his head. He raises one hand in interrogation, and in answer his accuser buffets Christ's face. In the next space Caiaphas is more formally enthroned, hands on knees, his elbows out. Christ is pushed forward by the same accuser, his wrist held as he gestures quietly to the high priest. Pilate too is enthroned, with his legs loosely crossed. He raises a hand, his forefinger questioning, to which Christ's answering gesture shows his whole palm to Pilate, denying any knowledge of his fault. Finally he is brought before the most formidable of these judges, Herod. Like Caiaphas, he has his arms akimbo on his knees. Like Pilate his leg is crossed, but here menacingly and formally laid across his lap. No gesture from Christ can answer the accusing stare. Only St Luke mentions the judgement by Herod, describing how Christ was mocked by him and returned to Pilate. St Luke adds that from this time Herod and Pilate were made friends, and once again Christ is shown to be betrayed by his own people.[37]

The narrative is fully explained by gesture and pose, the four judges identified with the aid of captions next to each medallion. But above the whole miniature runs a caption which provides the meditative context and, with it, the key to the interpretation of this whole Passion series. It is the only completely intact caption to these prefatory scenes, and reads: *a prime len amena iesu devaunt anne le prestre i lu demanda de sa doctrine. un sen ribaut lu duna une bufe*. It is that introductory phrase '*a prime..*' that locates the meaning. It links the historical events of the Passion, occurring as they did during the course of a single day, to the daily celebration of the canonical hours. To the

66

37. f32 Prime of the Virgin, Full page prefatory miniature. Opening a new quire with
Prime, the text is prefaced by four vesica shaped medallions set about with decoration. The
caption, *a prime len amena iesu devaunt anne le prestre i lu demanda de sa doctrine, un sen ribaut lu dona
une bufe* identifies the beginning of Christ's judgement with the canonical hour of Prime.
Clearly Annas asks a question. Taken through the twists and turns of judgement he is
examined by Caiphas, Pilate – who wears a red round cap – and finally Herod crowned
and enthroned. The opening phrase of the text begins below: Deus in adiutorium meum.

67

rite of the Hours of the Virgin is added a rite of meditation on the Passion of Christ.

It was just before the time that this manuscript was made, that a rite of meditation on the Passion was composed by St Edmund of Abingdon.[38] St Edmund had a house of his own in Oxford early in the thirteenth century. This house, it is thought, stood on the site of the present St Edmund Hall, next to the church of St Peter in the East.[39] The rite he devised was based closely on the gospel accounts of the events of the Passion, focusing on the sufferings of Christ. Such meditations were not unusual and, promoted particularly by Franciscan writers, had became popular before the end of the century for clergy and laity alike. These meditations of St Edmund focused firmly on the timing of the day of Passion, structuring the events of that day around the canonical hours, to which he had a special devotion, and attaching another episode drawn from the life of Christ.[40] The meditations were prescribed to be said before each of the canonical hours, beginning with the Betrayal at Matins. At Prime, Christ was sent before Pilate; at Terce he went before Herod and was condemned by Pilate. By the hour of None, Christ was crucified. By Compline, he was entombed.

The canonical structure to the devotional day for the thirteenth-century layperson seems entirely natural in this series of meditations by St Edmund. With this structure, these meditations and the whole phenomenon of the popular adoption of the hours, became a way of life: a familiar pattern for the laity. By the end of the century, a devotion to the Passion of Christ on this canonical pattern had become a most important aspect of lay worship.[41]

With a turn of the page the concentration returns to the Virgin, and the text of Prime. The page begins with the hymn for inspiration from the Holy Spirit, **Veni creator**. In its historiated initial a whole new story opens, which is to be told in the next ten historiated initials, flowing over right up to the beginning of Sext, lasting through half the devotional day. It tells the most popular of the stories of the Miracles of the Virgin, the tale of Theophilus, and it shows a different side to the devotion to the Virgin.[42] So far her importance has been established because she was miraculously conceived and then miraculously chosen to be the Mother of God. The imagery at Lauds has shown her fulfilling that role. But the devotion to the Virgin has always had its pragmatic side, and her miraculous intervention on behalf of her faithful was a developing aspect of her cult. From the beginning of the

---

(*Opposite*) 38. ff.32ᵛ–33 Prime of the Virgin, Hymn, Psalm 1. This opening shows the start of the text of Prime with the first two episodes of the story of Theophilus. Although urged by his fellows, Theophilus refuses to take on the episcopal throne, *theofle de estre [eveske] il refusa*. Theophilus turns away to reject the throne. He is next shown impoverished wandering barefoot in a simple shift, his hand to his head in a gesture of despair, *theofle enpovri*.

twelfth century, stories of her miracles were being written down, and numerous manuscript copies of the Miracles of the Virgin survive, mostly dating to the thirteenth century and later. These may be elegantly written and illustrated, including a whole sequence of stories. But sometimes the odd single miracle may be found written on a flyleaf or in the margin of a quite different text, witness to their everyday familiarity.[43]

William de Brailes writes the Theophilus story in pictures, with only identifying captions to help the narrative along. It was a familiar enough story at this time, and numbers of depictions of Theophilus survive.[44] William de Brailes used the story on another occasion, where it was equated with the idea of the Wheel of Fortune.[45] There it is linked to the Ages of Man, from his birth to death, and is seen as a parable of man's changing fortunes. This may be so, Fortune may have played a part, but it is the intervention of the Virgin which changes the outcome, reversing the wheel.

Theophilus has only himself to blame for his ill fortune. In this first initial, to the **Veni creator** hymn summoning the Holy Spirit, he rejects the bishop's throne, which stands empty and gleamingly gilded. Urged to accept, he nevertheless gestures his decline. Declining through humility, the new bishop heaps humiliation upon him, and deposes Theophilus altogether from his priestly function. Illustrating the first of the psalms of Prime, the **Beatus vir**, Psalm 1, he is sent off into exile and poverty, wearing only a thin shirt, barefoot, and leaning on a stick: 'Blessed is the man who hath not walked in the counsel of the ungodly, nor stood in the way of sinners, nor sat in the chair of pestilence'. *(fig.38)*

Repenting the foolishness of humility, he is tempted to regain worldly recognition, and rashly pledges his soul to the devil. Illustrating **Quare fremuerunt**, he kneels before the devil, and confirms the contract with a properly executed charter which, as the caption makes clear, was written with his own blood: *theofle fet humage au deable e lui escrit chartre de sen propre sanc*. Entitled 'CARTA TEOFOLI', a huge wax seal hangs from it. The importance of the written charter in this transaction, the necessity of the written word to establish the unbreakable nature of this contract, shows how literate and legalistic the world of the thirteenth century was becoming.[46] With his rash promise in writing, his fate is undeniably sealed, both in blood and wax. For a while fortune smiles. Illustrating the capitulum, **Verba mea auribus**, the devil, quite properly, keeps his side of the bargain. Theophilus is reinstated and, filling the initial space, he is grandly dressed. Seated on a throne with his legs arrogantly set apart, he takes on the posture of power. *(fig.39)* *(fig.40)*

To end the hour of Prime is the moment of personal prayer, addressed directly to the Virgin, **In omnibus requiem**. A prayer appealing for the aid of the Virgin, its direct approach is echoed by Theophilus. As described in the caption, *theofle se repenti a nr dame cria merci*, he repents the sacrifice of his *(fig.41)*

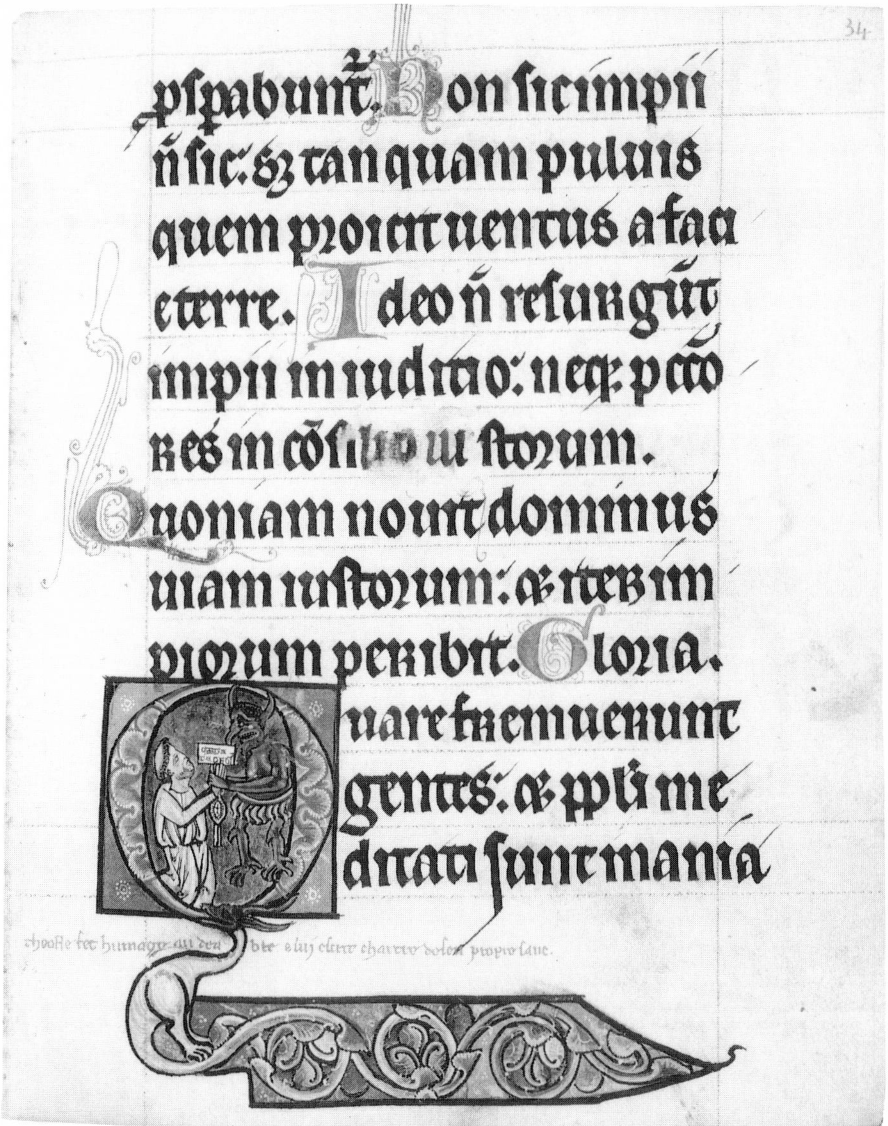

39. f.34 Prime of the Virgin, Psalm 2. With the second psalm of Prime, Quare fremuerunt, Theophilus pledges his soul to the devil in return for reinstatement to his former wealth and power. Still simply dressed he kneels before the devil and hands over an elaborate and properly sealed charter, CARTA THEOFOLI. The caption describes the circumstances, *theofle fet humage au deable e lui escrit chartre de sen propre sanc* – written in Theophilus's own blood.

(*Above left*) 40. f.36 Prime of the Virgin, Psalm 5. The third psalm sees the fortunes of Theophilus restored, and he is enthroned in power, his hands firmly set on his knees, his body swathed in rich robes. There is no surviving caption.

(*Above right*) 41. f.38 Prime of the Virgin, Capitulum. A small semi-roundel is the only image of the illustration of the 'I' of **In omnibus requiem**, but here Theophilus repents, kneeling before an altar, his hand stretched out in supplication. At the top of the page the caption reads *theofle le repenti a nr dame cria merci.*

soul. Kneeling before an altar, his arms stretched out before him, he begs the assistance of the Virgin.

As the story pauses at the end of Prime the wheel of fortune is at rock bottom. Theophilus has made his contract. Sealed so firmly he cannot, surely, find salvation now.

Terce

Well into the devotional day now, the hour of Terce would have fallen at about midday. Introduced once again with a meditation on the Passion, it is at the hour of Terce that the final judgement and condemnation of Christ took place, and the opening meditation concentrates on the role of Pilate.[47] The full page miniature is divided again into four medallions but, despite the elaborate frames, they need to be read as two scenes only.

In the top pair of scenes, Christ is again brought before Pilate, following the text of St Luke, where Herod is said to have: 'put on him a white garment and sent him back to Pilate'.[48] Pilate is enthroned in the left medallion, his

fig.42

72

42. f.39 Terce of the Virgin, Full page miniature. Opening Terce of the Virgin with four medallions, the judgement of Christ continues, quizzed across the barrier of decoration by the enthroned Pilate. Beneath, as Pilate washes his hands, Christ is turned away, to the mercy of the Jews. Although the caption at the top of the page has been cut away, the lower ones survive, *pilate leve sa meins*, and *les giues le geugerent*.

pose of power reinforced by a group of four similarly seated companions. Pilate's forefinger is again raised, but this time questioning Christ's accusers. Across the barrier of the medallion frame, Christ is brought forward by the habitual accusing figure, now accompanied by two others. Christ's pose is not of fear, nor does he gesture denial. By this point in St Luke's account indeed, he had little to fear from Pilate, who declared: 'You have presented unto me this man as one that perverteth the people. And, behold, I, having examined him before you, find no cause in this man, in those things wherein you accuse him.'[49] It is in St Matthew's gospel that the next episode is told, depicted here in the third of the medallions. 'And Pilate, seeing that he prevailed nothing, but that rather a tumult was made, taking water, washed his hands before the people, saying: I am innocent of the blood of this just man. Look you to it'.[50] Pilate stands, firmly turning his back on Christ, while a servant pours water over his hands from a jug. And with that, 'Look you to it', the accusers take him, according to the caption: *les giues le geugerent*. As they lay hold of Christ, their accusing forefingers are silent, and turning him away

43. f.39ᵛ Terce of the Virgin, Psalm 119. The first psalm of Terce, **Ad Dominum** finds Theophilus kneeling in supplication before the Virgin, who has appeared before him, *[nr da]me apert a theofle*.

74

44. f.40ᵛ Terce of the Virgin,
Psalm 120.
The Virgin physically recovers the
charter from the devil. The
caption, though much trimmed,
emphasises the importance of the
charter, *tout la chartre*.

from the presence of Pilate, the responsibility is clearly theirs, that of the
Jews. Pilate's hands are clean.

Again it needs a turn of the page to begin the text, though the opening line
Deus in adiutorium is fitted beneath the miniature. The Theophilus story is
taken up again in the initial to Psalm 119, Ad dominum in tribularer, 'In my
trouble I cried to the Lord: and he heard me'. Here Theophilus kneels again,
depicted much diminished in size, but this time before the figure of the
Virgin herself, his prayer heard. And in illustration to Psalm 120, Levavi
oculos, she answers his prayer with a hand to hand battle with the devil,
physically wresting the charter from him, and punching him firmly on the
nose. With Psalm 121, Letatus sum, 'I rejoiced at the things that were said to
me: we shall go into the house of the Lord', the Virgin returns the charter to
Theophilus, who remains on his knees before her.

The capitulum, Ab initio, follows this psalm of celebration, and now Theophilus is empowered to break his contract with the devil. No blood or wax
can prevail against the power of the Virgin's intercession, and he burns the
damning written charter on a great bonfire, its leaping flames reminiscent of
the fringes of the skirt of the devil himself.

This seems to bring the story to a close, though the question of the final
deliverance of Theophilus must remain. The last historiated initial of Terce
to the prayer, Concede nos, 'Grant us', is not part of this sequence. Instead the
figure of a kneeling tonsured man intrudes. William de Brailes, in a pink and

fig.43

fig.44

fig.45

fig.46

45. f.41ᵛ Terce of the Virgin, Psalm 121.
The Virgin restores the charter to Theophilus, who kneels before her once more, [nr dam]e la rent a theofle.

white striped habit, raises his hands in supplicatory prayer. In response, the hand of God emerges from the cloud of heaven and touches him reassuringly on the side of his face. In the tiny red caption the illuminator identifies himself: *w. de brail' qui me depeint*.[51]

fig.46
fig.1
plate 1

At this point in the devotional day Susanna's attention is directed to supplicatory prayer once again – the final act of each of these hours services. And as she prays, she is reminded of William de Brailes, who designed and painted this book. It seems that with this small image he looks for her intercession. Like a scribe's colophon which asks for the remembrance of those who read his work, de Brailes reminds us through his painting, his self-portrait and his signature. Like Giselbertus who prominently signed his sculptured tympanum at Autun, or like Sir Christopher Wren at St Paul's, the work is his memorial.[52]

(*Opposite*) 46. f.42ᵛ–43 Terce of the Virgin, Capitulum, Prayer. This opening at the end of Terce sees the destruction of the charter, burnt on a fire with two contrasted birds in the extensions to the initials. The caption reads, *theofle la art*. Facing this image, in a small scale initial, only 2 lines in height, is the supplicatory *w. de brail' qui me depeint*, with the hand of God reaching down to touch him beneath the chin. This image interrupts the Theophilus tale, and illustrates the personal supplication of the prayer, 'Grant us, thy servant'.

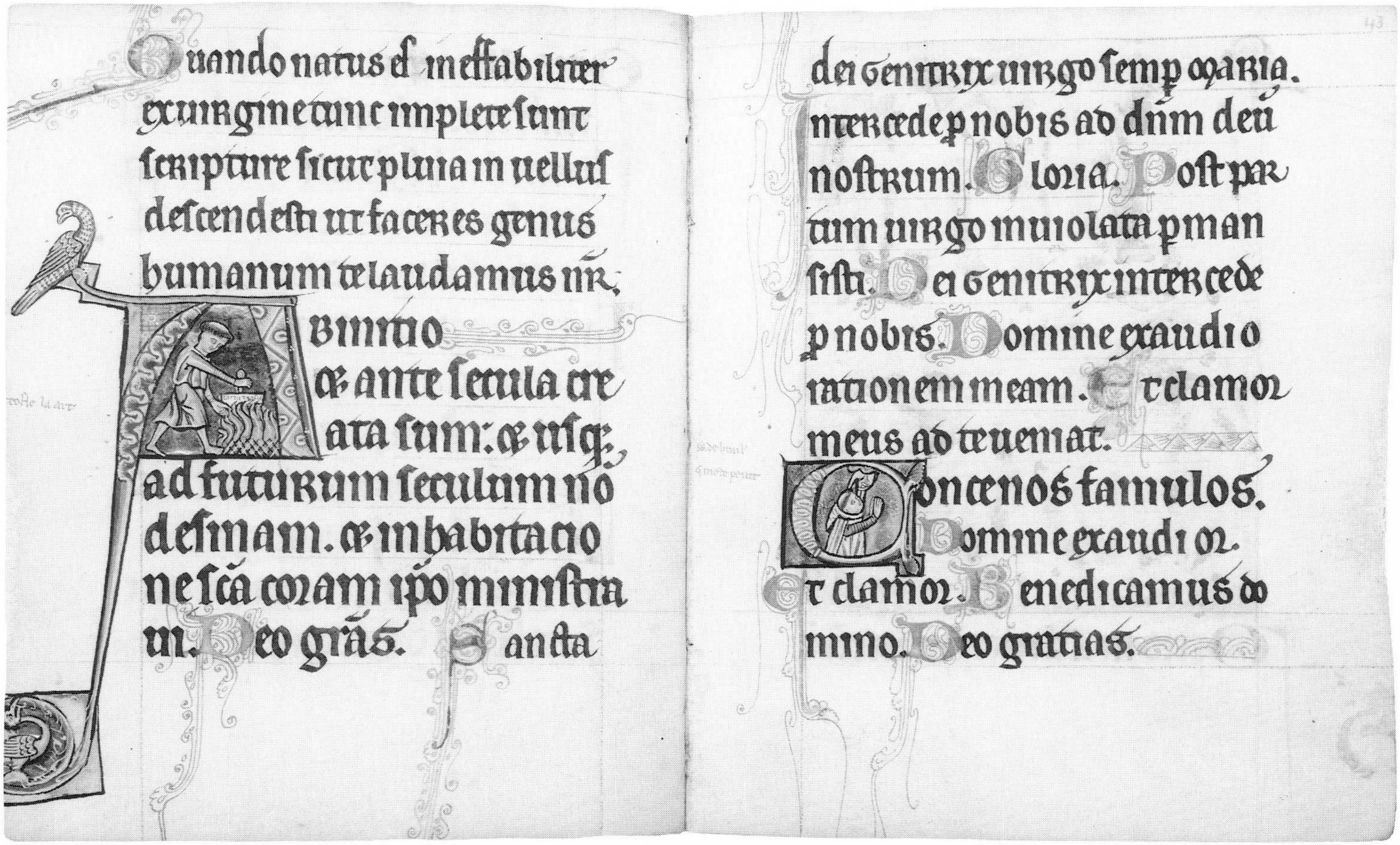
Quando natus est ineffabiliter
ex virgine tunc implete sunt
scripture sicut pluvia in vellus
descendisti ut faceres genus
humanum te laudamus deus noster.
Ab initio
et ante secula cre
ata sum: et usque
ad futurum seculum non
desinam. et in habitatio
ne sancta coram ipso ministra
vi. Deo gratias. Sancta

43
dei genitrix virgo semper Maria.
Intercede pro nobis ad dominum deum
nostrum. Gloria. Post par
tum virgo inviolata perman
sisti. Dei genitrix intercede
pro nobis. Domine exaudi o
rationem meam. Et clamor
meus ad te veniat.
Concede nos famulos.
Domine exaudi or.
Et clamor. Benedicamus do
mino. Deo gratias.

47. f.43ᵛ Sext of the Virgin, Full page miniature. Sext begins with four incidents of the Way of the Cross. The legend of the Wandering Jew, who was doomed to wander until Christ's second coming, is described in the caption, the beginning of which has been trimmed, ...*regarde e dit e tu remeines ici desque ieo reveine*. The start of the caption, by analogy with Prime, might have begun, *a sext*. The story continues with the carrying of the cross, the disrobing of Christ and Christ's isolation before the cross, awaiting crucifixion.

Sext

Returning to her devotions at the hour of Sext, at about three o'clock in the afternoon, Susanna's book opens at a grand double page spread, with a full-page miniature facing the beginning of the text. With this miniature, Susanna resumes her meditation on the Passion. At Sext, she retraces the journey from judgement to Calvary, finally to share in Christ's isolation before the Crucifixion.

Yet the first episode of this journey is no gospel theme. It tells the story of a Jew, one of the crowd who had pressed about the condemned figure of Christ, and had struck him as he left the presence of Pilate. This Jew wears the white cowled robe of a venerable and honoured Jewish priest, as it was worn by Annas the judge (at Prime on f.32). The Jew raises that terrible forefinger of accusation as Christ stops and turns back to him. Enough of the caption remains to interpret the scene: *.. regard et dit e tu remeines ices desque ieo reveine*: Christ's words have doomed the Jew to wander the earth until the Second Coming.[53]

This, the legend of the Wandering Jew, had been told to the monks of St Alban's in 1228 by a visiting Armenian bishop. It was re-told at St Alban's in

fig.47

plate 8
fig.48

fig.37

48. f.43ᵛ Sext of the Virgin, Miniature, single medallion. The Wandering Jew wears the robe of the High Priest, and his forefinger is raised to challenge Christ. Christ stands tall and turns back to him. His gesture is less emphatic, but it is a gesture of total certainty.

the *Flores Historiarum* of Roger of Wendover, which was written no later than 1236.[54] When Matthew Paris came to write his illustrated chronicle (the *Chronica Maiora*) of St Albans, between 1240 and 1253, he incorporated Roger of Wendover's material as well as the latest up-to-date information, telling the legend again, together with a marginal drawing of the Jew confronting Christ carrying the Cross.[55] To the Armenian bishop, and perhaps to the monks of St Alban's and their chroniclers, it was a contemporary event that they were recording: the telling of a tale by an honoured visitor.

William's use of this episode as part of the Passion meditation is very different. Here, placing the Wandering Jew back at his origins as if he were part of the gospel accounts, the legend links the historical events of the Passion, and particularly the ill-usage and abuse of Christ by his people the Jews, with contemporary life in thirteenth-century England. While a part of the meditation at Sext on the story of the Passion of Christ, it has relevance too in the contemporary manifestation of that Jew still wandering: a warning that any Jew might be just that Jew.

The journey to Calvary, according to the gospel accounts, has Christ bearing his own cross. The second episode of the meditation at Sext shows it lain on his shoulders as he strides firmly forward. Pushed from behind by a still mocking persecutor, he is helped forward by a figure who takes up the cross, looking up into Christ's face. This figure, Simon of Cyrene, is named in three of the four gospels. They tell how he was pulled out of the crowd of onlookers to help Christ take the weight of the cross.[56] The importance of Simon was more than as just part of the narrative. His appearance is a reminder of the role of the worshipper as sharing in the Passion of Christ: the Christian duty to help with Christ's burden. This burden can be shared by all Christian penitents: an act of charity here personified by Simon.[57]

fig. 47

Arriving at Golgotha, the meditation moves through the moments of preparation for crucifixion. The public removal of Christ's garments, as described in the caption: *il departent sa robe*, has his red tunic held to the left, while the blue robe that was restored to him after the Judgement by Pilate is pulled from his outstretched arms by a figure on the right. And finally, the cross erected behind him, Christ stands dressed in a skimpy white tunic, with only two persecutors who hold in readiness the hammer and the nails. In each one of these scenes, he is isolated from his followers. Only the charity of Simon of Cyrene offers any mitigation of this solitary journey.

Returning to the hours, the story of Theophilus resumes accompanying Psalm 122, **Ad te levavi**, 'To thee have I lifted up my eyes; who dwellest in heaven'. This is an image of the fulfilment of trust. It affirms the constancy of the devotion of Theophilus to the Virgin, and it confirms the power of her intercession to save souls, even those for whom a battle with the devil was required. Theophilus is dead, but his soul is secure, with the Virgin standing

plate 9   by to wrap it in her arms. Raising up her eyes, she lifts him to the hand of
God: 'who dwellest in heaven'. To the eyes of Susanna, the putting aside of
such a binding legal charter as that entered into by Theophilus would have
constituted a miracle indeed: a salvation only possible through the intercession of the Virgin. The moral of the Theophilus tale is an encouraging one:
the power of trust in the Virgin to save man from even the bleakest of
situations.

Trust, particularly trust in the face of adversity, is the theme of the nine
psalms of Terce, Sext and None. These, Psalms 119–127, begin the Gradual
Psalms series.[58] In the second psalm of Sext, Psalm 123, Nisi quia Dominus,
this theme is expressed in verses 5 and 6: 'Our soul hath passed through a
torrent: perhaps our soul had passed through a water insupportable. Blessed
be the Lord, who hath not given us to be a prey to their teeth.' Like the tale of
Theophilus, the story told in the following thirteen historiated initials is
miraculous, an equally impressive testament to the value of trust in devotion
to the Virgin.

fig.49   It is a poor priest who is the hero of this next story. He is no grandly-named
Theophilus, who fell victim to ambition. Indeed, it is the priest's ignorance
that is his downfall. The caption to the first episode, introducing Psalm 123,

(*Left*) 50. f.45ᵛ Sext of the Virgin, Psalm 124.
With the third psalm the priest is deprived of his office by the archbishop, Thomas Becket, as described in this caption, *sein tomas le erceveske le suspendi*.

(*Opposite*) 51. f.46ᵛ–47 Sext of the Virgin, Capitulum, Prayer
The historiated initial to the capitulum shows the priest begging Thomas to reinstate him. He kneels with his hands raised high above his head. But Thomas cannot help, and gestures with his open palm over the bar of the initial, *ne poet aver reles*. Facing this image of supplication is another. Illustrating the incipit to the prayer, is *w de brail'* again, kneeling with his hands raised in supplication, a gesture echoing that of the priest.

says this clearly: *un prestre chanta de notre dame e ne saveit neet plus*.[59] The priest is shown properly vested in alb and chasuble, devoutly kneeling and intoning the familiar words of the Mass of the Virgin: SALVE SANCTA PARENS, written neatly in liturgical script on a scroll next to his mouth. But he did need to know more. Since 1215 and the resolutions of the Lateran Council, the ignorant priesthood was under attack – the attack of education – led by reforming bishops.[60] No such ignorance as this could be tolerated in Lincoln diocese, under the care of a bishop like Robert Grosseteste. William de Brailes, of Oxford in the diocese of Lincoln, would have been well aware of the requirements, both to teach the faith and to perform the essential liturgical functions of the priesthood. This included a great deal more than the ability to chant just one mass.[61]

The consequences of failure for this poor unnamed priest, are revealed in the next caption: *sein tomas le erceveske le suspendi*. Not just any bishop visits, but St Thomas Becket, whose shrine in Canterbury was the most important in England, and whose cult was still developing.[62] Becket, wearing his mitre, is grandly arrayed in an elegant blue scapular, covering a white alb decorated with a red and white spotted border. Solemnly he holds out his archiepiscopal cross. Vested in all this pomp and authority, he stands tall over the poor

fig.50

Deus in adiutorium meū.

52. f.47ᵛ None of the Virgin, Full page. Facing the opening of None of the Virgin is the climax of the Passion story – the Crucifixion itself. Three separate aspects of the story are identified. The carefully balanced narrative above fills the space of two medallions, and the caption now reads *len le crucifia*, although the trimmed off opening perhaps identified the canonical hour – *a none*, with the crucified Christ balanced by two figures attending to him, the one who offers him the sponge of gall described *le lui offre buerre*. The good and bad thieves hang on either side, and two groups of onlookers, apparently the believers and non-believers, extend into the distance. Below, the medallion in which the Virgin is entrusted to the care of St John, is paired with the conversion of Longinus and a standing figure, who also affirms his faith.

priest, and suspends him from office. The words of Psalm 124, Qui confidunt, 'They that trust in the Lord shall be as Mount Sion', would have provided some necessary comfort at this moment of disgrace.

fig.51

The priest returns to St Thomas in the initial to the capitulum, Et sic in Syon, this time kneeling before him to beg for reinstatement. But in vain. *Ne poet aver reles* is the verdict of St Thomas.

At the end of the hour of Sext, as at Terce, supplication is the theme: this priest is surely in need of prayer. But William de Brailes interrupts the narrative here to insert his own image once again, interposing himself as the suppliant. As at the end of Terce, he depicts himself as all prayer: hands raised high to God. Yet in this image, accompanied by the simple signature *w de brail'*, there is no comforting hand of God to reach down to him.

None

With the late afternoon comes the hour of None. And at None, as we are told in St Edmund of Abingdon's meditations, Christ died on the Cross.[63] It is the central moment in the story of the Passion. It represents the central tenet of Christian belief and the meditative theme at this moment is complex. Opening her book of hours at None, Susanna was conducted through this meditation by the imagery of the Crucifixion. In contrast to the devotional image

fig.33

accompanying the suffrage to the cross on f.27v – an image evoking the 'sign' of the cross – the Crucifixion here is narrative, devotional and meditative, and its complexity is shown in three separate images.

fig.52
plate 10

Like a panorama of Golgotha, the narrative theme spreads across the whole top half of the page and, in contrast to his isolation during the episodes at Sext, Christ is now the centre of much activity. Simply described in the caption: *len le crucifia*, Christ is raised high on the cross while his feet are nailed together, crossing over one another and lending his body a twist that is almost graceful. He is offered a sponge on the end of a long stick by a figure with an upturned face of evil countenance, again described: *le lui offre beurre*. On either side hang the thieves; loosely hanging indeed, suspended from their crosses by their elbows, their arms threaded through large holes in the horizontal cross bars, their feet dangling free: a murderously effective version of the stocks. The thief crucified on the right of Christ, young and beardless, turns his face towards him, as described by St Luke with the words: 'Lord, remember me when thou shalt come into thy kingdom'. He on Christ's left, grizzled with sin, turns his face away.[64]

The cross of Christ extends through the frame of the miniature and is partly cut off by the trimmed page. So too is the title, but enough remains to show that it read: HIC EST JESUS NAZAREN REX IUDEORUM. In the gospel accounts this title is said to have been written in Greek, Latin and Hebrew, so that all the world could understand. In William's image the statement is clear. Unlike the common abbreviation of this title: 'INRI', it is written in full as a 'formal' statement in Latin and in a Gothic liturgical hand. This inscription, written by Pilate, is seen as a testament to Pilate's own belief in Christ where, following the text of St John's gospel, he answers the chief priests of the Jews with 'What I have written I have written'.[65] And leading the group of onlookers on Christ's right is the Centurion, his forefinger raised; not here the terrible forefinger of accusation, but an equally emphatic one of affirmation: 'Now the Centurion, seeing what was done, glorified God, saying: Indeed this was a just man.'[66] Meanwhile the group on the left of Christ remain unmoved. Headed by a well-dressed figure, they look on passively.

With the raising of the cross of Christ, the questions of belief that surround this most important of moments are raised also. The conversion and the affirmation of belief of the figures on Christ's right, the malice and the rejection of Christ's sacrifice by the unthinking onlookers on his left spell out the choices for the faithful Christian.

No doubts are raised in the medallions below. Secure devotional imagery, the imagery of affirmation, underpin the narrative. Christ's mother Mary raises her hand, accepting rather than mourning here, and accepting the care of St John, as described: 'When Jesus therefore had seen his mother and the disciple standing, whom he loved, he saith to his mother: Woman, behold

53. f.49 None of the Virgin, Psalm 126.
Following the first psalm of None, illustrated by another rejection of the priest's cause, the next historiated initial reveals how the devotion to the Virgin of Thomas himself was rewarded by her gift to him of a hair-shirt to be worn in secret, as told in the caption, *nr dame vest un here a sceint thomas*.

thy son. After that he saith to the disciple: Behold thy mother'.[67] Christ's head is bowed and his eyes closed in the last of these three images. It is entirely a statement of faith: the soldier's spear revealing the blood and water of Christ's side: 'But one of the soldiers with a spear opened his side; and immediately there came out blood and water'.[68] The Centurion appears again here, bareheaded now in a simple tunic, but his forefinger does not waver. 'And he that saw it hath given testimony; and his testimony is true. And he knoweth that he saith true; that you also may believe.' Through these three images, the narrative and the devotional, Susanna's faith is affirmed. Like the Centurion, she too had seen it and believed.

plate 11

With her faith confirmed in this opening meditation at None, she may turn to the text and the continuing saga of the ignorant priest. The next three psalms continue the sequence of Gradual Psalms. With In convertendo, Psalm 125, the poor priest tries yet again to urge his case with St Thomas. The bishop is unflinching – a rule is a rule, and the priest must know his masses. But St Thomas too has need of penance and, in the initial to Psalm 126, Nisi Dominus, the Virgin helps him into a huge hair-shirt. This image bears witness to his private and hidden holiness, and to his special favour with the Virgin. Described in the caption, *nr dame vest un here a sceint tomas*, he kneels, small in scale himself now and without the vestments of power, to receive the gift of penance from the Virgin herself.

fig.53

Illustrating Psalm 127, Beati omnes, 'Blessed are all they that fear the Lord:' the priest takes to the water in his despair, rowed by a solitary oarsman in a boat with a dragon's head prow. Perhaps his goal is the education that would earn him his priesthood again, best found overseas in the schools of Paris. Maybe he just follows the journeys of St Thomas, himself constantly crossing

fig.54

54. f.49ᵛ None of the Virgin, Psalm 127.
Seeking release from his ban, the priest travels overseas. *[il pa]se mer [pur aver r]eles*. He is seated low in the dragon-prowed boat, and looks anxiously up to the oarsman, who fights with the swell.

55. f.50ᵛ None of the Virgin, Capitulum.
Arriving, the priest again kneels before St Thomas. But, despite his devotion to his office, he can make no further claim, and St Thomas again rejects his request, *ne pet aver reles*.

the Channel. Yet it is certain that Thomas cannot get rid of him: a pesky and persistent priest indeed. Once again, illustrating the capitulum, Et radicavi, the priest is there, kneeling before him, and again *ne pet aver reles*.   fig.55

This capitulum finishes imperfectly, as a pair of folios have been cut out of the manuscript here, and the prayer that should follow, Concede nos, is entirely missing. Judging by the way this narrative is told, there is no missing episode here, as it continues on in the illustrations to Vespers without an apparent break. The image accompanying the prayer would have been, following precedent, another self-portrait of William de Brailes. Alternatively it may have been here that a portrait of the patron herself was first introduced. It might even have had a caption, revealing her name.

Whatever illustration has been lost, it is plain that the narrative sequence of the priest was interrupted. This pause must again have provided the interval needed for some moments of private intercessionary prayer.

Vespers

Gathering around the hour of Vespers, the evening of the devotional day, was a cluster of rites. Extra prayers, the recitation of the psalm sequences, and in particular Vespers of the Office of the Dead, would have made this a time of prolonged kneeling for the devout lady. She would have needed an extra volume too as, in this first book of hours, the Office of the Dead was not included.[69]

There can be no doubt that the first part of the rite at Vespers would have been a meditation on the Passion of Christ, like each of the other hours. But this first page of Vespers has been cut out, and the exact course of the Passion meditation set out for Susanna remains uncertain. As it was told in the gospel, on the evening of the day of the Passion it was necessary to hasten the removal of the body of Christ, before the start of the sabbath.[70] As it was set out by St Edmund of Abingdon, the theme for meditation at Vespers was similar; that Christ was taken down from the cross.[71] The role of Joseph of Arimathea, of Nicodemus, and of the mourning women anointing the body of Christ – all central to this narrative – would have been shown. Yet it would have been in the design, the style and the gesture of William de Brailes's figures that the focus of the meditation at Vespers was developed. To cut out this page was to cut out not just pictures and decoration but the entire devotional rite of the Passion at Vespers.

The text for Vespers of the Virgin has lost only the opening versicle and response. With the historiated initial for the first psalm, Psalm 121, **Letatus sum**, the tale of the priest is taken up again. It resumes with a revelation. His devotion to the Virgin is evident in his ability to manage only the mass dedicated to her. Now this devotion is rewarded, and she appears before him as he prays. The token of her care for him is there in that appearance; a token of special favour that must surely impress even St Thomas enough for the priest to earn his right to reinstatement. With her appearance, she provides her favoured priest with proof of her visitation. According to the caption she

fig.56

56. f.53 Vespers of the Virgin, Psalm 121.
Now, with the first psalm of Vespers, 'I rejoiced at the things that were said to me', the Virgin appears to the priest. He kneels, cut off by the horizontal bar of the 'L' on which the Virgin herself stands, tall and commanding as she speaks St Thomas's secret. The caption survives in full, *nr dame aparut au prestre lu dit quil aut a scein tomas a scele enseine que lu vesti une here*. With this revelation she gives the priest the proof he needs to establish his claim for reinstatement, and reason enough to rejoice.

reveals to him the secret of St Thomas and his hair-shirt: *notre dame aparut au prestre lu dit quil aut a scein tomas a scele enseine que lu vesti une here.*

With this, the means to prove his special stature to St Thomas, the priest again chases after the bishop. Illustrating Psalm 122, **Ad te levavi**, he crosses the sea again: *il pase*, in the same little boat, oarsman battling with a heavy swell, the sail flapping loosely. fig.57

The battle was worthwhile. Triumphant now, the priest stands tall in his next encounter with St Thomas. Illustrating Psalm 123, **Nisi dominus**, the priest's victory must be assured: 'If it had not been that the Lord was with us, when men rose up against us; perhaps they had swallowed us up alive: when their fury was enkindled against us; perhaps the waters had swallowed us up.' Where the priest was short before, constantly on his knees, now he stands tall, his forefinger assertively raised before the bishop's face to disclose his secret: *le prestre dit les ensenes a scein tomas*. He gives not just a verbal account. From his other hand rises a scroll containing the all-important written verification of his revelation. St Thomas is convinced. Such a clear sign of favour cannot be denied, and the priest's determination and faith must be rewarded. fig.58

In illustration to Psalm 124, **Qui confidunt**, 'They that trust in the Lord shall be as Mount Sion', his stature overtops St Thomas, who now kneels before the priest, begging forgiveness as the hand of God reaches down in fig.59

57. f.54 Vespers of the Virgin, Psalm 122. Full of secret knowledge the priest again crosses the sea, *il pase*. In illustration of the second psalm of Vespers, his eyes are lifted 'unto the Lord our God, until he have mercy on us'.

58. f.54ᵛ Vespers of the Virgin, Psalm 123. Standing tall the priest declares his knowledge of St Thomas's secret, who listens intently gesturing acknowledgement of the truth, *le prestre dit les ensenes a scein tomas.*

blessing. The priest is released from his ban at last, and may again be a priest as before.

The last of these psalms at Vespers, Psalm 125, In convertendo, 'Then was our mouth filled with gladness and our tongue with joy', shows the priest's joy in the elevation of the Host – although, according to the caption, it was still only the Mass of the Virgin that he celebrates: *le prestre rechante de notre dame.*[72] Such is the power of the devotion to the Virgin. She cannot ensure his better education or enable him to know all the masses. But not even St Thomas can deny his worthiness, with such proof of his special favour in the eyes of the Virgin.

Proof once more is provided by the next image, accompanying the capitulum, Beata es Maria. Just as the soul of Theophilus reached heaven by the power of the Virgin, so too the soul of this poor priest achieves eternal bliss. She stands by his dead body and, taking the small naked figure of his soul in her hands, she lifts him directly up to the hand of God.

No supplicatory prayer follows the capitulum at Vespers. But the service is completed with the immensely popular hymn in praise of the Virgin, Ave maris stella.[73] Three clerics sing. An image frequently used in the illustration of the psalter to accompany the psalm, Cantate domine, shows three monks

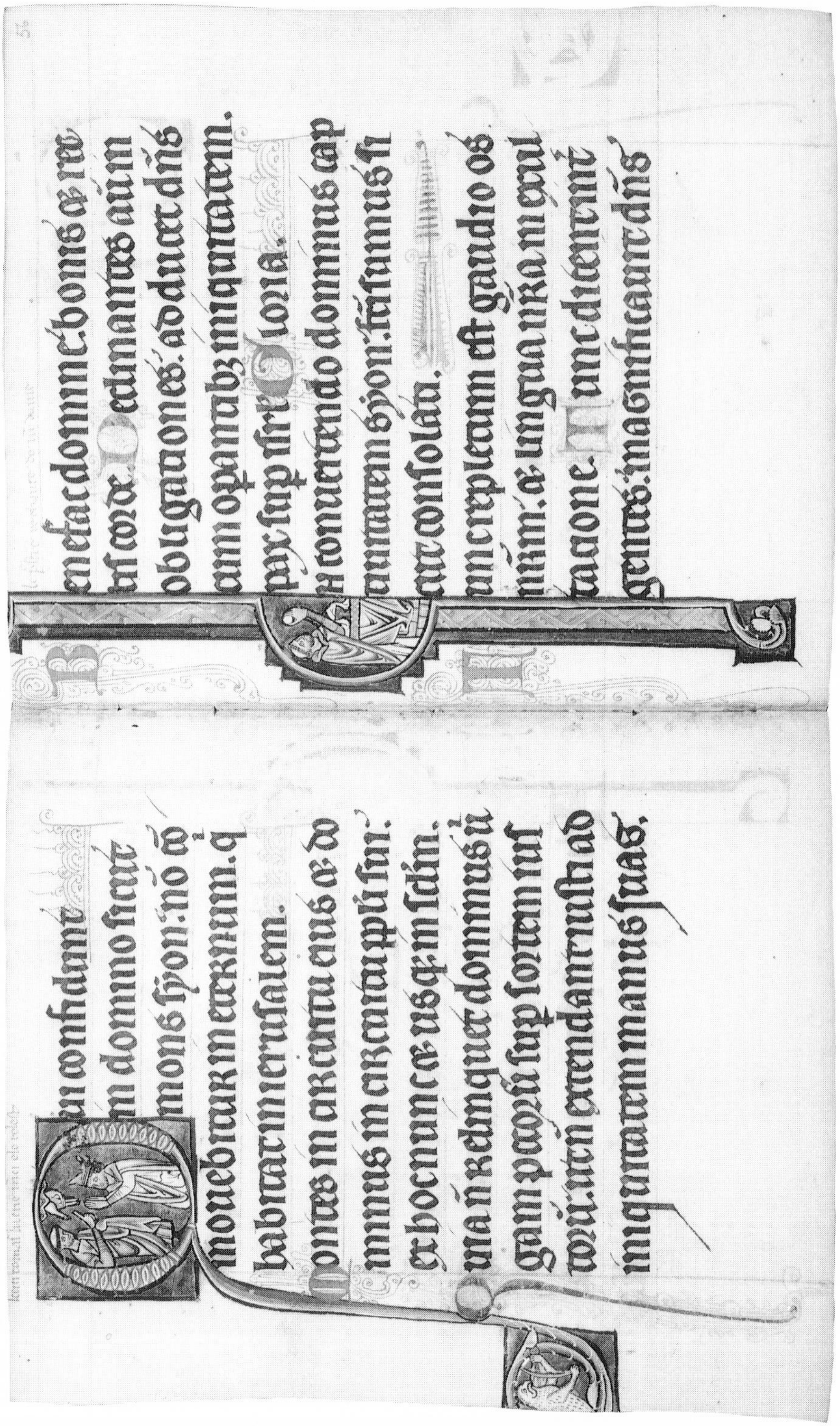

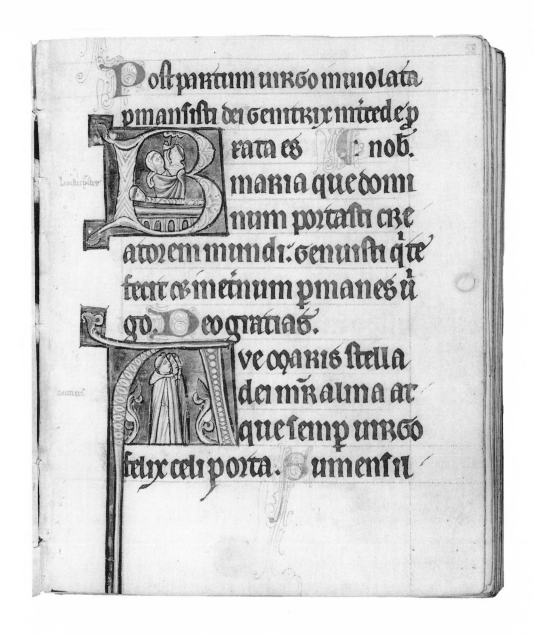

(*Opposite*) 59. ff.55ᵛ–56 Vespers of the Virgin, Psalms 124–5. This opening, of the last two psalms of Vespers, shows the priest now fully in command. St Thomas kneels in apology, *scein tomas lu crie merci e le relest*, his apology accepted by the hand of God. Once again the priest celebrates Mass, elevating the Host in praise, despite the caption which affirms he still offers only the Mass of the Virgin, *le prestre rechante de nr dame*.

(*Above*) 60. f.58 Vespers of the Virgin, Capitulum, Hymn. With the capitulum of Vespers the soul of the priest is raised up from his death bed by the Virgin to a hand from heaven which firmly grasps him. Like Theophilus, this security comes from devotion to Mary. Below, singing a hymn to her praise, 'Hail, star of the sea,' three clerics sing, as described, *cantaurs*.

singing in just this way.[74] The colourful assortment of their garments here – a figure in white with a pink hooded mantle stands in front of one in blue and a third in bright pink – does not argue for a solemn liturgical ceremonial, nor does it suggest that these singers belong to any particular religious order. But, like William de Brailes in his self-portraits, they do wear the tonsure. Evidently they are clerks, or *clerici*.

The identification of the term *clericus* with *litteratus*, in contrast to the identification of *laicus* with *illiteratus*, was commonplace by the mid-twelfth century, persisting through the thirteenth.[75] Matthew Paris describes Paulin Peyver, who died in 1251, as '*miles litteratus sive clericus militaris*': a 'knightly clerk' indeed, literate and even learned but, with a wife and children confirming that he had no pretensions to the status of cleric, one of the clergy.[76] A sure sign of a *clericus* is his tonsure, and maybe it is simply in that sense, as the sign of literacy, that these three singers wear their tonsures. In that sense too, William de Brailes, a married professional illuminator, wears his: a sign of distinction, like the bald pate of a professor of today.

The three clerks here sing the Ave Maris Stella, a hymn full of evocative imagery of Mary's special role to guide the faithful safely to heaven. Coming   fig.61
here, at the end of the two narratives that demonstrated her power to save both Theophilus and the nameless priest, their song was one of praise and thanksgiving. Furthermore, their appearance here serves as punctuation, marking the end of the miracle legends, returning the narrative to the life of the Virgin.

61. f.58 Vespers of the Virgin, Hymn.
The three in multi-coloured habits wear their tonsures as signs of literacy and clerical status.

fig.62

fig.21

62. f.59 Vespers of the Virgin, Canticle.
With the Magnificat, the death of Mary is announced by the Angel's emphatic gesture across the vertical of the 'M', holding aloft the palm of death. The caption survives in full, *quant nr dame deveit deuier le aungle deu lui nuncia.*

The hour of Vespers ends with words spoken by the Virgin herself. The familiar canticle, the Magnificat, is an exultant hymn of praise, 'My soul doth magnify the Lord, and my spirit doth rejoice in God my saviour', the words of the Virgin spoken at her meeting with her cousin Elizabeth.[77] Her faith in her own salvation is affirmed: 'Because he has regarded the humility of his handmaid; for, behold, from henceforth all generations shall call me blessed'. The image here begins the narrative of the end of her life. Once again she is greeted by the angel.[78] William uses the initial 'M' to create a double-celled room, just as he had used the vertical bar of the 'T' for the Annunciation on f.11. The angel's long wings wrap around the initial frame as, carrying the palm heralding her death in one hand, he greets the Virgin. His gesture now is emphatic and unequivocal reaching across the barrier to poke the tip of his forefinger into the cell where the Virgin stands clutching her book and gesturing her acquiescence. The greeting is the news of her approaching death.

The joyful words of the Magnificat continue: 'Because he that is mighty hath done great things to me: and holy is his name. And his mercy is from generation unto generations, to them that fear him'. For the Virgin, just as for Theophilus and the ignorant and humble priest, death is the way to heaven. And after this, at the end of Vespers of the Virgin, Susanna would turn to her Office of the Dead.[79]

Compline

With Compline, the final rite of the devotional day, Susanna could take her lamp and go to bed. She would end her day with prayers in her chamber, just as she had begun it there with Matins.[80] Night-time prayer would have begun with the final meditation on the day of the Passion, conducted through the imagery of William de Brailes. But, just as at the opening of Vespers, this miniature page has been cut out. Nevertheless, the meditation can be reconstructed. Meditation at Compline would have been on the final events of the Passion, the anointing of the body of Christ and the Entombment within the sealed doors of Joseph of Arimathea's tomb. Certainly they would have centred on the events of the Entombment, just as Vespers centred on the Deposition.[81]

Yet to link the Entombment of the body of Christ with prayer at night was to evoke the fear of death. A constant theme of night-time prayer is for the granting of a good death if, by any chance (and such a chance was always in mind), the hour of death was to come during the darkness. The means by which such meditation was depicted by William de Brailes can only be imagined. Yet the theme of death continues into the illustration of the historiated initials.

This theme starts with the final initial of Vespers, illustrating the Magnificat, which had announced the Death of the Virgin. Just as at Matins the Annunciation scene in its final initial represents an iconographic introduction to the story which was to be told in the initials at Lauds, so here too the angel, who appears to the Virgin at the end of Vespers, is the herald of the legends of her death, to be told in the initials of Compline. Again an angelic announcement moulds the break between the Hours, and again it implies the short interval that elapsed between the hours of Vespers and Compline.[82]

fig.62

fig.21

Turning from the meditation based on the Entombment, Compline of the Virgin opens with Psalm 12, Usquequo domine, 'How long, O lord, wilt thou forget me unto the end? How long dost thou turn away thy face from me?'. The caption: *les apostles saluent nr dame*, describes the scene. Miraculously summoned and brought from every part of the world where they had been preaching the message of conversion to Christianity, the apostles gather to honour the Virgin. They confirm that she was not 'forgot unto the end'. Seated, almost enthroned, she accepts their greeting, all thirteen of them, including St Paul, reminiscent of her role as 'Ecclesia', symbol of the Church.[83] Certainly she is honoured here as the Mother of the Church, the Church which was being established by the missionary travels of the apostles. It is a celebratory psalm which it illustrates. Starting with that cry of tribulation, 'How long wilt thou forget me?', it ends in joy: 'My

fig.63

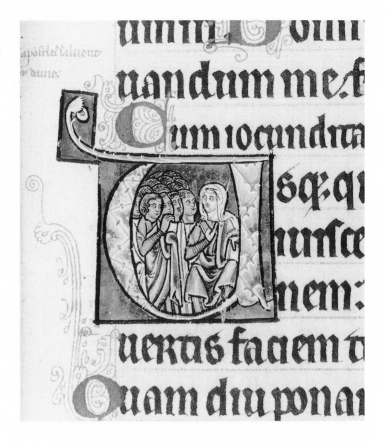

63. f.60 Compline of the Virgin, Psalm 12.
The opening full page illustration to Compline of the Virgin has been removed. Now the illustration of Compline opens with the assembly of the apostles, summoned from the whole world to honour her before her death, *les apostles saluent nr dame.*

heart shall rejoice in thy salvation: I will sing to the Lord, who giveth me good things'.

With the next psalm, Judica me, Psalm 42, the story of the Death, Assumption, and Burial of the Virgin unfolds in a sequence of six episodes, in a rich and elaborate page design, placed so as to make the story plain. Up the vertical border to the left of the text the Virgin rises to heaven while, travelling along the lower border, her body is borne in procession to her tomb. At the axis of these two narratives the Virgin lies on her death bed.

plate 5

Three attendants watch over her. Her eyes are closed, and she has come to the end of her journey. Standing tall is a white-habited figure, extending a lily in his hand, witness to her eternal purity.[84] Upwards, her soul is borne to heaven in the enclosing arms of an angel. Her head is veiled, but otherwise only her praying hands, palms extended in the *orans* gesture, cover her small naked body. Once in heaven however, she is full-sized and richly robed, and is enthroned on the right hand of Christ, who reaches up to place the crown on her head.[85] In this small medallion, the bodily presence of the Virgin in heaven is made plain.

fig.64

On earth, beneath the text, two of the apostles, dressed identically, carry

97

64. f.61 Compline of the Virgin, Psalm 42. The full story of her death and assumption fills the margin of the page but here, in the half-medallion at the top, is the last episode in the story, her coronation by Christ, her hands extended in acceptance. As the caption makes clear, it was through her bodily assumption that she was brought to heaven and her coronation, *ce est lasumption nr dame quant les apostles la porterent al val de iosefaz.*

her to the valley of Jehosophat, while disbelieving and mocking Jews disturb the procession. One of these, leaping and writhing, has his hands firmly stuck to the pall that covers the bier, to be released only by faith. Eventually the body of the Virgin is entombed, laid in a vaulted sarcophagus, and completely shrouded. Her body is attended by the same trio that watched over her deathbed, the tonsured figure now swinging a thurible of incense. His companions too have acquired haloes, their belief established by these events.

But the power of the Virgin does not end with her death and her enthronement in heaven. She leaves relics, and in the following four initials the power of the pall from her coffin is established, both for conversion and for cures. In an echo of the theme of Psalm 128, **Sepe expugnaverunt**, nine Jews are struck blind: 'The wicked have wrought upon my back: they have lengthened their iniquity. The Lord who is just will cut the necks of sinners: fig.65 let them all be confounded and turned back that hate Sion.' Crowded into the initial space, crushed together by the restraining horizontal of the 'S', their eyes are sightless, their expressions bewildered. As the caption explains: *le giues aveoglerent.*

The next psalm once again supplies a suitable text. Psalm 130, **Domine non est** ends with the verse: 'Let Israel hope in the Lord: from henceforth now and forever.' And in the historiated initial that begins it, one of the nine Jews, hoping in the Lord, cries for mercy from St Peter. The caption supplies fig.66 the detail: *un de giues crie merci a scein pere. sein pere lui demande si il creit en ihu, il dit*

65. f.61ᵛ Compline of the
Virgin, Psalm 128.
The Jews, disbelieving but
present at her burial
procession, are here struck
blind, as described in the
caption, *le giues aveoglerent.*

66. f.62ᵛ Compline of the
Virgin, Psalm 130.
One of the blinded here
begs St Peter to cure him.
With the pall from the
coffin of the Virgin and the
confession of faith from the
Jew, the cure is achieved.
The caption explains, *un de
giues crie merci a scien pere.
sein pere lui demande si il creit
en ihu, il dit oil. [sein] pere le
baut [du dra]p dunt le cors
[nr d]ame fu covert . . .d sas
ous veit.* It is the affirmation
of belief in Jesus that counts.

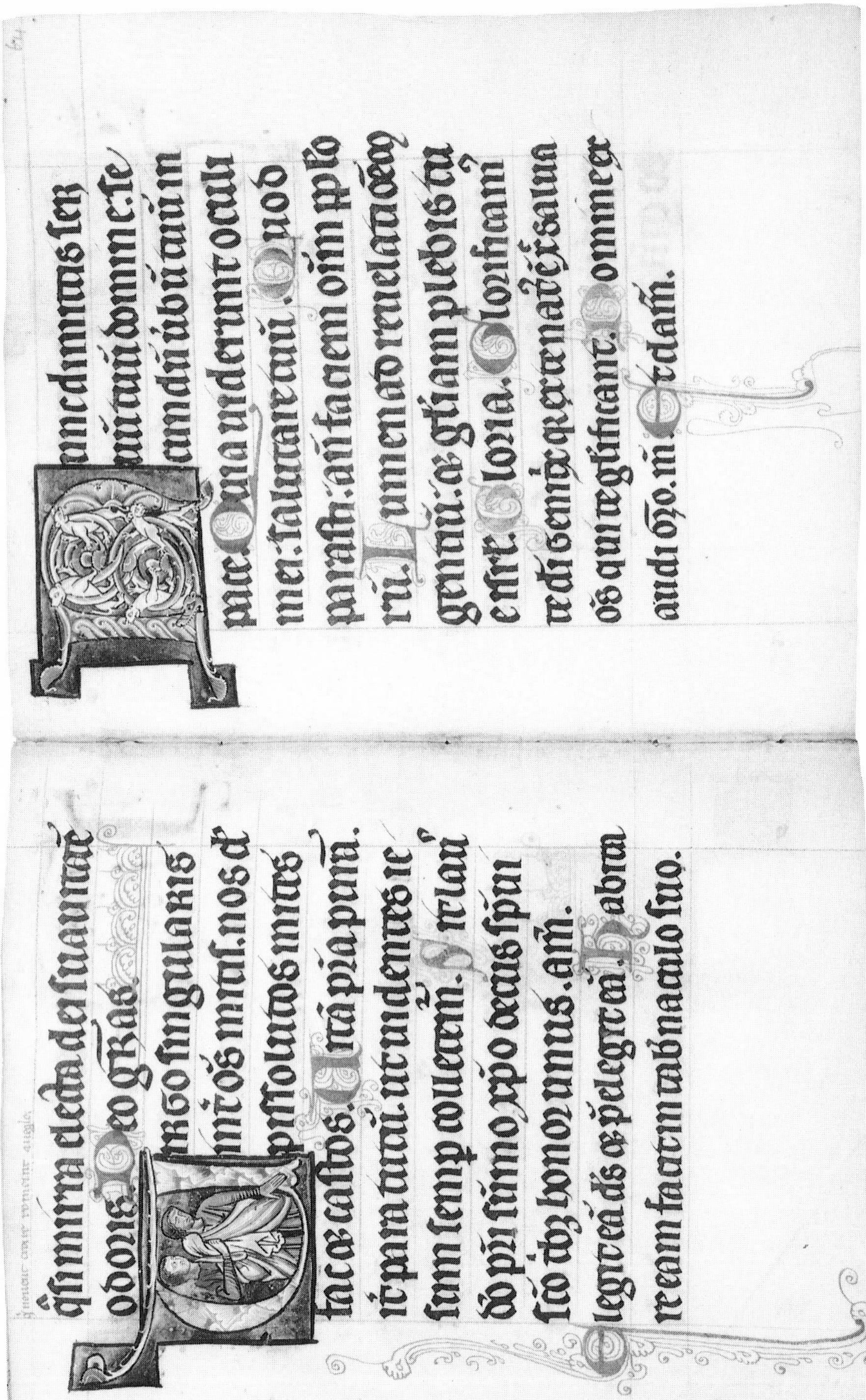

oil. sein pere le baut [du dra]p dunt le cors [nr d]ame fu covert ...d sas ous veit. His sight is seen to be restored, and with it the efficacy of the Virgin's pall is established. Yet, as the caption makes clear, the cure was the result of the declaration of faith that St Peter so firmly demanded. It is that declaration that is required. To be cured is the reward of faith, not simply the power of the cloth itself.

That this is so is fully demonstrated in the next two initials. The converted Jew successfully cures one of his compatriots by holding the pall to his eyes, illustrating the capitulum, **Sicut cynamomum**. But he fails with another. Steadfastly this stubborn Jew refuses to believe: *qui ne veut creire remeint avegle* and,

fig.67 despite the miraculous pall, remains blind. This last image begins the hymn, **Virgo singularis**: it is only through faith in the Virgin that such cures may be made.

This whole series of images is based on legend, though a legend that, by the thirteenth century, was seen to be as true as the gospels. These legends lent great support to the cult of the Virgin, and provided the foundation for the belief in the Assumption of the Virgin and the belief in her coronation in heaven. Finding their way into the iconography of the Virgin's life, they became (as here) visibly true.

However, there is nothing in the Gospels to underpin these legends. Mary disappeared from the Gospel accounts at the foot of the Cross, as she was given into the care of St John.[86] It was to Mary Magdalen and to the apostles that the gospels record Christ's visitations after the Resurrection: 'To whom (the apostles) also he shewed himself alive after his passion by many proofs, for forty days appearing to them and speaking of the Kingdom of God.'[87] Only once is the Virgin Mary mentioned again: 'All these were persevering with one mind in prayer, with the women and Mary the mother of Jesus.'[88] The continuance of Mary's story relies on these apocryphal legends, various and conflicting though they are.

From the second century onwards the legend developed, partly based on fragments of narrative, partly based on tradition. The legend that gained greatest popularity in the west was based on a Latin fragment, apparently written as an epistle from Melito, bishop of the church of Sardis, now known, cautiously, as the Pseudo-Melito.[89] It was the Pseudo-Melito version that William de Brailes followed most closely in his sequence of images.

The gathering of the apostles is an essential episode in this narrative, with an important role for St Paul. In this version of the legend, the key figure accompanying the Virgin is St John, summoned first to her side, and later

(*Opposite*) 67. ff.63ᵛ–64 Compline of the Virgin, Hymn, Canticle. Opening the **Virgo singularis** this statement of faith is seen to be essential. The cured Jew who cured his unbelieving Jew through establishing new faith (in the initial to the Capitulum, not illustrated) is shown now to fail, *qui ne veut creire remeint avegle*. On the facing page the **Nunc Dimittis** opens with a fine decorative initial of entangled lions.

given the task of carrying the palm before the bier. In Peter's words to John he also reminds him of his special position: 'Thou only of us art a virgin chosen of the Lord, and has found such favour that thou didst lie on his breast: and when he hung for our salvation on the tree of the cross committed her unto thee with his own mouth.'[90] That white-robed figure, attending her at her death and bearing the lily, is St John, dressed, so it seems, in the garb of a Cistercian, the white habit of purity. In the scenes that follow, William de Brailes spells out his interpretation of Mary's death. Just as the interpretation of the Immaculate Conception was essential to her position as Mother of God, so too the interpretation of the events of her death and assumption were needed to verify her theological position and her true existence in heaven, ever ready to supplicate for man and to plead for mercy at the Last Judgement.[91] Without doubt the image that de Brailes presents is of her assumption, as it is told in the caption: *ce est l'asumption nr dame quant les apostles porterent al val de iosefaz*. The achievement of the assumption is clear, leading to her coronation in heaven.

But the question of how her bodily presence in heaven was achieved is not resolved in this sequence.[92] However, its importance to the cult of the Virgin is attested by the long-established celebration of the feast of the Assumption of the Virgin on 15 August. It was obviously an essential, triumphal, end to the life of the Virgin, complete and in glory.

It was completed in glory in the sequence of events that was set out in the Pseudo-Melito text. Her soul was raised to heaven, passed into the arms of an angel by Christ himself. Three days later, her soul was re-united with her body, again on the orders of her son, and angels carried her to heaven, body and soul.[93] It is this, in essence, that is the tale depicted by William de Brailes, but the Assumption of that shrouded body is not shown. Mary's soul ascends, lifted by the angel. Then, without explanation, William simply depicts her in heaven in body also, crowned by Christ as the Queen of Heaven, the culmination of the narrative and a devotional image which was vital to establish her credentials.

Meanwhile her funeral procession continues. This procession carried her body to the tomb that had been set aside for her. From the seventh century, when this part of the cult of the Virgin was developing substance, an empty tomb in the valley of Jehosophat, outside Jerusalem, was identified as hers and became the focus of pilgrimage.[94]

The miracles associated with the disbelieving Jews are a vital part of the narrative of the Pseudo-Melito. The leaping, writhing figure of William's image is identified there as 'a prince of the priests of the Jews'. It was he who urged his companions to overthrow the bier, and: 'forthwith his hands dried up from his elbows and clave to the bier'. This Jew then debates with Peter, pleading for release, granted only when he makes a complete statement of

68. f.64 Compline of the Virgin,
Canticle.
Entwined and entangled lions.

faith in God, the Son of God, and the Virgin herself. Armed with this faith he may cure his companions who had been blinded by angels, only if they too proclaim the faith. They see and therefore they believe.

New believers multiply, and to see this story unfold in pictures with the passage of the evening prayer at Compline was to proclaim the truth of the legend. By the 1240s, when William de Brailes was devising his programme of illustration, the legend of the Death of the Virgin had become established.[95] In William's design, the sequence focuses on the essentials of the story, leading the eye upwards to heaven in praise, and following the course of the narrative as it unfolded on earth. He designs his sequence simply. Evidently the Virgin has power to save; evidently she is there in heaven.

The end of the devotional day has not quite come. But with the Nunc dimittis, the end of Compline is near: 'Now thou dost dismiss thy servant, O Lord, according to thy word in peace', the words of Simeon on receiving the infant Christ at the Presentation.[96] One of the very few decorative initials fig.68 in the manuscript opens this text. But it is a sprightly invention, with four little white lions cavorting among the foliage stems.[97]

And finally Susanna, surely the servant of the Virgin, goes in peace with a final prayer. In the historiated initial to the Graciam tuam a young woman kneels upright, her hands raised before her, her head thrown back, her gaze towards heaven. Her costly pink robe is covered by a scarlet cloak, with a neat white hat over her flowing brown hair. No caption remains to tell us her name, but she is surely the lady for whom William de Brailes created this book. She may also have been shown in the initials to the prayers at None and Vespers, before those pages were brutally cut out. Perhaps her portraits there had captions which identified her by name, like the first two images of William de Brailes himself. Maybe, like William's self-image at the end of Terce, she too once had the support of the hand of God. But not here. With this final supplication to the Virgin ending her devotional day, Susanna prays alone.

fig.6
plate 2

The Penitential Day

No devotional day can pass without penance. Sin is inescapable. To return to the all-important state of grace, penance – together with confession and contrition – is essential. The laity of the thirteenth century was, it seems, being told of these needs by everyone; by its parish priests, by the preaching of the new mendicants and by the bishops, all encouraged by the resolutions of the Lateran Council of 1215. Indeed, recently the spiritual welfare of the laity had developed new significance in the life of the Church. It was acknowledged that the laity, despite its freedom from any Rule, needed to be subject to the rules of the Church. The Church needed to ensure that Christian folk were kept within the structure of the parish and the diocese. The urgent task for the Church in the thirteenth century was to reinforce its role as all-important to everyone, and to organise and establish the laity within the body of the Church.[98]

Paradoxically it was sin that provided a framework of control for the clergy. Only through the offices of the Church, through the sacraments, could sinful man make his way to heaven. In the succeeding centuries, it was chiefly penance and that hope of salvation that maintained the fabric of the Church, both spiritually and materially. It was the penance of the laity which paid for the upkeep of the parish church, which erected chantry chapels, which donated the vestments and which paid the clergy through the commissioning of memorial masses.[99] Penance sent lay folk on pilgrimages, paying their way to salvation through alms to support the shrine of their destination, whether that of St Thomas Becket at Canterbury, St Edmund at Bury, or St Frideswide at Oxford.[100]

But confession to a priest was a rare event, even though the Lateran Council had prescribed that all laity should confess annually. The penance prescribed by the priest, and the consequent gift of absolution, was therefore a high-point, not a regular solution to daily sin. For everyday penance the key devotional text was the sequence of seven psalms extracted from the psalter, and believed to have been composed in response to King David's own needs for penance. These Penitential Psalms were said daily as part of the Divine Office by the monks, clerks and nuns who lived according to a Rule. For them, the focus on penance was part of the day's routine that would be fitted into the pattern of the Office, usually said after the Office at Prime.[101]

For the laity, the Penitential Psalms were an important remedy against the temptations of everyday life. While the work of God, the *Opus Dei*, of the religious communities required a constant routine of praise and worship, the devotion of the laity was altogether more pragmatic, searching for individual salvation and for a personal solution to sin. The daily recitation of these seven psalms went some way to providing this. The imagery of the Hours of the Virgin had already demonstrated the power of supplicatory prayer to the Virgin, through obtaining her personal intercession with God. To illustrate the power of penance in the Penitential Psalms, William turned to the model of King David himself, author of the psalms. Comfort lay in the manifestation of David in these historiated initials, as much tempted by sin and redeemed by penance as any thirteenth-century layperson.

Psalm 6, **Domine ne in furore**, starts the sequence: 'O Lord, rebuke me not in thy indignation, nor chastise me in thy wrath'. Grasped by a dragon's mouth, the initial encloses King David and Nathan the Prophet, and it is Nathan who rebukes David in his indignation, who chastises him in his wrath. Nathan's forefinger is raised in that gesture so characteristic of William de Brailes – the finger of accusation. David shifts uneasily on his throne, his head tilted up to Nathan, his sceptre propped on one knee, and his feet hanging slackly over the edge of the initial frame. Nathan wears a halo, David merely a crown. The whole top line of the page is taken up with the caption which sets the scene: *le prophete demaunde a davi un iugement de un riche hume qui aveit l. owales. un sen povre veisin n'aveit que une sule. le riche le ravi. queu jugement en serreit. dit davit meetre le vif en tere. dit le prophete vus l'estes.*[102] It is only a moral proposition that Nathan puts, but he draws David on to condemn himself. It was not a lamb that was stolen by David, but a woman: Bathsheba. Nathan reveals that he knows of David's sin. As the caption says, 'the prophet tells him, you are he'. These are the words of Nathan's bony forefinger.[103]

The Book of Kings relates the story of David sighting Bathsheba taking a bath, and then, having seduced her, ridding her of her husband, Urias the Hittite, through subterfuge.[104] But it is not William's aim to tell this part of the story. Penance, not sin, is his theme.

It is penance that illustrates Psalm 31, **Beati quorum**. David is buried up to his chest in the earth, fulfilling the punishment that, as the caption said, he himself prescribed for the sinner in Nathan's proposition: *meetre le vif en tere*. He reaches up in prayer to heaven and, in the words of the psalm, forgiveness is at hand: 'Blessed are they whose iniquities are forgiven: and whose sins are covered.' His sins indeed are buried, and Nathan's words to David in the Book of Kings: 'The Lord also hath taken away thy sin', echoes the theme of forgiveness.[105] But still he must pay. His son, Bathsheba's boy, will die. The

plate 12

fig. 12

plate 13

fig. 69

story is told in the Book of Kings. In penance he fasts and prays: 'and David kept a fast, and going in by himself lay upon the ground. And the ancients of his house came to make him rise from the ground: but he would not.' There he stayed until, on the seventh day, the child died. 'Then David arose from the ground, and washed and anointed himself ... went into the house of the Lord: and worshipped.'[106] The Lord had forgiven him and, as he is buried in the ground in William's image to Psalm 31, this forgiveness is made clear by an angel reaching down to him from Heaven. It is spelt out in the caption: *davi se mist en tere desque deu le repela*.

In the New College Psalter, William again shows David buried in the ground as a consequence of this same sin. The image illustrates Psalm 101, Domine exaudi, one of the liturgical divisions of the psalter, and fifth of the sequence of the Penitential Psalms.[107] Enthroned, and with his hand raised in blessing, the forgiving and merciful God overlooks all. David's temptation in spying Bathsheba bathing is shown here, as she sits and demurely dabbles her feet in a bath. David's accusation by Nathan is shown just as in the de Brailes Hours, and below is David, buried in the ground and reaching upwards to God in heaven in his penance.

fig.5

It seems that it is William's own invention to inflict this penitential burial on David. His real punishment is the death of his son. But, in his penance, the bible tells how David lay upon the ground, fasting, and no-one could raise him until after the boy's death. William's interpretation of these words was to envisage him not just lying on the earth but buried within it. Quoted as such

70. f.69 Penitential Psalms, Psalm 37.
Inspired by God, David continues his penance by composing the seven penitential psalms, *la cumenca les vii psaumes*. His signed scroll runs directly into the text of the psalm.

in the caption, it conflicts with David's declaration to Nathan, as told in the Book of Kings, that the rich man should 'restore the ewe fourfold: because he did this thing and had no pity'. No such restoration is attempted in William's sequence. Yet in his hands David's punishment is evoked through this image of abject penance in the face of sin. It is surely that first line of the psalm, Beati quorum: 'Blessed are they whose iniquities are forgiven' that forms the source of the angelic release shown coming down to David.

The third psalm opens with that same request: Domine ne in furore, Psalm 37. Like the first of the Penitential Psalms it is full of the anguish of the sinner: 'I am become miserable, and am bowed down even to the end: I walked sorrowful all the day long. For my loins are filled with illusions: and there is no health in my flesh'. But it is at this moment of anguish and despair that, in William de Brailes's account, David begins to compose the Penitential Psalms, writing his way to salvation. He kneels in prayer and, with the support of the divine hand from above, begins to write. Signing his name DAVIT at the top of the scroll, the caption defines his work: *la cumenca les vii psaumes*.

In the midst of that psalm of anguish, Psalm 37, comes the line: 'For I am ready for scourges', and in the next image David is scourged. Still crowned, his cloak is pulled up over his shoulders, revealing his bare back. He is exposed for scourging in only a pair of flouncy white drawers and black stockings, in illustration of Psalm 50, Miserere mei Deus: 'Have mercy on me, O God, according to thy great mercy. And according to the multitude of thy

fig.70

fig.71

107

71. f.72 Penitential
Psalms, Psalm 50.
Illustrating the fourth
psalm, David, still
crowned, is scourged.
Once again blessed by
God, the scene is simply
captioned, *disciplines*.

72. f.78 Penitential
Psalms, Psalm 129.
The fifth psalm shows
the manuscript's owner
in prayer (see plate
15). With the sixth
psalm, De profundis
David kneels, his hands
raised up before him, in
a small-scale two-line
initial, captioned,
reclamer deu.

tender mercies, blot out my iniquity.' Accompanied by the simple caption *disciplines*, William has again designed a double celled room from the structure of the initial 'M'.[108] This time it encloses the figure of a tonsured cleric who grasps David's outstretched hands in front of the central column of the room, while his right arm reaches above David's bowed head to apply the scourge. David's awkward crouching pose is one of willing surrender, a pose of penitence that is reinforced by the hand of God reaching down in blessing. Two young dark-haired men wait their turn, watching, one clutching his cloak over his otherwise bare shoulder.

plate 15   But for the penitential woman, prayer should be enough. Matching the last caption in simplicity, this next reads: *oreisuns*. Kneeling in prayer is Susanna, accompanying the psalm that is, perhaps, the most supplicatory of all the seven: Psalm 101, Domine exaudi orationem meam, 'Hear, O Lord, my prayer: and let my cry come unto thee. Turn not away thy face from me: in the day when I am in trouble, incline thine ear to me'. The praying lady, in the midst of David's penance, once again returns attention to the present. David is the example. It is David's words that form the text with which to pray, but it is Susanna's devout attitude that is essential to her absolution: her own sincere penitence.

The captions that accompany the final two images to these seven psalms set the devotional emphasis. *Reclamer deu* shows David begging to the Lord
fig.72   for mercy in Psalm 129, De profundis clamavi: 'Out of the depths have I cried unto thee O Lord, Lord hear my voice.' Ending with the ever-hopeful 'Because with the Lord there is mercy: and with him plentiful redemption', David's psalms of penance speak of trust as well as anguish. With the final
fig.73   initial showing King David still in prayer, the caption tells of petitioning:

73. f.79 Penitential Psalms, Psalm 142. The seventh psalm again shows David in prayer, and this three-line initial shows him reaching upwards in a request to God for mercy, *suent requere*.

suent requere. The last penitential psalm, Psalm 142, **Domine exaudi**, is full of hope. Out of the anguish comes at last. 'Thou wilt bring my soul out of trouble: and in thy mercy thou wilt destroy my enemies. And thou wilt cut off all them that afflict my soul: for I am thy servant.' Again William depicts David, kneeling in hope, the servant of the Lord. The story told in the Book of Kings ends: 'And he sent by the hand of Nathan the prophet, and called his name: Amiable to the Lord; because the Lord loved him.'[109]

They are a powerful set of psalms. Old Testament wrath bubbles through these texts, but always the sweet imagery of forgiveness is there to provide the hope, even the certainty, of salvation. The series of images echoes this. David is caught by Nathan's 'indignation' and 'wrath', but he admits his fault: he confesses. His contrition is clear as he subjects himself to that same punishment he marked out for the rich man of the parable that Nathan proposed. Not content, however, with the angel's gesture of release as he wallows in that mud, he sets to, with God's help, to write the Penitential Psalms. The fulfilment of his penance is through the discipline, punishment and undoubted humiliation of his public scourging.

For Susanna the meditation on these things, together with her own sincere penance through the recitation of David's psalms, is surely enough. And at the end it is possible for David to pray quietly too, begging for mercy and petitioning the Lord, but in some security now of his forgiveness. The imagery echoes the all-important penitential requirements laid on the thirteenth-century laity: confession, contrition and punishment as the essential route to penance and absolution.

The Litany of the Saints

Kyrie eleison: 'Lord have mercy' is the cry that opens the Litany of the Saints. The same cry opens the introit at the celebration of the mass, in preparation for communion. In the devotional day set out in the de Brailes Hours, it follows the Penitential Psalms. After penance comes the cry for mercy. Directly to the Lord, and for aid and intercession from the company of the saints, the litany storms heaven. The new text is marked by a large, four-line high, historiated initial. The 'K' of **Kyrie** frames the enthroned Christ, his right hand raised in judgement, with a book tucked under his left arm. It is a powerful image. Christ is a dominating figure, filling the initial to overflowing. This opens the text with a truly devotional image which directly addresses the reader, a rarity in William's design. The caption presents the purpose of both image and text: *deu merci e tuz sas scienz* and, following the thrice repeated **Kyrie**, the invocation of the Litany of the Saints begins.

The ancient form of the Litany had been established in the monastic Office centuries before. The form in which it was to be written caused no

plate 14

hesitation. Following the calling on God's mercy, Christ is invoked, and God in his three-personed role is called upon: Father in heaven, the Son redeemer of the world, the Holy Spirit, and then, in unity, the Trinity.

Chief among the saints is the Virgin, and she too is called upon in her various roles – as simply herself, Sancta Maria; as Mother of God, Mater dei genetrix, and as the most important of Virgins, Sancta virgo virginum. The archangels (two of whom have appeared in the illustration) are called upon, followed by a collective invocation of all angels and archangels.[110] In the highest medallion of that image of the hierarchy of All Saints illustrating the fig.35 suffrage after Lauds, the Virgin was shown grouped with the angels.[111] Invoked now just as she was depicted, the angels define her heavenly setting. Her role to intercede for sinners as felix coeli porta, blessed gate to heaven, is made plain.[112]

Invoking Omnes beatum spiritum ordines, the litany moves into the orderly plate 7 sequence of saints as they were set out in that image at Lauds. The intermediary role of St John the Baptist, neither fully an Old Testament figure nor a New Testament saint, is marked by placing him in a section to himself, followed again by a collective invocation to the prophets and the patriarchs of the Old Testament.

The next section of the litany is devoted to the apostles and evangelists, each listed individually, beginning with St Peter and ending with St Luke. In the All Saints image, this group is simply captioned as *apostles*, though in the litany both apostles and evangelists are called upon collectively to ora pro nobis, pray for us. Collectively too, the disciples are invoked, those nameless New Testament figures, ever-present in the gospel accounts. Invoked too are the Innocents, the male babies of Jerusalem murdered at the order of King Herod in his attempt to destroy the King of the Jews.[113] Twenty of the many martyrs of the Church are selected to be individually called upon. St Stephen, as the first Christian martyr, is almost invariably called upon first in any litany, and he heads the list here. The list also includes English martyrs, notably St Alban, St Oswald, St Edmund (king of East Anglia), St Edward (king and martyr), and St Thomas Becket. The martyrs end with St George – not English but already a popular saint in England.[114] Finally, a collective petition evokes that crowded image of countless martyrs as they were depicted at Lauds.

Below the martyrs on the gilded column of the saints is the roundel dedicated to *confessurs*, and eleven of that company are selected for invocation in the litany. Most important is St Gregory, who heads this list; his role in the conversion of the Anglo-Saxons and the foundation of the English Church ensured his priority, quite apart from his position as pope and doctor of the Church.[115] Other confessors who were especially venerated in England are invoked here – notably St Augustine, St Dunstan and St Botulf – and the list ends with the popular but legendary figure of St Julian.[116] As well as the collective invocation of all confessors, there is a special call to Omnes monachi et heremite, all monks and hermits.[117]

The lowest medallion of the All Saints image shows the company of women, always called virgins, whatever their life stories might tell. Twelve virgins are called upon in the litany. Beginning with that most crucial of female saints St Mary Magdalen, the most prominent of virgins are invoked here, including St Katherine and St Margaret. St Anne is not included, but her cult was only just beginning at this time.[118] The final four virgins were all familiar, but would have been specially chosen for the patron. St Frideswide is first of these, of course, as the most important local saint of Oxford, later formally adopted as Oxford's patron. She is celebrated in virtually all the calendars and the litanies of these manuscripts made in Oxford.[119] St Mildred's cult centred mainly on Canterbury, as her relics had been translated to St Augustine's in the eleventh century. St Radegund, a sixth century French queen-saint, had five ancient churches dedicated to her in England, though her cult was limited and her appearances in litanies rare. St Helen, mother of the Emperor Constantine, was sometimes believed to have been born in England. She was particularly venerated in and around York because of Constantine's visit there. Associated too with the finding of the True Cross, she was certainly a woman to be admired and a saint to be venerated and invoked, Ora pro nobis. And collectively, Orate pro nobis, the Virgins are invoked together. Omnes sancti vidue et continentes is followed by the collective call to All Saints, and the litany is at an end.

Regularly recited, this sequence must have been intensely personal. These chosen saints were the focus of Susanna's daily devotion: those to whom she could look for intercession with God, those from whom she might request special favours for special needs. The saints whose shrines she had visited would be here. She would have known the shrine of St Frideswide in the saint's own foundation in Oxford, by this time an Augustinian priory.[120] The miracles reported at the shrine of St Thomas at Christ Church (Canterbury) following the translation of his relics into the new and elaborate shrine in 1220, attracted pilgrims from all over the country, certainly from Oxford. They climbed on their knees to the new eastern end of the choir, newly set about with Thomas's life and miracles depicted in the brilliant colours of the stained glass windows.[121] While in Canterbury other shrines were open to

(Opposite) 74. ff.87ᵛ–88 Litany, Collects. The litany creates a supplicatory mood, with the opening initial of Christ blessing beginning a sequence of petitions. At the end the collects or prayers are illustrated by prayer. Susanna is first kneeling, then prostrate, but both times she is blessed by God. As she falls prostrate, so the 'P' of the initial which enclosed her is balanced precariously on the head of a female acrobat, trimmed by the binder.

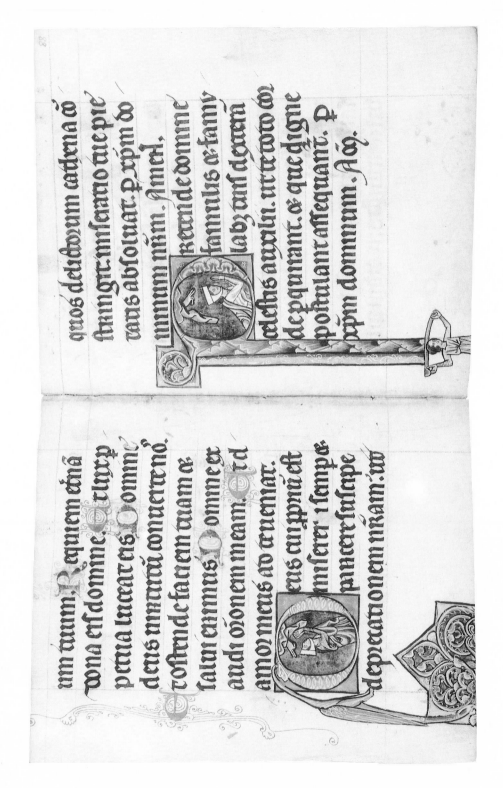

quos delictorum catena co(n)-
stringit: miseratio tue pie-
tatis absoluat. P(er) xp(istu)m dominum n(ost)r(u)m. Amen.

Recande d(omi)ne
famul(us) et famu-
lab(us) tuis dsignam
delictis aug(us)tii. ut te toto cor-
de p(er)quirant. et que digne
postulant assequant(ur). P(er)
xp(istu)m dominum n(ost)r(u)m. Am(en).

...tuam. Requiem eterna(m)
dona eis d(omi)ne. et lux p(er)-
p(etu)a luceat eis. O(mn)e
de(us) misericordi: co(n)uerte no(s)
ostende faciem tuam et
salui erimus. D(omi)ne exaudi o(rati)onem meam. et
clamor meus ad te ueniat.

...eius culpa p(re)m(ic)t(ur)ir est:
miserer(e) i(n) semp(er)
pan(cer)e suscipe
deprecationem n(ost)ram: uo

the pilgrim, including that of St Mildred, either at St Augustine's Abbey or at the hospital of St Gregory.[122]

Calling on the saints as a part of the passage of the devotional day would have been entirely natural. However shadowy the reality, these saints represented the continuity of Christian belief, from the apostles and St Stephen dating back to the earliest period of Christianity, through to such near-contemporaries as St Thomas.[123] They recall the establishment of Christianity in England through St Gregory and St Augustine, and the monastic tradition is celebrated through St Benedict, founder of the Rule, and St Dunstan, reformer of the English communities in the tenth century. Saints providing special services, such as St Julian the Hospitaller, patron of ferrymen, guardian of river-crossings, would have had special importance in a city circled about with rivers and tributaries.[124] The litany celebrates and requests all at once. The attributes of these chosen saints would have been constantly in Susanna's mind as she called upon this vivid company.

And the calling goes on. Still invoking this whole company, the specific petitions begin: Ab omnis malo libera nos, free us from all evil; Ab immentibus peccatorum, from unending sin – again this constant fear. Specific petitions follow for delivery from the devil and from illness, and then come the petitions for the good things of life – all these everyday requests and aspirations are intimately connected with calling on the saints. Petitioning God through the saints was clearly a route strewn with hope. Legend upon legend, image upon image, provided the evidence that this was the way.

75. f.88ᵛ Litany, Collect.
Finally the figure of W de Brailes re-emerges. Characteristically he prays, in illustration of the last of the series of collects. He no longer needs to be introduced with a caption.

The collects, special prayers, follow the litany and, as with the collects at
the end of each of the hours, William depicts both his patron and himself in
the historiated initials. Standing with her hands raised high above her head,
Susanna reaches to heaven with her prayer, **Deus cui proprium**. Her red robe,
her cascading hair, her smart white hat, mark her out. This time the hand of
God reaches down to touch her in his blessing. She is there with the next
prayer too, **Pretende domine famulis**. But this time she is prostrate in her request
and her elbows rest on the edge of the initial, her face turned to the ground.
The hand of God is there again, so it seems her requests are heard. Finally
William reappears, kneeling again in prayer, **Deus qui es sanctorum tuorum**, a
personal request for help, **per nos famulos tuos**, and he prays for eternal rest for
all the dead.

fig.74

fig.75

The passage of the devotions has many pathways, stilling the anxieties of
the living and assiduously accumulating grace to assure salvation at the hour
of death. But, with the intercession of the saints ensuring that a clamour has
been raised in heaven, these last collects are essentially prayers for the living:
for Susanna and for the illuminator of her manuscript.

The Gradual Psalms

By degrees, by the steps of the Gradual Psalms, spiritual enrichment is
gained.[125] As a group, these fifteen psalms celebrate, petition, praise and
instruct. Through metaphor and through rich imagery, this series of short
psalms creates an atmosphere of dependence on God, in which to express joy
and gain comfort. An additional, sixteenth, psalm ends the devotional series
in the de Brailes Hours with the final shout of praise that is Psalm 150, **Laudate
dominum**, the last of all the Psalms of David.

The importance of the Gradual Psalms as a part of daily devotion was
established in the liturgical routine which in England was prescribed for the
reformed monasteries in the tenth-century *Regularis concordia*. Only in English
books of hours is this sequence of psalms regularly included, though even in
England they became rare in the fifteenth century.[126] As they were prescribed in the *Regularis concordia*, the sequence was said before Matins, as a
spiritual preparation for the rigours of the liturgical day. Sometimes, on feast
days, they would be said in procession, as the community moved around the
altar, pausing on its way to say each psalm.[127] In William's design, the
Gradual Psalms are written after the Penitential Psalms and the Litany.
Nevertheless they would have formed part of the morning's prayer, ideal
preparation for the day.[128]

Ad dominum in tribularer, 'In my trouble I cried to the Lord: and he heard
me', the sequence opens. Susanna kneels in prayer, her hands stretched
upwards crying to the Lord, who extends his hand downwards in reassu-

plate 16a

76. f.90ᵛ Gradual Psalms, Psalm 120.
The first of the Gradual Psalms has Susanna begging for mercy in her tribulation (see plate 16a). Here illustrating the second of the Gradual Psalms she refutes the charge of adultery laid against her. Dressed just as the manuscript's first owner (see figs 73–4, plate 2), her hands in the *orans* gesture, she calls on the witness of the Lord, ..*st eie de deu*.

rance. Echoing the words of the opening of the psalm, the caption describes her: *ele clama deu en sa tribulaciun*. She is dressed as always in the familiar pink robe, here covered with a blue cloak, and her hair falls down her back beneath the white hat. It is only with the continuation of the story in the next initial that she is identified as the biblical heroine Susanna, the subject of Chapter 13 of the Book of Daniel. The words of the caption, 'She cries in tribulation to the Lord' open the narrative story of Susanna and the Elders, a story of wickedness and deceit threatening the virtue of a young woman.

The next verse of that first psalm, Psalm 119, 'O Lord, deliver my soul from wicked lips and a deceitful tongue' echoes Susanna's cry, as she calls for deliverance from the wicked old men. The story told in the Book of Daniel is of a beautiful and virtuous woman, wife to Joakim. He is described as 'very rich and had an orchard near his house: and the Jews resorted to him because he was the most honourable of them all'.[129] Two of the 'ancients of the people' were appointed judges that year and, frequenting Joakim's house, they saw the beautiful Susanna walking often in the orchard alone. 'And they perverted their own mind and turned away their eyes that they might not look unto heaven nor remember just judgements'. These two lustful old men then hid themselves in the orchard to watch her wash herself in the shade of the trees, 'for it was hot weather', and her maids left her alone. 'Now when the maids were gone forth the two Elders arose and ran to her and said:

77. f.91ᵛ Gradual Psalms,
Psalm 121.
The third psalm sees the arrival of
Daniel, 'the Lord raised up the holy
spirit of a young boy, whose name
was Daniel' (Daniel 13, 45). Yet he
is tall in his wisdom, commanding in
his gesture, and examines the first of
the two Elders. The caption has
been trimmed but reads, *..eu veat un
des ... i les asamina .. dit quil les vit
suz ... nier* (perhaps *prunier*).

Behold, the doors of the orchard are shut and nobody seeth us and we are in
love with thee: wherefore consent to us and lie with us. But if thou wilt not we
will bear witness against thee that a young man was with thee and therefore
thou didst send away thy maids from thee.' Susanna refused, 'But it is better
for me to fall into your hands without doing it than to sin in the sight of the
Lord.' And of course the 'deceitful tongues' of the Elders were believed: 'The
multitude believed them as being the Elders and the judges of the people'.

With the opening of the next psalm, Psalm 120, Levavi oculos, 'I have lifted
up my eyes to the mountains, from whence help shall come to me. My help is
from the Lord, who made heaven and earth', Susanna stands falsely accused
fig.76 before a Jewish judge, marked as a Jew for the thirteenth- century reader by
his round hat. On either side he is flanked by two young men. Raising her
hands in the *orans* gesture of total innocence, in denial of the charge brought
against her, her eyes are lifted up too, 'And she weeping looked up to
Heaven: for her heart had confidence in the Lord'. She cried out 'Thou
knowest that that they have borne false witness against me: and behold I
must die, whereas I have done none of these things which these men have
maliciously forged against me'. And that help from the Lord, promised both
in the words of the psalm and in the narrative, comes in the shape of Daniel,
who urges that the word of the Elders should be tried further.

Beginning Psalm 121, Laetatus sum, Daniel stands before the seated judge
and, with his finger raised in accusation, examines the first of the Elders
fig.77 alone. Daniel demands an explanation, demands detail, 'tell me under what
tree then sawest them conversing together. He said: Under a mastic-tree.'
This is not the reply he gives here. Perhaps the caption read: *prunier*, a plum
tree.[130]

117

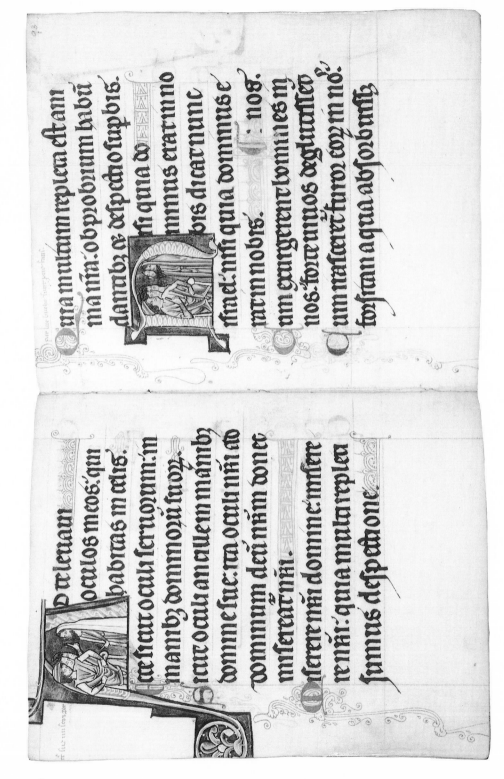

(*Right*) 79. f.94 Gradual Psalms, Psalm 124.

pur fausse crime sunt ars, and the Elders are burnt, prodded by Daniel by both his still-accusing finger and by a pitchfork.

At Psalm 122, **Ad te levavi**, the second Elder stands before the judge who watches as Daniel, from the back of the group, raises a finger to pose the question again. This time the answer differs: *[quils les v]it suz un serizer*, a cherry tree. And with Psalm 123, **Nisi quia dominus**, 'If it had not been that the Lord was with us when men rose up against us; perhaps they had swallowed fig.78 us up alive', the Elders stand condemned: *par lur buche sunt prove faus*, 'for Daniel had convicted them of false witness by their own mouth'. This time it is the Judge himself whose finger is raised.

It was seen to be a true judgement, and reward to Susanna for the trust in the Lord that she had shown in the opening image of this sequence. Psalm 124, **Qui confidunt**, makes the point: 'They that trust in the Lord shall be as fig.79 Mount Sion: he shall not be moved'. The false Elders are burnt in a flaming fire, while Daniel prods at them with a pitchfork. The imagery is of Hell, though the Book of Daniel says simply: 'And they put them to death'. In the words of Psalm 125, **In convertendo**, her rejoicing is made evident, 'The Lord hath done great things for us: we are become joyful' and 'They that sow in tears shall reap in joy'.[131] 'Innocent blood was saved in that day' rejoices the fig.80 Book of Daniel, and Susanna, the innocent and now dressed all in white, kneels again in prayer at the opening of Psalm 126, 'Nisi dominus.

(*Opposite*) 78. ff.92ᵛ–93 Gradual Psalms, Psalms 122 and 123. Accusing the other Elder, Daniel again launches the question with an upraised finger, though from the back of the group this time. Tentatively the Elder responds, raising his finger low at this side as he gives the wrong answer, *[quils les v]it suz un serizer*. On the facing page the two Elders are confronted and proved by the judges to have lied. It is the judge alone here whose finger is raised, *par lur buche sunt prove faus*.

The ultimate reward is Susanna's too. In the initial to Psalm 127, **Beati omnes**, 'Blessed are all they that fear the Lord: that walk in his ways', the soul of Susanna, her head enclosed in a great blue halo, is borne up to heaven by a pair of angels, her lifeless body left below, *l'ame susanna vet a deu*. Linked pictorially with its thirteenth-century owner, Susanna was the model of virtue to be followed. Hers is an uplifting story and, with its conclusion, the first nine steps of the Gradual Psalms have been ascended.

fig.81

The tenth step forms an interval; no illustration accompanies Psalm 128, **Sepe expugnaverunt**, 'Often have they fought against me from my youth: but they could not prevail over me'. A new story fills the remaining six initials, and with this we are fully back in the thirteenth-century present.

Psalm 129, **De profundis**, is a cry for mercy: 'Out of the depths have I cried unto thee O Lord'.[132] A burgess is the hero of this tale, a successful townsman who would have owned his own tenement in the town, and would have taken his share of the burdens of civic office.[133] Among these duties would have been the support of his parish church, contributing to necessary extensions or repairs, or donating items to its treasure.[134] It was not just generosity that encouraged such donations but the material demands laid upon the wealthy to ensure the health of their immortal souls. The generosity of this burgess is described in the caption: *un burgeis duna un chaliz a l'eglise scein laurenc*. And proudly, he places a very large golden chalice on the altar. Wearing an enveloping hooded cloak, and with his full head of brown hair,

fig.82

plate 16c

81. f.96 Gradual Psalms,
Psalm 127.
Her confidence rewarded, her soul
is borne up leaving her dead body
on the bier. Wrapped in a napkin
and borne up by angels, *l'ame
susana vet a deu.*

the chalice is given as witness of his prosperity: the image of the burgess in pursuit of his civic duty. But plainly he also follows the hopeful route to mercy, petitioning St Laurence, whose special concern is guaranteed through the dedication of the burgess's own parish church. Such gifts as a part of the penitential route would have been familiar to the burgess. In penance to expiate the sins of the past, they evoke an echo of verse seven of the psalm: 'Because with the Lord there is mercy: and with him plentiful redemption'. Such a gift would represent an insurance payment, a means to the assurance of certain death benefits.

Death itself is certainly assured. With Psalm 130, Domine non est, 'Lord, my heart is not exalted: nor are my eyes lofty', the burgess lies dead, *ci mirt le burgeis.* For Theophilus, for the ignorant priest, and for Susanna, the security
fig.82   of their souls is already all wrapped-up at the hour of their death. Without hesitation, the Virgin (or an angel) is at hand to wrap the soul in a napkin and pass it up to God's Heaven. Not so for the burgess. His soul hangs in the balance.

Psalm 131, Memento domine, which pleads with God to remember and fulfil his promises, contains fragments of hope: 'The Lord hath sworn truth to David and he will not make it void.' St Michael does his best: *[l'angle] et le*
fig.83   *deable pleident [pur sun] ame.* But the devil is winning. The small naked soul of the burgess stands hopefully with St Michael, separated from the horned and toothy brown devil by the central vertical of the letter 'M'. The argument is fierce, the gesturing forefingers do battle, and all the burgess can do is raise his right hand in a gesture of innocence and peace.

Yet the burgess evidently gave alms too. His charitable work extended to

(*Opposite*) 82. ff.97ᵛ–98
Gradual Psalms, Psalms 129
and 130.
A new story accompanies the
next group of Gradual Psalms,
beginning with the generous
burgess donating a chalice to
the Church of St Laurence,
presumably his own parish
church. The caption describes
this in detail, *un burgeis duna un
chaliz a l'eglise de scein laurene.*
And now the burgess lies dead,
ci mirt le burgeis.

(*Right*) 83. f.98ᵛ Gradual
Psalms, Psalm 131.
Fighting for the soul of the
burgess, the Angel and the
Devil bandy accusations, while
the burgess stands mute, unable
to defend himself. The caption
is cropped but read *[l'angle] e
le deable pleident [pur sun] ame.*

(*Right*) 84. f.100ᵛ Gradual
Psalms, Psalm 132.
Seeing the peril of the soul of
the burgess, the recluse, the
anchorite of the Church of St
Laurence, calls on the saint to
come to the aid of the burgess,
*une recluse vit une nuit le deable
peiser sun pecche e l'angle sun benfet
qui ne sufit mie.*

the support of an anchorite, walled up in the tower of St Laurence Church. This anchorite, whose life was dedicated to solitude and prayer, was reliant on brotherly love and alms and, in illustration of Psalm 132, Ecce quam bonum, 'Behold how good and how pleasant it is for brethren to dwell together in unity', this vigilant anchorite repays those kindnesses. Walled up in a rose-red tower, the hooded face of the recluse looks out. Extending a long arm and, praying for the soul of the dead burgess, the anchorite points upwards to heaven to alert St Laurence. As the caption explains, *une recluse vit une nuit le deable peiser sun pecche et l'angle sun benfet qui ne sufit mie*. The drama of the disputed soul of the burgess is played out in the sight of the 'recluse', and the plight of the burgess is plain, weighed in the scales of justice against the weight of his sins. The recluse succeeds in summoning St Laurence. With Psalm 133, Ecce nunc benedicite, 'Behold, now bless ye the Lord, all ye servants of the Lord', St Laurence appears. Outside the initial frame, just dropping in, he reaches over to place the golden chalice from the treasury of his own church into the scale-pan of the goodness of the burgess, *la vint sein laurenz si geta le chaliz as benfez que le chaliz brusa*. This is the scientific test. Despite the energetic efforts of the black and beastly devil, surreptitiously pulling down on the the pan filled with heaped up sins, the good deeds – with the burgess peering cautiously over the edge of the pan – now outweigh the sins. Through the combined efforts of the anchorite and St Laurence, the burgess has his security.

fig.84

plate 16b

85. f.101ᵛ Gradual Psalms, Psalm 150. After the intercession of St Laurence (see plate 16b) the soul of the burgess is safely taken to heaven, greeted by the blessing hand of God, [li an]gles la portent.

This is the last of the Gradual Psalms, and with this the ascent of the fifteen steps is achieved. But in William's design, a further psalm is added to the sequence, and the story reaches its happy ending. At last, and accompanying the shout of praise of Psalm 150, **Laudate dominum**, the death benefits accrue and the soul of the burgess is carried to heaven in triumph, wrapped in the napkin, borne up by angels. 'Praise ye the Lord in his holy places: praise ye him in the firmament of his power. Praise ye him for his mighty acts: praise ye him according to the multitude of his greatness'.

fig.85

And so the devotional routine, as it was set out for Susanna in about 1240 by William de Brailes in Oxford, is complete. The range of devotions had been part of the everyday expected routine. But never before, it seems, had these been written out in quite this way, so clearly intended for the devotional guidance of the laity. The incorporation of the illustration, with the captions identifying, explaining, elaborating and prescribing a meditative exercise, enriches the text beyond measure. This illustration is not simply a biblical narrative, nor is it a literal interpretation of the first words of the text. Its narrative unfolds with dramatic effect, and constantly, the words of the text find echoes in the illustration. Read as a whole, the text and both the narrative and devotional illustration reveal some of the details of everyday life and the commonplace concerns of faith and religious belief in thirteenth-century England.

Yet the text does not finish here. This is the end of the formal text of the book of hours, but immediately following is a sequence of prayers surely written at the request of Susanna. Her book was complete, leaving seven sides of parchment still empty. Ruling these left-overs with many lines, to provide at least twenty-eight lines of text, a different scribe in a small and less formal book hand wrote some extra prayers for her. Using up these final few folios of the last quire, she is straightaway reminded to pray for the Dominican friars, well-known to all residents of Oxford by this time. Three specific friars are named, and "*1 pater noster 1 ave marie par charite*" are prescribed. Evoking the sweetness of devotion to the Virgin, a prayer, **Duce dame seint marie**, begins a sequence of poetic **Aves** to the Virgin. Each **Ave** claims a special quality for her, and each celebrates her life and her importance as a model for all women. These **Aves** form a devotional summary of the cult of the Virgin. The cult of the saints too is celebrated in French prayers, including many more saints than those few invoked in the formal Latin suffrages after Lauds.

fig.86

These last few pages gave Susanna her chance to pray in her vernacular. While she has had the captions to encourage her meditation, the words of her devotional day have all been Latin, written large in the solemn liturgical script of William de Brailes's scribe. In later books of hours these French devotions often become a part of the formal text too. But these last texts are a

Jo ðen preir pur frere richart de neuere.
y p frere richart de westey. y p frere bel
meu degrimistū. e prut frere prechr̄
e menur̄ k deus meduut part delur praers
e delur benfez. e p tus me confessurs. pur
dur senurs uus ke uez chetelectre priez
p̄r̄ e p̄ mar.1. pater nr̄. 1. auemarie. par
charite. O ye dame seincte marie p̄ icele
grace ke us receutes en cel dur moz par le
angle gabriel. aue maria gracia plena dn̄s
tecum: requerez nost̄ fiuz ke il me enuert
grace par unt 10 pusse fere sauolūtte e la nost̄.
Aue mar. p̄ nr̄ a.

Aye seincte marie lamere au rei iesu. Seine
des aungeles e uere pleine de ducur. Que
esteile de mer de graunt respleclisur. eschele de
parais salu de pecheur. ue seincte marie la
uerge au rei iesse. De uus es panust la flur que
pleine: de bunte. De fozce de uigur y de humi
lite de cunseil de seintete e de pitee e dela pour
de deu par ke deble emacte. Gloriose reine eez de
mei pitee. Aye la tur au rei dauid. aue seincte
marie. De uus uint cele pere par ki murrut
golie. la parente adam de mort reuint
auie e merci de mei ki estes la duce amie.

Aye seincte marie ki estes le temple sala
mun. Auus trans mit le angele q̄ gabri
el adanun. nuus descendi ducement par

relaxed and informal devotion, the humanity of the Virgin and the presence of those special friars, *richart de neuerc, richart de westeu* and *bartelmeu de grimistun* kept constantly in mind.[135]

Suggesting Susanna

To own such a book in 1240 was a rare privilege. Kings, bishops, institutions and saints might own illuminated manuscripts, though even to these medieval owners a book was worth treasuring.[136] For an ordinary laywoman, young and unmarried, such a possession would have been a rarity throughout the Middle Ages. Susanna's was the first book of hours. More than that, Susanna's possession of an illuminated book comes at the beginning of their ownership by ordinary laywomen of her period.[137]

Like the grand books owned by such well-known historical figures as St Ethelwold, Henry of Blois, St Hugh of Lincoln, Robert de Lindesey and Giles de Bridport, or owned by famed abbeys and cathedrals – the Bury St Edmund's Bible, the Winchester Bible, or the *Chronica Maiora* of St Alban's Abbey – this little book of hours gains from the identification of the patron for whom it was made.[138] Susanna's presence explains its iconography and defines its context. And, just as is the case for those better known patrons, the manuscript itself reveals and explains its patron, Susanna. Just like some of those well-known patrons too, her identification has an element of supposition in it.

Suggesting Susanna still provides no historical existence for her. No Susanna has leapt from the archives of medieval Oxford to steal the supposition away. Yet perhaps this would be unlikely anyway. The archival records of this time deal mostly with property ownership, and the young and unmarried girl represented in these images is unlikely to have been a woman of property, though women are certainly recorded. Even so, putting the evidence of the iconography together as a whole, a little more detail can be filled in, a little more colour added to the circumstances of her life.

Inevitably the colour can be applied most securely to the details of her religious beliefs and her devotional routine. With the end of the day the devotional purpose of the interlocking of the imagery with the text, both formal liturgy and descriptive captions, enables the structure of the whole to be reviewed. Thinking back, the unfolding of the Passion story has taken only this one day, just as it did in the gospel accounts, and just as it is echoed in the liturgy of Good Friday. It tells of the day in which the Crucifixion of Christ can be seen as the centrepoint of the telling of the faith. Tracing the pattern of the day in step with Christ is the goal of such a meditative scheme. The story of the life of the Virgin, as William tells it, has a longer time-scale, enclosing within it the events of that one day, the day of the Passion. Each of the events depicted in William's iconographic programme for the Hours of the Virgin, whether part of the Passion or of the life of the Virgin, contributes to the establishment of the central truth of the Christian faith.

The narrative of the life of the Virgin does more than just tell the story. It uses the narrative frame to establish her credentials. The purity of Mary's Immaculate Conception is depicted; the power of her miracle working is established; and, through her Assumption and Coronation, her role not just as Mother of God but also as Queen of Heaven and Mother of the Church is seen to be true. By the device of William's design, interjecting the miracles between her early life and her death (the miracles illustrate the initials to Prime, Terce, Sext, None, and Vespers – the entire middle of the day), those miracles become a part of the narrative of her life. Yet, while Theophilus is a legendary figure of the early Church, St Thomas Becket's martyrdom in 1170 was almost within living memory. Certainly, the translation of his relics in 1220 to the shrine in Canterbury Cathedral, the goal of so many pilgrims, was a contemporary event. In the same way, the ignorant priest is representative of the thirteenth-century concern to establish a learned and literate clergy, able to read the Latin of any liturgy, not just the Mass of the Virgin. By enclosing these miracles within the narrative frame of her lifetime, the Virgin takes all mankind into her care – past, present and future. The narrative wizardry of William de Brailes makes all these images relevant to the thirteenth-century present.

Of great contemporary relevance was the question of the Jews. While their role as the chosen people of the Old Testament was maintained in the earlier Middle Ages, they had, in the latter part of the twelfth and thirteenth centuries, begun to be perceived much less favourably.[139] Throughout the illustrative narrative of the de Brailes Hours, the Jews are portrayed without sympathy. They are depicted as the caricatured tormentors of Christ at his Crucifixion, and as mocking, blind, and stubborn after the death of the Virgin. Most threateningly, however, the effect of the insertion of the story of the Wandering Jew into the narrative of the Way of the Cross is to bring the Jews of the gospels into the thirteenth-century present. Through the continued presence of that one Jew who was doomed to wander, the Jews as a whole remain a potentially malevolent force. The contemporary telling of this story at the abbey of St Alban's, and its appearance in that abbey's chronicle, was undoubtedly the root of its appearance here. But William's decision to include the story was not just one of many. Only in Matthew Paris's marginal illustration in the St Alban's Chronicle itself does the story get another depiction at this time.[140]

The role of the Jews in the legend of the Death of the Virgin is only partly malevolent, however. Confronted by the miraculous relic of the pall, they can be converted; though there are bound to be some who will stubbornly

dei genitrix virgo semp maria.
Intercede p nobis ad dnm deu
nostrum. Gloria. Post par
tum virgo inuiolata pman
sisti. Dei genitrix intercede
p nobis. Domine exaudi o
rationem meam. Et clamor
meus ad te veniat.
Concede nos famulos.
Domine exaudi or.
Et clamor. Benedicamus do
mino. Deo gratias.

W. de bril'
q mode peint

Plate 1 f.43 Terce of the Virgin, Prayer, CONCEDE NOS. *w. de brail' qui me depeint.*

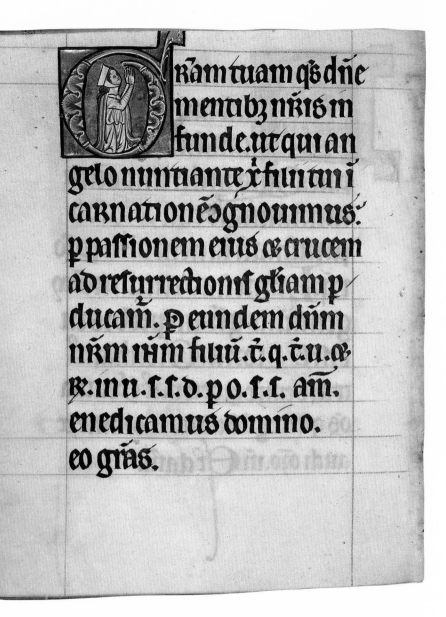

ꝗꝛaciam tuam qꝗ dñe
mentibꝫ nꝝis in
funde. ut qui an
gelo nunciante ꝛ filii tui i
carnationem ꞅgnouimus·
p paſſionem eius ꝛ crucem
ad reſurꝛeccionis gliam p
ducam. p eundem dñm
nꝛm iħm filiũ. t. q. t̃. u. ꝛ
ꝛ. in u. ꞅ. ꞅ. d. p o. ꞅ. ꞅ. am.
enedicamus domino.
eo gꝛas.

Plate 3 The manuscript in the hands, open to show ff.27ᵛ–28 Suffrages to the
Holy Cross and St Laurence.

Plate 4 f.1 The opening of Matins of the Virgin, DOMINE LABIA MEA APERIES. The four medallions show the Betrayal; the Scourging of Christ, with Peter's first denial; Mocking of Christ, with the second denial; Spitting at Christ, and Peter's third denial; and the remorse of Peter outside the frame of the initial.

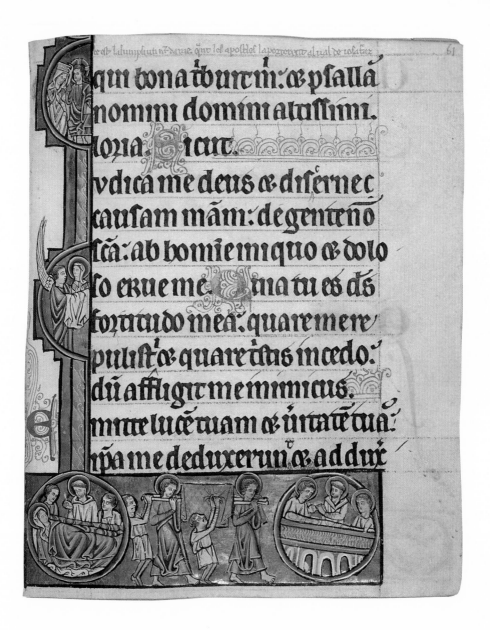

Plate 5 f.61 Compline of the Virgin. Psalm 42, JUDICA ME. The Death of the Virgin, mourned by St John; her soul lifted to heaven; her Coronation in heaven by Christ; the burial procession and the unbelieving Jews; the veneration of her entombed body.

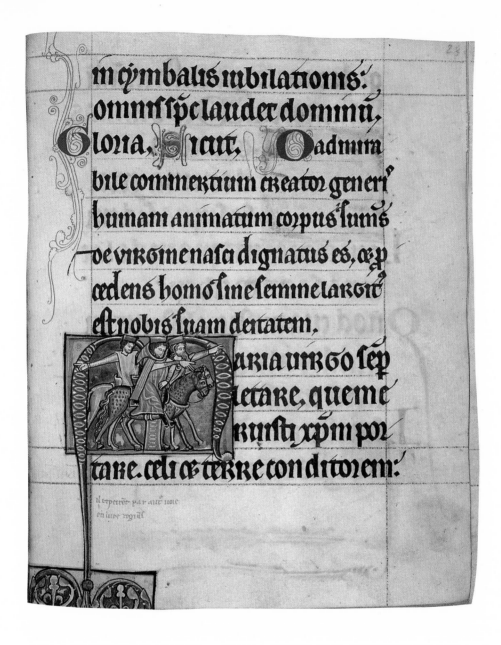

m cymbalis iubilationis:
omnis spc laudet dominū,
Gloria, Sicut, O admira
bile commextium creator generi
humani animatum corpus sumis
de virgine nasci dignatus es, & p
cedens homo sine semine largit
est nobis suam deitatem.
ARIA VIRGO sep
letare, que me
ruisti xpm por
tare. celi & terre conditorem:

il repetit par aut note
on une vigint

Plate 6 f.23 Lauds of the Virgin. Capitulum, MARIA VIRGO. The Magi return home
separately.

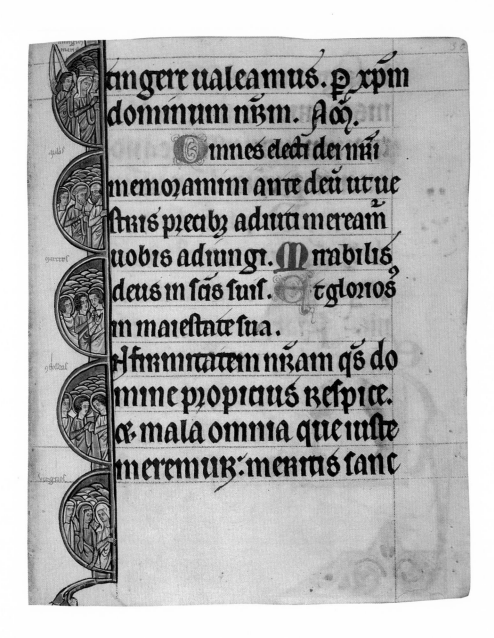

gere ualeamus. p xpm
dominum nrm. Aoñ.
Omnes electi dei ñi
memoramini ante deu ut ue
stris precibz adiuti meream
uobis adiungi. Mnabilis
deus in sas suis. Et glorios
in maiestate sua.
Hfirmitatem nram qs do
mine propicius respice.
æ mala omnia que iuste
meremur: meritis sanc

Plate 7 f.30 Suffrage to All Saints, IN FIRMITATEM. Angels with Virgin Mary, Apostles, Martyrs, Confessors, Virgins.

Plate 8 f.43ᵛ Opening of Sext of the Virgin. Full page miniature with medallions, the Wandering Jew; the Way of the Cross; Christ stripped of his garments; Christ before the cross.

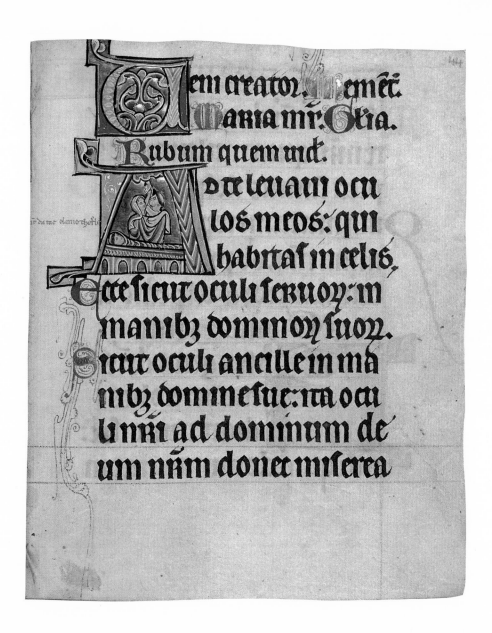

eni creator. ... emē.
Maria mr. Gra.
Rubum qtem mid.
d te leuaui ocu
los meos: qui
habitas in celis,
Ecce sicut oculi seruoy: in
manibz dominoy suoy.
Sicut oculi ancille in ma
nibz domine sue: ita ocu
li nri ad dominum de
um nrm donec misera

Plate 9 f.44 Opening of Sext of the Virgin. Facing the miniature, the start of the text has a decorated initial to the hymn VENI CREATOR. Illustrating Psalm 122, AD TE LEVAVI, the Virgin raises the soul of Theophilus to heaven.

Plate 10 f.47ᵛ Opening of None of the Virgin. Full page miniature with narrative
Crucifixion with the thieves and, in the two medallions, Christ crucified between Mary
and St John; Crucifixion with two witnesses.

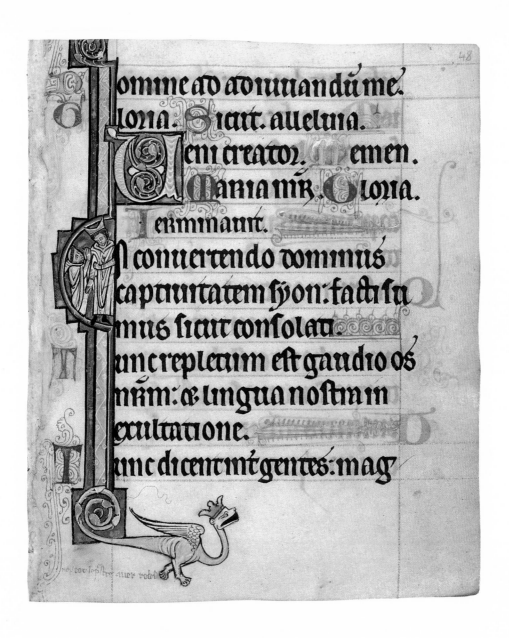

omine ad adiuuandũ me.
loria. Sicut. alleluia.
Veni creator. emen.
Maria mr. Gloria.
Terminauit.
N conuertendo dominus
captiuitatem syon: facti su
mus sicut consolati.
unc repletum est gaudio os
nrm: & lingua nostra in
exultatione.
unc dicent intgentes: mag

Plate 11 f.48 Opening of None of the Virgin. Facing the miniature, the start of the text has a
decorated initial to the hymn VENI CREATOR. Illustrating Psalm 125, IN CONVERTENDO.

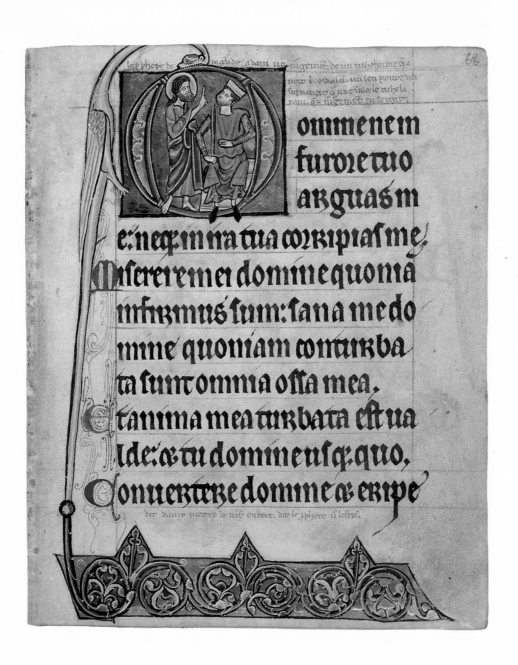

Plate 12 f.66 Opening of the Penitential Psalms. Psalm 6, DOMINE NE IN FURORE. Nathan contrives to make David pronounce sentence upon himself for his sin with Bathsheba.

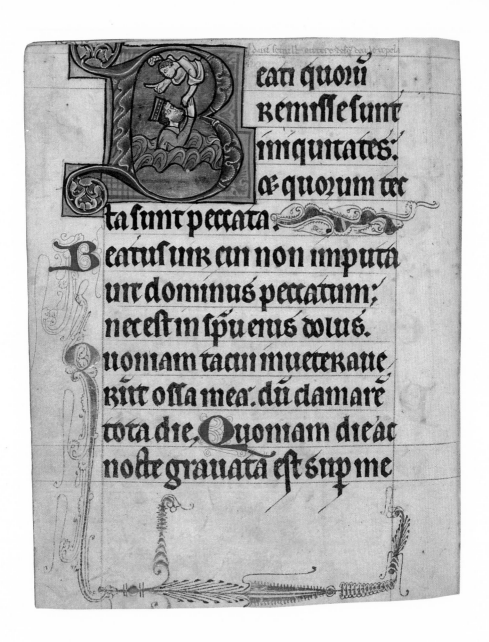

eati quorū
remisse sunt
iniquitates:
æ quorum tec
ta sunt peccata.
Beatus uir cui non imputa
uit dominus peccatum;
nec est in spu eius dolus.
Quoniam tacui inueterauc
rūt ossa mea. dū clamaré
tota die, Quoniam die ac
nocte grauata est sup me

Plate 13 f.67ᵛ Penitential Psalms. Psalm 31, BEATI QUORUM. David, according to his self-prescribed punishment, is buried in the ground.

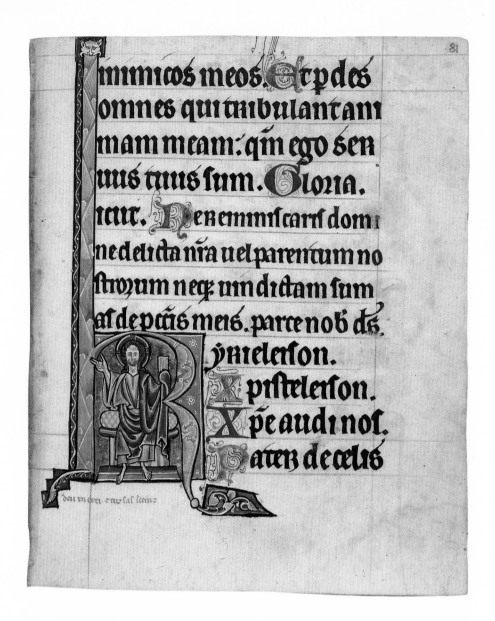

inimicos meos. Et pde
omnes qui tribulantani
mam meam: qm ego ser
uus tuus sum. Gloria.
retur. Ne reminiscaris dom
ne delicta nra uel parentum no
strozum neq um dictam sum
as de pctis meis. parce nob ds.
yrieleson.
pristeleson.
Xpe audi nos.
Pater de celis

den morr. ou sal scontz

Plate 14 f.81 Opening of the Litany, KYRIE. Christ enthroned.

Plate 15 f.75 Penitential Psalms. Psalm 101. DOMINE EXAUDI. The patron, Susanna,
prays in penitence.

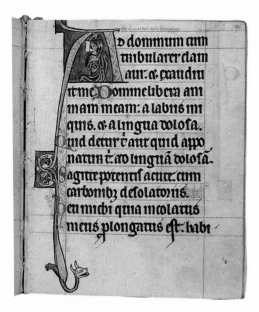

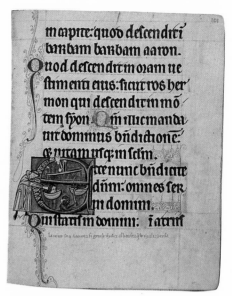

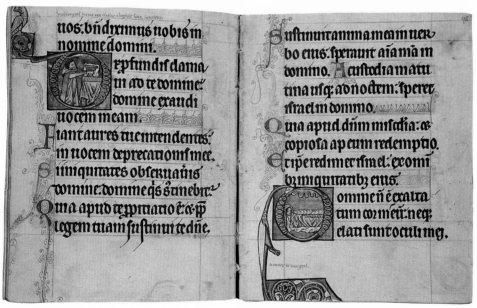

Plate 16a (*Top left*) f.90 Opening of the Gradual Psalms, Psalm 119, AD DOMINUM. Susanna kneels in tribulation. Accused of adultery by the Elders, she prays to the Lord for help to prove her innocence.

Plate 16b (*Top right*) f.101 Gradual Psalms, Psalm 133, ECCE NUNC BENEDICITE. Summoned by the anchorite of the church dedicated to him, St Laurence adds the weight of the golden chalice to guarantee the burgess's passage to heaven.

Plate 16c (*Above*) f.97ᵛ–98 Gradual Psalms, Psalm 129, DE PROFUNDIS. The burgess donates a chalice to the church of St Laurence. Psalm 130, DOMINE NON EST. The burgess lies dead.

stick with the old religion.[141] Furthermore, as William tells it, the story of Theophilus excludes the intermediary Jew who urged Theophilus on. Theophilus here makes his pact directly with the devil, and the chance for a deeply anti-semitic interpretation was passed over.

In the towns of England, from the end of the twelfth century, the Jews represented a commercial threat, and a number of measures were taken to single them out. Statutes prescribing peculiarities of dress and enforcing the wearing of badges of identification were imposed by Henry III.[142] Hints of this anti-semitism are here, clearly visible in the imagery of this manuscript. They depict the seeds of an anti-semitism which culminated eventually in the expulsion of the Jews in 1290.

This, like the other themes made visible in the choice and composition of the imagery, is all part of the currency of the thirteenth century: for the lady living her life in relation to her Church and her role as a citizen of Oxford. Evidently, she took this role seriously. William de Brailes added a leaf to her manuscript, at a point after the folios were ruled and counted out.[143] This added leaf celebrated St Laurence, martyred on his grid in a particularly large-scale historiated initial, identified by a large red rubric – the only formal rubric in the manuscript. This special evidence of devotion to St Laurence is multiplied by the sequence of scenes in the Gradual Psalms which tell the tale of a burgess who lived in the parish of St Laurence. He gave to his church, he contributed to the upkeep of its anchorite, and ultimately he received his reward through the intervention of St Laurence.

Susanna, too, surely lived in the parish of St Laurence. The burgess, clearly a thirteenth-century burgess, was probably known to her. Possibly he was her father. The miraculous deliverance of his soul would have been told to the whole parish by the anchorite or recluse himself, relating his vision of the struggle for the soul of the burgess, and the timely arrival of St Laurence. No anchorite in constant need of alms would have let such a vision remain untold.[144]

Just to the west of the city of Oxford, standing on a rise just above the water of the river Isis, is the old church of St Laurence, North Hinksey. Its fabric is mainly twelfth century: it certainly stood there when Susanna's book was being made. It has been suggested that this church was originally a chapel or monk's cell for the use of travellers crossing the ford, or in winter taking the ferry across the meadows to Oxford.[145] The invocation to St Julian the Hospitaller and ferryman in the litany of Susanna's Hours, would therefore fit a manuscript made for a lady in a parish like this, dependent on the ferryman to make the journey to the city.

So Susanna's devotion to St Laurence can be explained. But how could she have permitted her manuscript to be chopped about, even before it was bound? No complete explanation presents itself. Yet the addition of the prayers to Dominican friars may provide a clue. The building of a huge Dominican friary in Oxford had begun as early as the 1230s. Certainly Oxford housed Dominican scholars and friars by then, including no doubt the three named in Susanna's book – Richard of Newark, Richard of Westey and Bartholomew of Grimston.[146] These three were there to be prayed for, perhaps acting also as spiritual advisers to de Brailes and Susanna, organising a devotional programme for her day.

While clearly the Hours of the Virgin was a necessity to Susanna's day, the selection of the 'Use' of the text would not have been obvious as early as this. Existing contemporary texts of the Hours of the Virgin all differ widely in their details. These variations include their antiphons and capitulae, with variations in the responsory and even in their choice of psalms. In nearly all the English dioceses except York and maybe Hereford, the Hours of the Virgin had settled down by the fourteenth century, accepting the Use of Sarum. By the middle of that century there were only occasional variations from the formula. Earlier on, variability can be expected.[147] The de Brailes Hours has a notable variant in the inclusion of the psalms of the Use of York at Prime. But apart from that, its psalms are standard Use of Sarum, as are the antiphons and capitulae, the best indicators of different Usage even at an early date.[148]

The leaves that were cut out of the de Brailes Hours included the start of Vespers, and here the additional leaves altered the Use of the Hours. Inserted into the collation in place of its opening miniature were three of the psalms of the Use of Rome. Written by a scribe with an Italianate hand, on finer and thinner parchment than the rest of the book, they would always have stood out, despite being neatly tucked into the original sewing. If their purpose had been to transform the manuscript to the Use of Rome, then the job was inefficient. Many more texts needed to be changed, including those Use of York psalms at Prime. But perhaps this change was enough to satisfy a Dominican friar. His order used the Use of Rome, so this change would have enabled Susanna to say her Vespers according to the Dominican usage, maybe in the company of those named friars. It might even have been a Dominican who wrote these pages for her: a friar might well be expected to write in an Italianate hand. Pandering to Susanna, the ruling and penwork flourishes were copied. But permitting such mutilation was surely to pander to the Dominican.

The links between this manuscript and the Dominicans are established by those final prayers. William also had already established links, as he had clearly worked for a Dominican (or for those closely connected with the Dominicans) in the organisation of the writing and executing most of the illumination of a little bible, containing the text of the Mass of St Dominic.[149]

To the non-liturgical mind of the twentieth century, the loss of two full-page miniatures is still inexplicable. Nor is it easy to account for the shortening of so many of the captions to nearly eliminate the meditative 'text' that accompanied those Passion scenes. These two pieces of mutilation all but destroyed that Passion devotion altogether. Yet explanation there must be, while the addition of those extra three psalms was also undoubtedly done for a serious contemporary purpose.

This explanation has not told the full story of the de Brailes Hours, colour and circumstance and all. It has, however, placed Susanna, the patron, in her parish of St Laurence at North Hinksey, clearly in relation to William, the maker, in Catte Street. Their relationship was evidently a cooperative one, allowing her to ask that her own namesake and her own parish saint should be celebrated. Yet the importance of the Dominicans to her devotional life is clear also, and she must have welcomed the addition of the individual prayers and the vernacular verses to the Virgin at the end of her little book. Even so it was surely hard to follow the instruction to lose her Passion pictures to refine her Use. And she must have fallen out forever with her binder.

4. The Book of Hours in thirteenth-century England

There is no earlier book of hours than the de Brailes Hours, but plainly there were others of its kind. Experimental as it is, there is nothing random about the selection of texts. These are the texts for an educated and devout laity, just the sort of people who the resolutions of the Fourth Lateran Council had urged the clergy to care for. Simply written, they focused on the devotion to the Virgin. The humanity of the Virgin is stressed in the hymns selected and in the prayers. Her emotional reactions, and her joys and sorrows, are the joys and sorrows of ordinary people, particularly of women and mothers. It is a devotion based on empathy which, together with the other textual ingredients of these books of hours, gives encouragement to the laity and substance to their hope of salvation.

The de Brailes Hours uses its special mixture of imagery and text to make these hopeful points. No other book of hours of the thirteenth century is as carefully focused and designed. But they all share the simple daily routine of prayer to the Virgin and the saints. This is both the novelty of the book of hours and the key to its enormous popularity over the next three hundred years. Thousands of books of hours were made. In the fifteenth century, many were imported from France and Flanders where mass-produced but lavish manuscripts were designed for the English market, employing the 'Use of Sarum' text.[1] In England, it was the Reformation that finally ended the book's existence. With Edward VI's injunction in 1549 for the confiscation of 'popish rituals' and the books that went with them, many books of hours were destroyed – both manuscripts that would have been passed from generation to generation and the many printed versions that, from Caxton's earliest edition of the primer, had been an evergreen on every publisher's list.[2]

This successful formula, as it was seen in the de Brailes Hours, was the first fully developed statement not just of a new type of book but of a newly important devotional routine for the laity. It structured the day, echoing the monastic regimen in its regularity if not in its complexity. The appearance of both William de Brailes and Susanna in the initials to the prayers at the end of the hours and the litany, gives a glimpse of this book in use: a part of the devotional life of the contemporary laity.

This glimpse suggests the importance of a private devotional life not dominated by church-going. And this impression is borne out by every other feature of the book: its small size, its large script, its many small images. This

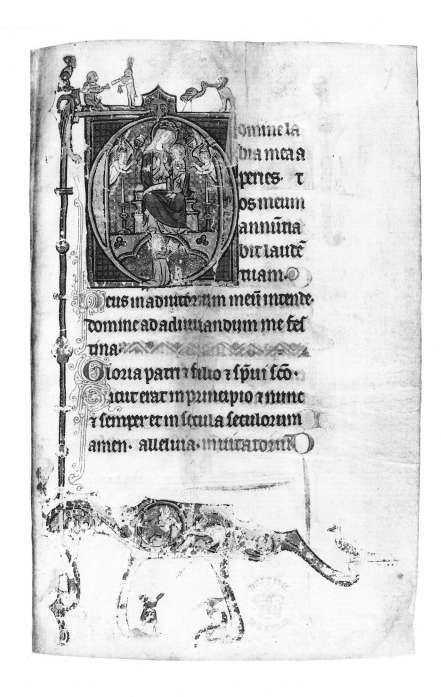

The manuscript text within the illumination reads (in medieval Latin script):

omine la
bia mea a
peries · τ
os meum
annūna
bit laude
tuam ·

Deus in adiutoriū meū intende
domine ad adiuuandum me fes
tina ·

Gloria patri τ filio τ spui sco ·
Sicut erat in principio τ nunc
τ semper et in secula seculorum
amen · alleluia · inuitatorium

87. The Egerton Hours. London, British Library MS Egerton 1151, f.7.
At Matins of the Virgin the lady owner of the manuscript is shown kneeling
beneath the throne of the Virgin and Child, holding up before her the
book of hours that guides her prayer, and structures her day.

was the pattern for the book of hours in the thirteenth century. The lady owner of a book of hours of about 1260, the Egerton Hours, is depicted with fig.87 just such a small book in her hands, praying and reading in privacy.[3] So too does the owner of the Vienna Hours, possessor of both a penance roll and a book of hours for her solitary prayer.[4] For Lady Cobham, a devout lady of figs.96–7 the fourteenth century, her Hours were said in her chamber, before 'speaking with any stranger', as it was recorded in the funeral sermon preached for her in 1344.[5] Much earlier, the *Ancrene Riwle* had stressed the importance of the Hours, said in privacy, for the anchoress. It was the recitation of the Hours of the Virgin in solitude that was seen to be the pivot of a day, set about also with a repertoire of other devotions, to create a complete inner life of prayer.[6] For all these women, laywomen and anchoresses alike, this was a private and personal routine, to be savoured in peace, with the aid of a personal book of hours.

By way of contrast, the pattern set by the large-scale lay psalters of the beginning of the century was also followed, notably in the hybrid psalter-hours, but also in two of the surviving thirteenth-century hours manuscripts, the Salvin Hours and the Walters Hours.[7] This grander type of hours continued to be made occasionally through the fourteenth century, and was the ancestor of the display books of hours of the collectors of the fifteenth century, among them the 'Grandes Heures' of Jean de Berri. Despite the magnificence of such manuscripts, their personal nature was still evident in their individually designed programmes of text and illustration, often making reference to their patrons.[8] The formula for a book of hours was, by this time, established and predictable, but adaptable in every way.

This adaptability was reflected from the very earliest of these manuscripts through the selection of the individual texts to be included, such as different Hours services or prayer sequences. Among the eight surviving English books of hours dating to the thirteenth century, there are as many as fourteen separate texts.[9] Some of these may be found only once (for example, a specific set of prayers meditating on the Passion), where others will occur regularly (including the Office of the Dead). The organisation of the de Brailes Hours might have been a pattern to follow, with devotions to the Virgin and the Passion, and the psalm sequences reflecting both penitential needs and spiritual ambitions. But from the very first, these early books of hours of the thirteenth century were individual and experimental. Each developed as a result of specific influences, whether these were the influences of the artistic tradition of illuminating devotional manuscripts in the centre or 'workshop' where they were made, or the dictates of patrons. While even the very earliest books of hours are readily identifiable as such, the pattern which all thirteenth-century books of hours shared was wide open to adaptation.

It must have been about ten years after the de Brailes Hours was completed that the next book of hours to survive was made. The Marston Hours dates to about 1250, and was patterned on the same scale; a small book written on only ninety folios in a large-scale script. Unlike the de Brailes Hours it was modest in its illustration, small historiated initials opening only the main texts. Even more modestly, it consisted of just two texts – the Hours of the Virgin and the Hours of the Holy Spirit – which were written together, each Hour of the Spirit following the corresponding Hour of the Virgin. Like the de Brailes Hours, where the devotion at each Hour began with the meditation on the Passion and then moved easily into the text of the Virgin with only a turn of the page, the owner of the Marston Hours had her text set out with the devotional arrangement at each Hour complete. Similarly also, the illustration forms two integrated but separate series. The Hours of the Virgin is illustrated with an Infancy cycle. A further layer of devotional interest is added as each of the Hours of the Holy Spirit is illustrated with a scene of the Passion.[10]

This small gathering of two illustrated texts has a personal and intimate quality. Seen as a separate devotional book, it would have formed the perfect supplement to a psalter, ideal for the use of someone following the devotional precepts set out in the *Ancrene Riwle*. This 'rule', although originally written in the early thirteenth century for the spiritual guidance of three secular women enclosing themselves as anchoresses, had a wide popularity. Written first in English, it survives also in both French and Latin versions, and in many manuscripts. A most important element in the setting out of the devotional practice in Part I of the *Riwle*, was the structuring of the day according to the canonical divisions of the Hours. It was clearly the expectation of the author of the *Riwle* that the anchoresses would have a copy of the text of the Hours of the Virgin, for he does not provide it. Moreover, it was his expectation that they would have copied this out for themselves. To add the Hours of the Holy Spirit to this pattern was suggested as a desirable option, although this text too is referred to, not given. The anchoresses were obviously dependent on an exemplar for these texts. The devotional pattern that they lived by prescribed these texts to be said just as they were written out in the Marston Hours: the Hours of the Holy Spirit intermingled with the Hours of the Virgin, each at the appropriate Hour of the day.[11]

Compilation in stages was a characteristic of many of these early books of hours. Before the end of the century, two further texts, the Penitential Psalms and the Litany, were added to the original Hours of the Virgin and of the Holy Spirit in the Marston Hours, together with collects and some prayers in French. These additions were made for a woman who kneels in prayer at the opening of the second of the Penitential Psalms. Perhaps it was always her book, expanded to include further devotional essentials as they seemed necessary, like Susanna's additions to her devotional routine.

Similar additions were made to another of the thirteenth-century hours manuscripts, the Harley Hours, datable to some twenty years later, about 1270. The original part of this manuscript already included the Penitential Psalms, and here the manuscript's lady owner is depicted, this time seen kneeling before the enthroned Christ. The additions were not made until the fifteenth century, by which time the expected texts would certainly have included the Office of the Dead. This Office, added together with a range of other texts, was simply written, and had no further illustration.[12]

That some of these early books of hours were compiled in stages is suggested also by their illustration. Two distinct styles, by more than two separate illuminators, are evident in the Salvin Hours. This large-format manuscript, made in Oxford in about 1270, consists of only three hours services, together with an astonishingly comprehensive suffrage list after Lauds of the Virgin. Indeed the text of the Salvin Hours is as remarkable as its illustration. No portrait-image or dedication introduces the original owner of the manuscript, though it was undoubtedly planned to be a luxury volume. As the Salvin Hours includes neither sequence of psalms, nor calendar, litany or Office of the Dead, it has the texts that would ideally supplement a psalter. Built itself on the lines of a large-scale psalter, the Salvin Hours opens grandly, with a unique interpretation of the well-known image of the Tree of Jesse, the characteristic opening illustration to Psalm 1 of a fig.88 psalter. The owner of the hours must have relied upon a companion psalter to provide the other elements of a devotional routine, possibly also opening with a Tree of Jesse, although it would have had a more conventional company in its branches.[13]

The thirteenth-century book of hours, while complete and free-standing, would only rarely have provided every need of its original owner, as such books were gradually to do later in their development. Even by the end of the thirteenth century, there is still no standard format for a book of hours which would be the model for either the English makers of such books or for the English people requiring them.[14]

Yet examples of completeness, to a textual pattern worthy of the fifteenth century, do exist. The Egerton Hours of about 1260 perhaps approaches this

(*Opposite*) 88. The Salvin Hours. London, British Library MS Add. 48985, ff. 1ᵛ–2. The Tree of Jesse, with eight episodes of the Infancy cycle framed within its branches, opens Matins of the Virgin. On the facing page the versicle **Deus in adiutorium** opens the Passion cycle, which occupies the main initials of each Hour and continues into the full-page opening of the Hours of the Trinity. Reflecting the text, the image opening the Hymn, **Venite exultemus**, shows the Holy Spirit coming to enlighten the Apostles. The page design, with its 22 lines of text and elaborate decorative border, is built on the lines of the large-scale psalter.

89. The Egerton Hours, Compline of Holy Spirit, f.93ᵛ
The Dove of the Holy Spirit lending inspiration to the mundane task of
straightening the pillows for bed at the end of the day, at Compline.

most clearly, with a calendar and a complete sequence of the devotions expected – apart, that is, from the absence of the Gradual Psalms, otherwise found regularly in English books of hours.

Of all these devotions it was the hours texts that lent the structure to the devotional day, as was clear for the laity and, more formally, in the rules for anchoresses. Always the Hours of the Virgin came first, but other hours services were becoming part of this routine too. Only the Hours of the Holy Spirit were also mentioned as central to the anchoresses' routine. But by 1270, the Hours of the Trinity had been written into two manuscripts. One of these, a book of hours which contains prayers added by a contemporary hand for the soul of a lady called Beatrice, perhaps the Beatrice who was a daughter of Henry III, also contained hours services of St John the Baptist and St Katherine, and a text of the Hours of the Passion of Christ.[15] For all these texts, the devotional day was to be divided into the canonical hours – as the French rubrics make quite clear. As the same psalms were called for in the St John Hours as in the Hours of the Virgin, the scribe has economised by requiring the reader simply to refer to the correct place in that text.[16] Perhaps this economy might have been followed in practice too, with lessons, antiphons and responsory for each of the different services said separately, but omitting the repetition of the psalms themselves. This integration of one hours service with another imitates the integration of the different series of illustration, seen both in the Marston Hours and in the de Brailes Hours, and emphasises again the importance of the canonical timing of the hours.

Linking the hours with the day of Christ's Passion had been the way to achieve this structure to the day in the de Brailes Hours, from the Betrayal at dawn to the Crucifixion at None. But in the Egerton Hours, and later in the Walters Hours, these links were made explicitly in the text of the Hours of the Passion.[17] A formal set of services dedicated to the Passion, the hours each began with a series of devotional couplets which linked the sufferings of Christ with each of the canonical hours. This form of the Hours of the Passion is introduced as *del nun iesu pur nus crucifie* in the Egerton Hours and is accompanied by guidance to add certain prayers and to obtain certain indulgences. The Beatrice Hours has a text of the Hours of the Passion too, again with the title *del nun jesu*, but the text is quite different.[18] In the Walters Hours there is a further Passion text, though this is in the form of a series of prayers to be said at the canonical hours. Whatever the form of the text, the meditative theme as set out by St Edmund at the beginning of the century is there: the canonical day linked with the passage of the day of Passion.

Yet, even more emphatically, the canonical pattern of the devotional rite is stated in the illustration to both the Hours of the Virgin and the Hours of the Holy Spirit in the Egerton Hours. In these small historiated initials it is just a day in the life of its owner that is chronicled, and the passage of the hours themselves defines the routine. Both hours sequences follow the same routine, though the Dove of the Holy Spirit is in constant attendance as the fig.89 day passes with the Hours of the Holy Spirit. Initials have been cut out, so that the sequence is not complete, but it is clear that Prime is the time to get up, Terce is for prayer, kneeling formally and in company, None is for fig.90 singing and dancing, Vespers is for more prayer, and Compline is evidently bed-time. The sequence of the hours has a role as a time-keeping routine for ordinary people, in addition to its canonical status. The presence of the enthroned Virgin and Child at Matins of the Virgin, with the tiny figure of the reading praying woman enclosed beneath the throne, acts as a dedication initial, stepping out of the time-keeping function. But coming before the fig.87 greeting of the dawn which illustrates Prime, the sequence implies that Matins was seen as a night-time service. No illustration marks the start of Lauds, just as only a minor initial opens Lauds in the de Brailes Hours. The night-time Matins of the Virgin must have been instantly followed by Lauds, and the prayer before dawn would not have ended until the completion of the sequence of suffrages to saints which follows Lauds.[19] The *Ancrene Riwle* suggests that the opening of the night-time devotions might be performed by the anchoress kneeling on her bed, her arms raised above her head.[20] For the rule-free laity, this would have been unlikely. But the start of the daily devotion must always have been followed in the chamber and in solitude, although not as early as three in the morning, as was suggested for the anchoress. These illustrations to the hours set out the routine of the medieval day, with devotions at each hour, but particularly at Terce and Vespers – clearly the hours for more formal prayer.

Into the structure of the hours services, the sequences of psalms would be inserted. In monastic practice the Gradual Psalms were the opening routine, if Benedict of Aniane's precepts were followed. In the thirteenth century, however, the rule for the anchoresses would certainly have corresponded more closely to lay practice. The *Ancrene Riwle* suggests that the anchoress would say these psalms at Terce. The Litany of the Saints, the Penitential Psalms and the Gradual Psalms all follow Terce of the Virgin and are followed by devotions before the Cross and other prayers. Echoing the prescribed routine of the anchoress, the illustration to Terce of the Holy Spirit in fig.91 the Egerton Hours shows three clerics at prayer before an altar, their vestments gaudy and their tonsures proudly worn. Furthermore this image of a group at prayer before an altar suggests that Terce was a time to go to the chapel for prayer with the household, breaking the solitude of the devotions.

Vespers in the Egerton Hours also shows people at prayer. Vespers of the Virgin was evidently accompanied by the singing of two clerics, to join the evening prayer of the kneeling woman. As well as the recitation of both

90. The Egerton Hours, None of the Virgin, f.47.
Dancing to the music of the afternoon, at None of the Virgin.

Vespers, of the Virgin and of the Holy Spirit, the Office of the Dead was also said at Vespers, as well as its other main service, said at Matins.

This Office was the regular routine of prayer for the dead, and formed no part of a funeral. Despite this, the Office of the Dead illustration in the Egerton Hours shows a service conducted around a coffin, which is an illustrative formula that becomes very commonly used. Moreover, this illustration includes lay figures, both men and women, in addition to the clerics singing the funeral service. The dead depended upon the living to carry out their intercessory role diligently: a complex routine of prayers, offices and masses for the dead.[21] Frequently written into the calendar of the liturgical and devotional books were obits to remind the living of the anniversaries of the dead. At the very beginning of the fourteenth century, a book of hours includes many obits of the de Vere family, some written at the same time as the calendar itself, some added later.[22] There is no calendar in the Beatrice Hours, but prayers for Beatrice's soul – reminders to the next generation who inherited her book – have been added to the text. In the Egerton Hours, depicted in the initial to the Office of the Dead, the living are present at the service, as a reminder of the vital task of intercession required both of the professional clerics and the lay men and women of the family.

In its very different way, the illustration of the Egerton Hours defines the structure of the passage of rites for the devout owner just as was the case in the de Brailes Hours. Even more than in that manuscript, the routine set out is demanding, with the addition of both the Hours of the Holy Spirit and the Office of the Dead. It also included a complete text for the Hours of Christ Crucified, rather than simply illustrated hints for meditation, as in William's design. It was almost equal in its devotional demands to the rule followed by the anchoresses; and for the laity who would have had all the demands of daily life to satisfy as well, it adds up to an astonishingly rigorous routine. To add even further to this, as was the case for the owner of the Beatrice Hours, made the demands overwhelming.

However, just as for Susanna, the demands of the daily use of these books of hours would have been eased by the programme of imagery that led the devout through the day. Further, just as in the de Brailes Hours, the imagery did not simply ease the routine, but enlarged and developed the meaning of the devotions for their owners. Even though no other English book of hours of the thirteenth century was planned with so complex a programme of iconography as the de Brailes Hours, the existence of the simplest illustration was important. It was this that set the scene and provided a focus for the devotional routine. Confirming this, the role of illustration is perhaps most evident in the Beatrice Hours where no imagery remains. It was never a lavish manuscript, but at the Matins initial of each of the major hours texts an historiated initial has been removed. These spaces and cut out pages

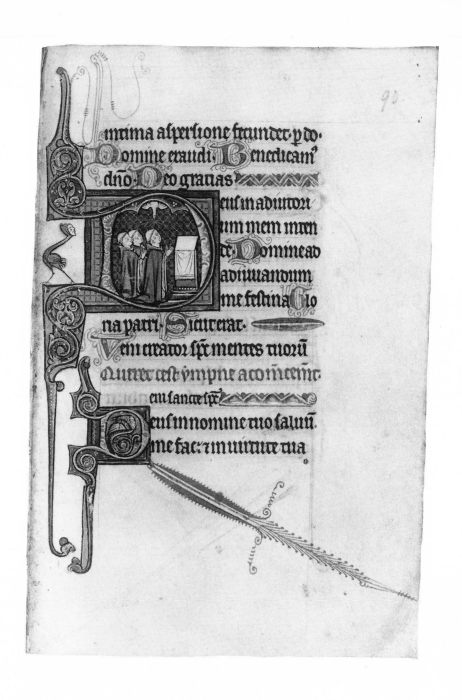

91. The Egerton Hours, Terce of the Holy Spirit, f.90.
Terce is evidently the hour for formal prayer, conducted here before an altar by three tonsured clerics, who receive the blessing of the Dove of the Holy Spirit.

92. The Harley Hours. British Library MS Harley 928, ff.3ᵛ–4 Prefatory miniatures venerating the Virgin and the life of Christ open the illustration of this small-scale book of hours. Out of order, the Nativity precedes the Visitation. Each image is accompanied by prayers on the reverse of the miniature.

(*Opposite*) 93. The Salvin Hours, Sext of the Virgin, f.35 The links with the design of the de Brailes Hours stand out firmly here. While Christ is mocked following his judgement, Peter denies his Lord and the cock crows the betrayal, perched on a decorative pinnacle. Peter suffers the agony of remorse, and as in William's version, is excluded from the initial frame.

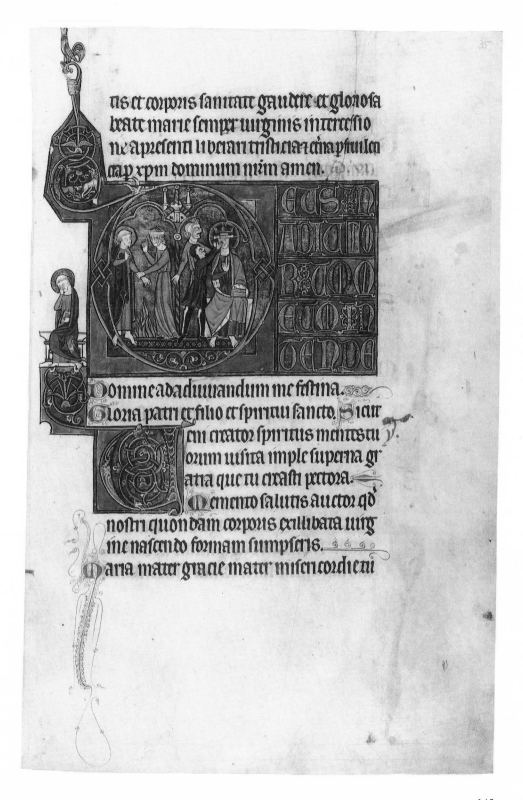

tis et corporis sanitate gaudere et gloriosa
beate marie semper virginis intercessio
ne a presenti liberari tristicia et eterna perfrui
letica p xpm dominum nostrum amen.

Domine ad adiuuandum me festina.
Gloria patri et filio et spiritui sancto. Sicut
erat creator spiritus mentes tu
orum visita imple superna gra
tia que tu creasti pectora.
Memento salutis auctor qd
nostri quondam corporis extibata uirg
ine nascendo formam sumpseris.
Maria mater gracie mater misericordie tu

emphasise the loss. It leaves the prayer routine without that extra layer of meaning; the devotional focus has gone.

The importance of the image in setting the mood for prayer was long understood. The illustration of a psalter text was commonly augmented with a series of pictorial pages that acted as a preface. Often these were historical, of Old and New Testament narratives, sometimes accompanied by descriptive texts. They would sometimes contain devotional or iconic images too – images akin to a Christ in Majesty or a Virgin and Child on an altarpiece or a wall-painting.[23] The pictorial preface did not become a part of the standard type of illustration for the hours in the long run. But even into the mid-fourteenth century, a few hours manuscripts adopted this model.[24] The preface to the Vienna Hours is a beautifully structured series of images telling the life of Christ in fourteen key episodes from the Annunciation to the Entombment. But the English artist who designed the historiated initials to conduct the worshipper through the text of this manuscript was not the designer of this highly organised scheme. It was a North French artist who painted these miniatures, though they were surely made to fit this manuscript, and their style dates them to much the same time.[25] As with the Marston Hours, it is evident that these hours manuscripts were being put together to their owners' special requirements. Only the Harley Hours, of this thirteenth-century group, has a preface of full-page miniatures painted in England. And even these six images have a text, each accompanied by a prayer in honour of the episode depicted. The life of Christ is celebrated, and his mother venerated through these images. They set the devotional mood, fig.92 anticipating the text.

Even though each one of these books of hours opens with the Hours of the Virgin, the imagery that accompanies the text may set quite different devotional moods.[26] William de Brailes's Hours concentrated first on the Passion, with the life and miracles of the Virgin integrated with the text. Sharing these iconographic features is the Salvin Hours, also made in Oxford, though some thirty years later. This has a similar devotional emphasis.[27] Each of the Hours of the Virgin is illustrated by an episode of the Passion of Christ, which provides a brief visual meditation on the events of the Passion, before moving fig.93 on to the textual devotion to the Virgin. Unlike the Passion scenes of the de Brailes Hours, these are not accompanied by captions linking the scene with the canonical hour nor, indeed, do they fit that scheme. Yet, just as in that designed by William, the pictorial narrative of Christ's Infancy is there too in the Salvin Hours, standing as a preface to the whole text. It is depicted in a series of tiny spaces among the branches of an elaborate Tree of Jesse in the fig.88 very first initial to the manuscript, a full-page initial 'D'. Looking just like the Beatus initial of a psalter, the unprecedented intrusion of this narrative into such a theologically significant image was a concession to the different iconographic requirements of a book of hours, chief of which was the establishment of the role and importance of the Virgin.[28]

The design of the Salvin Hours betrays a considerable uncertainty about both the contents of a book of hours and how it should be illustrated, evidence that there was as yet no established tradition for such books. The opening full-page historiated initial to the Hours of the Holy Spirit is also designed like a page from a psalter. But it contains scenes apparently left over from the Passion sequence of the Hours of the Virgin. Finishing off that narrative, the scenes seem to ignore the text that they preface. In point of fact the narrative includes the Pentecost, among the final events following the story of the Passion, but this apparently went unnoticed by the designer of the manuscript. Certainly, its relevance to the text it precedes failed to give this scene any greater prominence than the other episodes on this page.

The designer of the Salvin Hours, it seems, drew on a repertoire of stock images for the illustration of the manuscript. Images of popular saints – usually their grisly martyrdoms – were included in the pictorial prefaces of a number of contemporary psalters, made for a similar lay market, and the illuminators of the Salvin Hours made use of these same designs in the historiated initials to both the Hours of the Holy Spirit and of the Trinity. In the pictorial preface the function of such images was clear; to develop a devotion to these chosen saints, using the image in place of words. Here, linked tightly to a text through their inclusion in the first initial of the word of the text, their presence is confusing. The texts honoured the Holy Spirit or the Trinity; the initials provided a reminder of the saints.

Unlike the design of the de Brailes Hours, where the role of the illustration was to expand on and develop the words of the text, this use of illustration in the Salvin Hours seems arbitrary. While the designer made some use of the de Brailes Hours as an exemplar, once he was on his own and providing illustration for texts not included in the earlier book, he turned, without any of the care that de Brailes so clearly showed for the role of illustration, to the stock of images available to him. The Salvin Hours was a high-quality and lavish work. But this only demonstrates all the more clearly the lack of a tradition, making the need for the establishment of an exemplar all the more acute. Without such an exemplar, and in the absence of the control of a designer such as William, the tightly structured devotional link between text and image could become lost altogether.

As a result, to describe an expected series of illustration for these thirteenth-century books or to anticipate links between text and imagery is impossible. Sometimes, as with the Salvin Hours, it is through tracing the sources of the manuscript's imagery and noting its arbitrary quality that the flavour of the individual manuscript appears. The Harley Hours has a similar flavour, although seemingly even more arbitrary. With its devotional narratives tucked into the pictorial preface, Matins of the Virgin in the Harley Hours opens with the martyrdom of St Katherine. Three other services of the Hours of the Virgin also open with images of saints. But even this unconnected idea is not consistently followed. The sequence is not single-minded and, with the images of saints intruding, it leads the worshipper to celebrate the Coronation of the Virgin at Prime, and to contemplate the Ascension at Vespers and Pentecost at Compline. Both these last scenes would have been part of the sequence ending the illustration to the Hours of the Virgin in de Brailes's design, preceding Vespers or Compline. Both scenes occur in the Salvin Hours. fig.94

The design of the Harley Hours demonstrates the multiple possibilities that could be suggested to the maker of a book of hours in these early days, perhaps also reflecting the interests of its original owner. The woman who kneels before the enthroned Christ in the Harley Hours might have designed her very own series, to include her especially important personal saints. And the series of historiated initials in the Egerton Hours also shows the influence

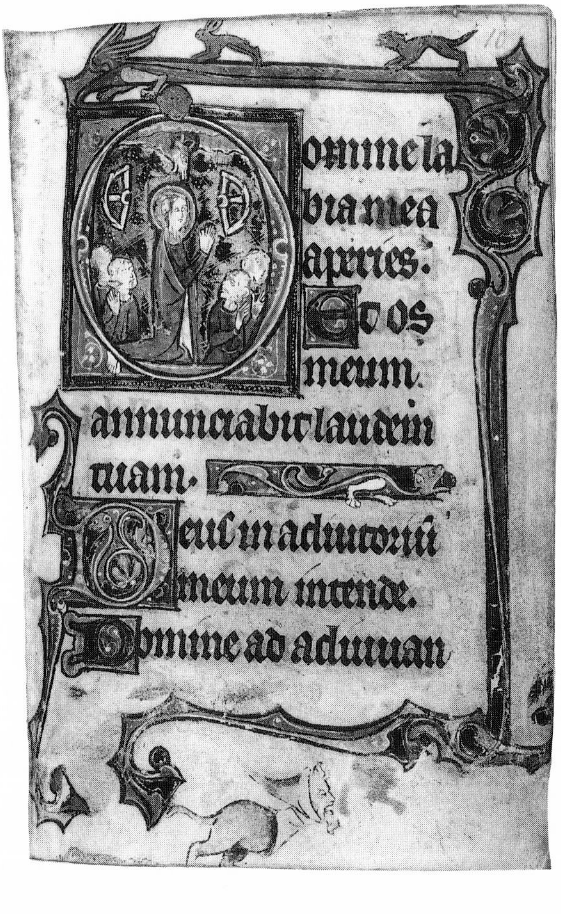

94. The Harley Hours. Matins of the Virgin, f.10
The opening of Matins of the Virgin celebrates the triumph of St Katherine over the torture of the wheel. Kneeling in praise, the wheels are seen to be powerless against her, crushing the onlookers who sought her death.

of the owner: the illustrations to her hours designed to mirror her life. These images of her daily life reflect the central role of the devotional routine, and the power of prayer to evoke the aid of the Holy Spirit. Constantly there in illustration to those hours, each part of the day is filled with his inspiration, fig.89 in prayer and even in such mundane tasks as straightening the pillows at bedtime. Only two initials in this manuscript step into narrative where, in direct illustration of the opening devotional couplets, the Betrayal of Christ illustrates Matins of the Hours of Christ Crucified and the Entombment opens Compline. These images come from a different tradition, which can be directly linked back to the purpose of the meditative pictorial devotion in the de Brailes Hours.

Even at the end of the century, no tradition had yet been established, and just about every possibility for illustration was exploited in the Walters Hours. A remarkable manuscript in every way, the problems of reconstructing the original text and illustrative programme of this Hours have been multiplied by the nineteenth-century rebinding, which cut the quires to pieces and reorganised the folios. The result is that the book opens with a Tree of Jesse initial which makes it look like a psalter, and the rest is a muddle. It is still lavish, however, despite some losses, as most of the illustration has been rearranged, not, as sometimes happened, cut out to be re-used in a scrapbook. Historical sequences accompany both the Passion texts, although the sequence of prayers of the Passion is illustrated with a mixture of narratives and devotional images, while the more familiar hours sequence has a simple narrative following the passage of the Passion, linked with the canonical hours. There is also a hint of a narrative series of images to accompany the Hours of St Katherine. One of the long sequence of lessons at Matins describes an episode from Katherine's life in which King Maxentius debates her fate with the doctors of Alexandria. This episode appears in the historiated initial which accompanies it, and indicates that there would have been further illustration here.

As well as all this formal iconographic richness there lurks an extraordinary sequence of marginal imagery in the Walters Hours, with the line fillers of the litany overtaken by large-scale figures, prominent among them St Stephen martyred by a stone in his head, but, incredibly, wearing a cruciform halo, the symbol of Christ. A nude figure of Adam fills one whole page fig.95 of line-endings, and a pair of chess-players occupy a large framed space to the right of the invocation of the saints. In the margins of the Office of the Dead, the funeral procession of Renart the Fox is played out, with rabbits and hares solemnly performing the liturgy in parodied precision. Symbolic birds and beasts turn up suddenly, in a margin or at a line ending. Even the scribe is depicted hauling into place a psalm verse that he had omitted in his copying, one long finger pointing to the spot, the verse itself lassooed on the end of a

rope.[29] But the devotional purpose of the manuscript is proclaimed by the many images of people in prayer. Lay men and women, clerics and acolytes all appear: sometimes together, sometimes in solitude, and sometimes with the figure of Christ or the blessing hand of God.

In de Brailes's Hours, only the moments of private prayer were illustrated with depictions of lay figures, either William or Susanna. Wrapped in the narrative, these devotional moments stood out, creating an image that spoke directly to the owner of the manuscript. In the Walters Hours, these praying figures create this same contact. And, in its particular canonical context, the idea was also exploited in the Egerton Hours. But in the Vienna Hours, this image of prayer dominates. It is the main theme of the historiated initials to the text. And while the first two initials, at Matins of the Virgin, show a laywoman in prayer, a variety of figures, dressed to identify themselves, inhabit the initials to the Hours of the Virgin, including each of the nine lessons of Matins. They include men and women, some of whom are crowned, some tonsured clerics wearing various coloured robes, and a black-habited nun. Found in a variety of settings, they are all essentially engaged in prayer – the community of the faithful in its many different guises. Interspersed with these people there are occasional images which would fit into a narrative series, such as the Visitation, the Nativity, the enthroned Christ. But the emphasis is surely on the importance of prayer, as an example for the owner of the manuscript, its regular user. This owner dominates the two final images of the Vienna Hours, reading from a prayer roll at the initial to the

figs.96–7 Penitential Psalms, and kneeling before a book at the opening of the Gradual Psalms. As in Susanna's Hours, the presence of the 'donor-portrait' is not surprising.

In the future story of the book of hours the donor-portrait was only to be expected.[30] But it is an expectation that depends upon a modern understanding of a book: that it is primarily a personal object for individual reading and private study. By the mid-thirteenth century this would not have seemed exceptional. Yet it was a change in perception that was not much older than the century itself. Illuminated liturgical books in the twelfth century were, of their nature, grand ceremonial objects. Mostly part of the furnishings of the ecclesiastical centres of power, they were predominantly community books, in common ownership. They were books to be shared, or books to be admired. For the really great twelfth-century

(*Opposite*) 95. The Walters Hours. Baltimore, Walters Art Gallery, ff.28ᵛ–29, Litany. While the litany invokes the saints, the imagery is not directly related it seems. The image of Adam holding the apple of the original sin confronts the face of Christ with the cruciform halo but with the wound of St Stephen. Without that original sin, neither the sufferings of Christ, nor those of Christ's martyrs would have been required. The image of the chess-board brings to mind the conflict in man as a result of the temptations of life.

bibles their role was similar in importance to the possession of the relics of the local saint.

In contrast, books of hours were designed, in the wake of the newly developed portable bible, to be used by an individual and to be carried about. Such bibles and books of hours were clearly personal, to be tucked in a pocket, to be brought out for regular consultation, and, in the case of the hours, to be used in the creation of the devotional day. While the bibles were written in tiny script in two columns, the owners of the early book of hours had a more accessible volume. The format as it was first seen in the de Brailes Hours, with its large clear script written in a single column, became common to most of these thirteenth-century hours manuscripts, laying out the devotional routine simply and clearly. Such a manuscript was a most satisfactory personal possession.

From the start their owners appear. Susanna's pink robe, her smart white hat and her flowing hair, insist that she was not dedicated solely to her faith, though no doubt religion was a highly important part of her life, structuring her day and providing its backbone. Each time William de Brailes depicts Susanna she is shown in prayer. She is always alone: an independent young woman of style and some substance, if not of great wealth or nobility. As early as this in the thirteenth century, few middle-class women are accorded this level of reality.

Indeed, at this date even aristocratic laywomen are largely invisible. Early in the century, the aristocratic landowning lady might appear on her personal seal. But, with her name and title inscribed around the frame, such images were designed primarily as identification – as a sign, a personal signature. Evidence of the letters that they wrote and the conduct of the affairs of their household and estates, the seal served a specific purpose.[31] The image portrayed in the pages of a manuscript had quite a different function. Two psalters, one in Berlin and the other at St John's College (Cambridge), dating to the very beginning of the century, contain images of crowned women, perhaps Isabella, queen of King John, who himself appears with her in the Berlin manuscript.[32] Both contain the text of the Hours of the Virgin, and both are copiously illuminated by the same artist, who may have been one of the Oxford community of illuminators. To find an artist or patron in prayer in the illumination of a manuscript is not unprecedented, but such images remain extremely rare before the mid-century.

Before the end of the thirteenth century, ordinary laywomen were portrayed in five more of the eight surviving books of hours made in England.[33] An obviously aristocratic lady of the family of the Bohuns of Midhurst, in Sussex, opted for a grandly illustrated psalter in about 1270. She appears three times in the illustration, and is identified by her armorials. Twice she is shown conventionally in prayer, but in a full-length portrait together with

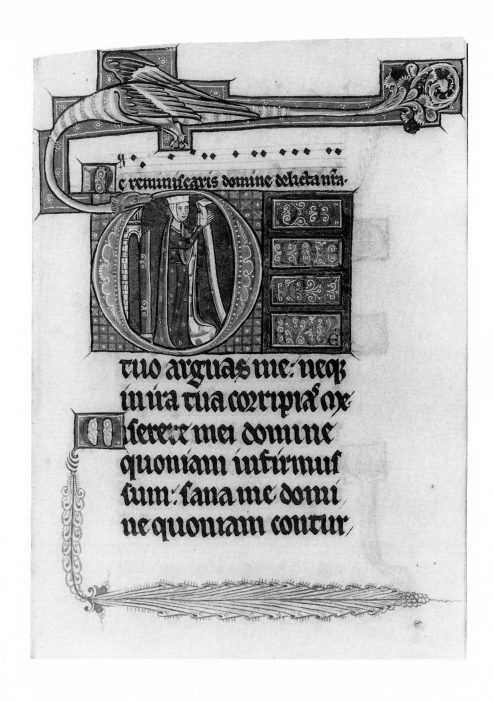

96. The Vienna Hours, Penitential Psalms, f. 153. Her penance roll in her hands, the lady owner of the manuscript stands outside the church door. The small scale manuscript is elaborately decorated, with the swooping dragon, clothed in decoration, grasping the initial in its mouth.

153

97. The Vienna Hours, Gradual Psalms, f.173ᵛ. Reminiscent of the image of Jacob
wrestling with the angel as sometimes found as illustration to Psalm 80 in a psalter, it is a
dragon and a man who wrestle here, forming the 'A' for **Ad dominum**, and enclosing the
woman as she prays privately, with the aid of her book of hours.

154

her little daughter, she is shown in a pose of maternal elegance rather than piety. Like the images of Susanna, the Bohun image is evidently a portrait of a living patron, not a posthumous image or memorial.[34]

Memorials of women at this date are also rare. An image in stained glass of Beatrix van Valkenburg, third wife of Richard of Cornwall, is an early example, witness to her donation of money for the glazing of the church of the Minorite Friars in Oxford, where she was buried in 1277.[35] Rather later, of 1310, is the first memorial brass to a laywoman, Margaret Lady Camoys. In the country church of St George at Trotton, just west of Midhurst, Margaret's gown was once studded with shields of arms, identifying her for all to see.[36] Unlike Susanna, Margaret's identity was secured both through heraldry (now lost) and by an inscription. Like Susanna, Margaret Camoys is portrayed alone, an independent woman made visible.

Portraits of the laity hardly exist until the late thirteenth century. And such depictions remained rare until the very end of the century when, with a rush, the laity emerged from the shadows, not just in illuminated manuscripts, but as memorials in commemorative panels of stained glass, on tombs and monumental brasses and, in the early fourteenth century, embroidered on church vestments.[37] The de Brailes Hours is the herald of this visible emergence of the laity: an aspect of the manuscript that has gone largely unnoticed because, after all, it was only to be expected in a book of hours that its lay owner should be depicted. The five other thirteenth-century books of hours to depict their first owners, all laity – the Marston, Egerton, Vienna, Harley and Walters Hours – each give the most prominent place among these donor-portraits to women. A sixth, the Beatrice Hours, was made for a woman, though she is not depicted. The very personal nature of these books of hours has created an obvious context in which their owners can become visible, and the expectation of the donor-portrait in such books is seen to be justified, even among these very early examples.

Unidentified, the owners of these hours kneel in prayer. Piety is their characteristic pose as they appear in these portraits in their books of hours, as is only suitable for images linked to prayers. But these book-owning women fig.96 are also depicted as readers. At the opening of the Penitential Psalms, the lady owner of the Vienna Hours stands before the open door of a church and reads from a penance roll.[38] Fashionable like Susanna she wears a similar fig.97 style of hat. With her hair falling down her back, and therefore surely unmarried, she reads from an open book at the beginning of the Gradual Psalms. And the owner of the Egerton Hours is shown kneeling too, with her fig.87 small portable book held up before her. It must surely be a book of hours that she holds.

The story, as told in the de Brailes Hours, is of a devotional routine for a literate and devout laywoman. The same story is told, with variations, by these other surviving thirteenth-century books of hours. While the book of hours was by no means used only by women, it is certainly in these manuscripts that literate women emerge most visibly during the thirteenth century. And it is in these books that the life of the laity, in relation to the life of the Church, also emerges. The giving of church plate to the parish church, and of alms to the anchorite, are depicted in Susanna's personal hours. The community of prayer shared by laity and clerks is a common image, particularly in the Egerton Hours and the Vienna Hours. Prayers for individual friars in the de Brailes Hours, together with the Austin Friars text of the Walters Hours, establish contacts between the town-based friaries and the lay owners of these books of hours. Moreover, the conversion of the laity into book-owners is central to the history of manuscripts in the thirteenth century. All these and other circumstances contributed to the immense popularity of the book of hours in later medieval England. But of one originating circumstance there is no reasonable doubt. The creation of the new book was William's own –

w. de brail' qui me depeint.

Notes

1 William de Brailes, illuminator of Oxford

1. Cambridge, Fitzwilliam Museum MS 330, leaf 3. See fig. 2 and Appendix 4, no. 19.

2. The de Brailes manuscripts are listed in Appendix 4, nos. 15–21.

3. Even within the individual manuscripts there is little firm indication of an intended destination. For example, while the calendar of New College MS 322 suggests a use within the Winchester diocese, the litany contains saints that were particularly important in the diocese of Canterbury. N. J. Morgan, *Early Gothic Manuscripts (I) 1190–1250* (London, 1982) catalogue no. 74.

4. C. M. Kauffmann, *Romanesque Manuscripts 1066–1190* (London, 1975), p. 15. Morgan (I), p. 14.

5. Described in Appendix 4, nos. 1–9. For this group of manuscripts, Morgan (I), p. 14 and cats. 23, 24, 28–32.

6. The variations are indicated in Appendix 4. See below, p. 16 and note 23.

7. St Frideswide's cult was given extra encouragement in 1180 when her relics were translated into a new shrine. Her translation was celebrated on 12 February. This feast in a calendar, together with her main feast of 19 October, is a sure indication of an Oxford importance, locating the origin of the manuscript. Morgan (I), cat. 24, p. 73, outlines the significance of these feasts as indications of an Oxford origin. See Chapter 3, note 120.

8. H. E. Salter, *Medieval Oxford* (O. H. S., 1936) pp. 41–2. Susan Reynolds, *An Introduction to the History of English Medieval Towns* (London, 1977). R. H. C. Davis, 'An Oxford charter of 1191 – the beginnings of municipal freedom', *Oxoniensia*, 33 (1968), p. 63. The existence of a municipal seal for Oxford, dated 1191, also confirms its independence. Colin Platt, *The English Medieval Town* (London, 1976), p. 129.

9. On exhibition in Oxford City Museum. Tom Hassall, *Oxford: The Buried City* (Oxford, 1987) p. 45.

10. The Abbey of Oseney was among the most important of the land-holders in Oxford at this time. H. E. Salter, *Cartulary of Oseney Abbey* (O. H. S., 1929).

11. H. E. Salter, *Map of Medieval Oxford* (Oxford, 1934). H. E. Salter, *Survey of Oxford*, edited by W. R. Pantin, W. T. Mitchell (O. H. S., new series, 14, 1960; 20, 1969).

12. Hassall, p. 19. Platt, pp. 51–57.

13. G. Pollard, 'The University and the Book Trade in Medieval Oxford', *Miscellanea Medievalia*, 3 (1964), pp. 336–44. A deed of *c.* 1210–20 provides clear evidence of the book trade in Catte Street, with a scribe, three illuminators and a parchment-maker all standing as witnesses, University Archives, WPB/F/46, catalogued in *Duke Humfrey's Library and the Divinity School 1488–1988*, Catalogue of an exhibition held at the Bodleian Library (Oxford, 1988), no. 1, p. 6.

14. Pollard, 'Book Trade'; Salter, *Survey*, vol. 1, pp. 65–130. *Duke Humfrey's Library* pp. 4–13. For the increasing importance of the written word at this time, M. T. Clanchy, *From Memory to Written Record* (London, 1979).

15. G. Pollard, 'William de Brailes', *Bodleian Library Record*, 5, no. 4 (1955), pp. 202–9. Pollard, 'The University and the Book Trade', p. 337.

16. For details of these documents, see Appendix 5.

17. *V. C. H. Oxfordshire*, 3, edited by H. E. Salter and M. D. Lobel (1954): The University of Oxford.

18. Christopher de Hamel, *A History of Illuminated Manuscripts* (Oxford, 1986) Chapter 4, 'Books for Students', pp. 110–134.

19. de Hamel, pp. 120–126.

20. J. Destrez, *La Pecia dans les Manuscrits Universitaires du XIIIe et du XIVe Siecle*, (Paris, 1935). G. Pollard, 'The pecia system in the medieval universities', *Medieval Scribes, Manuscripts and Libraries: Essays presented to N. R. Ker*, edited by M. B. Parkes, A. G. Watson, (London, 1978), pp. 145–161. De Hamel, pp. 126–130, pp. 134–5. *Duke Humfrey's Library*, pp. 4–6, no. 4, an Aristotle dating to before 1254, and no. 11, evidently a stationer's *pecia* of the the early fourteenth century.

21. *Duke Humfrey's Library*, no. 10, p. 10. S. J. P. van Dijk, 'An advertisement sheet of an early fourteenth-century writing master at Oxford', *Scriptorium*, 10 (1956), pp. 47–64.

22. No other names but that of de Brailes can be attached to specific manuscripts at present, but the

evidence of a prosperous bookmaking community is considerable. For details of the documents in which the name of de Brailes and these and other illuminators appear, see Appendix 5. *Duke Humfrey's Library*, pp. 4–5. Pollard, (1955), p. 209.

23. The variety of saints invoked in the litanies and marked in the calendars to be celebrated indicates links rather than creating definite liturgical destinations. For these manuscripts see Appendix 4, nos. 1, 7 and 4. This group is identified in Morgan (I), p. 14, where he catalogues them as nos. 23, 24, 28–32. The quantity and arrangement of illustration and decoration would have been to the requirements of their clients.

24. Even though the destinations of the de Brailes manuscripts are not so evidently far-flung, they were made for a range of customers.

25. Morgan (I), p. 13.

26. M. B. Parkes, 'The Literacy of the Laity', in *Literature and Western Civilisation: The Medieval Period*, edited by D. Daiches and A. K. Thorlby (London, 1973), pp. 555–77. Morgan (I), p. 13. Susan Groag Bell, 'Medieval Woman Book Owners: arbiters of lay piety and ambassadors of culture', *Signs: Journal of Women in Culture and Society*, VII, 4 (1987), pp. 742–68.

27. N. J. Morgan and L. F. Sandler, 'Manuscript Illumination of the Thirteenth and Fourteenth Centuries', in *Age of Chivalry* (London, 1987), pp. 148–56 (p. 148).

28. de Hamel, pp. 113–7, 134; Clanchy, pp. 104–5.

29. Indeed the surviving volumes of the de Brailes group are all of this format.

30. Salter, *Survey*, Map NE III. Among the records of the buildings of this area is a house called Glasen Hall, which stood at the south end of School Street, next to the tenement which changed hands with William de Brailes as witness. Glasen Hall was given to Oseney by John Pilet (who also once owned the neighbouring tenement) in 1235, and it had a Hall and two schools or lecture rooms. Salter, *Oseney*, vol. 1, p. 188.

31. J. R. H. Moorman, *Church Life in England in the Thirteenth Century* (Cambridge, 1945). Marion Gibbs and Jane Lang, *Bishops and Reform 1215–1272* (Oxford, 1934).

32. C. H. Lawrence, *St Edmund of Abingdon: a study in hagiography and history* (1960). Mother Mary Philomena, 'St Edmund of Abingdon's meditations before the canonical Hours', *Ephemerides Liturgicae* (1964), pp. 33–57. Edmund of Abingdon, *Speculum Religiosorum and Speculum Ecclesia*, edited by Helen P. Forshaw (London, 1973). St Richard of Chichester's special devotion to the Virgin is given visual weight through the attribution of the roundel of the Virgin and Child

in the Bishop's Chapel in Chichester to the period of his bishopric there, *c.* 1250.

33. A. B. Emden, *An Oxford Hall in Medieval Times* (Oxford, 1968), pp. 88–95.

34. *Fratris Thomae, vulgo dicti de Eccleston, tractatus De adventu fratrum minorum in Angliam*, edited by A. G. Little, (1951), p. xxx. Platt, pp. 159–160. Hassall, p. 43. R. W Southern, *Western Society and the Church in the Middle Ages* (London, 1970), pp. 284–290.

35. Platt, p. 159. Hassall, pp. 44–47.

36. Platt, pp. 160–163. Southern, pp. 289–292.

37. See pp. 126–7, 130–1, n. 146.

38. See pp. 9–10. self-portraits in both the de Brailes Hours and in the Last Judgement page in the Fitzwilliam Museum.

39. George Warner, *Descriptive Catalogue of Illuminated Manuscripts in the Library of C. W. Dyson Perrins*, 1920, no. 5, pp. 25–7, pl. vi e-k. Sothebys' sale, Monday 5 July 1976, Lot 81, where it is dated pre-1234 on the inference that it dates to before the canonisation of St Dominic. See Morgan (I), p. 115 where he refutes this argument, suggesting a date just after St Dominic's canonisation. Certainly the added text of the translation of St Dominic is a near-contemporary addition. The inclusion of liturgical texts with the bible creates a most informative volume. With its wealth of illumination, it could have been a lavish gift for a friar of the Oxford Blackfriars. *Duke Humfrey's Library*, cat. 3, p. 7.

40. New College MS 322. Appendix 4. In quire 13 the outermost bifolium, f. 113 and f. 122, was entirely painted by de Brailes, the large scale initial on f. 113 together with smaller scale historiated initials, decorative initials, line fillers and sprays into the border.

41. Historiated initials by de Brailes include four (ff. 28, 41v, 54 and 54v) which are pasted in on thin parchment, with the decoration continued from the initial onto the base folio, this decoration too being the work of de Brailes. Certain other psalters made in Oxford also have historiated initials stuck in.

42. These sets of leaves are both supplemented by others, found separately. See Appendix 4, nos. 18, 19.

43. The Hours of the Virgin is included in both Berlin, Kupferstichkabinett MS 78.A.8, and Cambridge, St John's College MS D.6. It is on an added section in a near contemporary hand in B L MS Arundel 157. See Appendix 4, nos. 5, 6, 2.

44. On f. 64ᵛ she kneels at the final prayer of the Hours of the Virgin. She appears again on f. 75, on f. 87ᵛ and f. 88. See Plates 2, 15, figs. 6, 74.

45. On f. 90. See Plate 16a.

46. It occurs in the Munich Psalter, Munich, Bayeri-

sche Staatsbibliothek Clm. 835 on f. 106, in six episodes. Appendix 4, no. 1, Morgan, (I), cat. 23.

47 Although the name Susanna does not occur regularly in the records of the thirteenth century, E. G. Withycombe in *The Oxford Dictionary of English Christian Names* (Oxford, 1977) records a great increase in number and variety of names at this time p. xxviv. 'Susanna' is recorded in Curia Regis Rolls in 1200 through 1213, Withycombe, pp. 273–4.

2 *Shaping the Book*

1. For the thirteenth-century book of hours, see Chapter 4 and Appendix 3. Four more English books of hours can be dated to the first decade of the fourteenth century, together with two that were made in France for English use. A further eight can be dated before 1330. Their survival rate would have been lower than that for contemporary psalters, since they were included among the prohibition on 'service books' at the Reformation. See my own unpublished thesis, C. M. Baker, *The Early Development of the Illustrated Book of Hours in England*, PhD University of East Anglia (1981), particularly Summary Table.

2. The shape of the book of hours has been described frequently, its characteristics based on the fifteenth-century manuscripts, mostly made in France or Flanders. L. M. J. Delaissé, 'The importance of Books of Hours for the history of the medieval book', in *Gatherings for Dorothy E. Miner* edited by Ursula E. McCracken, Lilian M. C. Randall and Richard H. Randall Jr. (Baltimore, 1974), pp. 203–25; John Harthan, *Books of Hours and their Owners* (London, 1977); Janet Backhouse, *Books of Hours* (London, 1985); de Hamel, Chapter 6, 'Books for Everybody', pp. 160–85; Roger S. Weick, *The Book of Hours in Medieval Art and Life* (London, 1988).

3. A brief history of the breviary is given in the Introduction to J. B. L. Tolhurst, *The Monastic Breviary of Hyde Abbey, Winchester*, Henry Bradshaw Society, 6 (London, 1930–42).

4. An early text of the Hours of the Virgin is found in B L MS Cotton Tiberius A III, an eleventh-century manuscript from Christ Church, Canterbury. It also contains the text of the *Regularis Concordia*. A facsimile of this text, together with another copy made for Winchester, is found in E. S. Dewick, *Facsimiles of Horae de Beata Maria Virgine*, Henry Bradshaw Society (London, 1901). The origins of the book of hours were discussed in V. Leroquais, *Les Livres d'heures manuscrits de la Bibliothèque Nationale* (Paris, 1927). Also E. Bishop, 'On the origin of the prymer', *Liturgica Historica* (Oxford, 1918) pp. 211–237. E. Hoskins, *Horae Beatae Mariae Virginis, or Sarum and York Primers* (London,

1901). Baker, pp. 20–1. For the cult of the Virgin, Marina Warner, *Alone of All Her Sex: the myth and the cult of the Virgin Mary* (London, 1976).

5. The use of the psalter as a private devotional book is easily established, yet the form in which the psalms were said is not entirely clear. Morgan (I), p. 15; J. A. Lamb, *The Psalms in Christian Worship* (London, 1962).

6. The timing of the Hours depended on the community, on its location, and on the time of year. D. H. Turner, 'The work of God', *The Benedictines in Britain* (London, 1980), p. 41, sets out the timing and routine for the Benedictine communities, with the proviso 'it is impossible to give a unified picture of the Benedictine *opus dei* in the Middle Ages'. M. M. Philomena, *Ephemerides Liturgicae*, pp. 33–57, discusses the origins of their timing. R. L. Poole, *Medieval Reckonings of Time* (London, 1935), p. 12, emphasises the variability of the timing of the canonical hours, following the system of variable hours depending on the day or night, and the season.

7. W. A. Pantin, 'Instructions for a devout and literate layman', in *Medieval learning and literature: Essays presented to Richard William Hunt*, edited by J. J. G. Alexander and M. T. Gibson (London, 1976), pp. 398–422. The timing of the lay routine is discussed in Wieck, pp. 39–44, although his account is drawn from fifteenth-century examples.

8. The popularity of the psalter in England declined slowly. Indeed it was not until the end of the fourteenth century that the book of hours outstripped the psalter, although by the mid-century in France, the psalter was in decline. Books of hours certainly did expand to satisfy the changing needs, both general and specific, of their owners. This quality of the book of hours is discussed in Delaissé, pp. 204–7, and in de Hamel, pp. 164–5.

9. As a small-scale volume it would have been easily possible to rule two text areas at a time. Prick holes at the gutter edge of each text area would therefore not be necessary. For a description of the process of preparing parchment, pricking and ruling, de Hamel, pp. 84–92. Prick holes in the gutter of the much larger New College Psalter demonstrate a more complex method of parchment preparation undertaken within the de Brailes circle.

10. As it is argued in N. R. Ker, 'From "above top line" to "below top line"', *Celtica*, 5, (1960), pp. 13–16, this feature is an indication of a date post-1200.

11. A standard English *textualis liturgica*, this same scribe can also be identified in de Brailes's most elaborate psalter, Oxford, New College MS 322. See Appendix 4, no 21.

12. This seems certain to have been added as a single folio, sewn through the fold, with the other half of the bifolium chopped neatly just above the sewing. See note 15, for collation and structure diagrams.

13. Described by Michelle Brown, British Library, as a contemporary *textualis rotunda*. She compares it with the descriptive captions of the *Chronica Maiora* of Matthew Paris, *c.* 1250–59, London, B L, Cotton Claudius D.VI. See Morgan (I), pl. 305.

14. This is a common format for contemporary psalters. Among the Oxford-made psalters associated with de Brailes, the Stockholm and New College Psalters both follow this pattern, as do most earlier Oxford-made psalters. It is rare among bibles.

15. The main section of the manuscript, the Hours of the Virgin, consists of 8 quires, with a blank folio at the end of quire 4, opening Prime on f. 32 at the start of quire 5, hence creating a sub-section of Matins-Lauds. The Penitential Psalms and Litany occupy quires 9–11, running together without a break. The Gradual Psalms begin on f. 90, the beginning of a new quire, leaving a whole blank verso following the collects after the Litany. The prayers are added onto the empty folios of the final quire. Essentially the three sections therefore are:
Hours of the Virgin Quires 1–8
Penitential Psalms and Litany Quires 9–11
Gradual Psalms Quires 12–13
Collation:
Quire 1 = 8 ff. 1–8
Quire 2 = 8 ff. 9–16
Quire 3 = 8 ff. 17–24
Quire 4 = 6 + 1 ff. 25–31
Six leaves with the addition of f. 28. This may be half of an added bifolium, from which one leaf has been removed. A stub remains before f. 28. The opening part of the text on f. 28 is not complete.
Quire 5 = 8 ff. 32–39
Quire 6 = 8 ff. 40–47
Quire 7 = 9 (3, –1, + 2, 4, + 1) ff. 48–57
Quire 8 = 8 (2, –1, 5, + 1) ff. 58–65
Quire 9 = 8 ff. 66–73
Quire 10 = 8 ff. 74–81
Quire 11 = 8 ff. 82–89
Quire 12 = 8 ff. 90–97
Quire 13 = 8 ff. 98–105

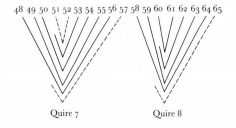

48 49 50 51 52 53 54 55 56 57 58 59 60 61 62 63 64 65

Quire 7   Quire 8

16. After the skin for the binding had been whittawed to whiten it, the skin could then be stained with kermes, a pink dye. Kermes-stained bindings occur quite regularly in the mid-thirteenth century. Described in Graham Pollard, 'The construction of English twelfth-century bindings', *The Library*, 18 (1962), pp. 13–14.

17. Revising Cockerell. In 1906 Sydney Cockerell described it as an Italian binding of the fifteenth century, reprinted as the entry in the catalogue of the Dyson Perrins collection, G. F. Warner, *Descriptive Catalogue of the Illuminated Manuscripts in the Library of C. W. Dyson Perrins* (1920), no. 4. p. 24.

18. Pollard, (1962), p. 3, note 5. He suggests that bindings of this date are almost invariably made of oak boards. Mirjam Foot, British Library, advised that the binding was consistent with the date of the text and illumination. This type of binding was used over a long period, and the de Brailes binding, in her view, has no features to verify a specific date, although the pin and strap fastening looked consistent with this date, and not much later. Pollard dates most kermes-stained bindings to *c.* 1250–1350, though noting one (B L MS Add. 15350) dating to *c.* 1150, Pollard, (1962), p. 14.

19. See note 15 above for the structural layout. For textual changes, see Chapter 3 below.

20. Cockerell, (1906), p. 14 considered these leaves to be Italian, and consistent with his view of the binding as Italian also. Michelle Brown, British Library, suggested comparisons with the *rotunda litterata Italiana Bononiensis* as seen in an English bible of *c.* 1240, Cambridge University Library MS Ee.2.23, itself connected to the de Brailes manuscripts. She considers the script of BL, MS Ashmole 1525 and Paris, Bibl. Nat. lat. 770 also comparable. See Morgan (I), pls 216, 115–20.

21. See discussion, pp. 103–4.

22. For discussion of possible reasons, see Chapter 3, pp. 129–31.

23. Both illustrative cycles interlock, illustrating the Hours of the Virgin. See Chapter 3, particularly pp. 45, 69, 75, 80, 87.

24. Lauds, in the routine followed by the monastic communities, followed Matins directly. Many English manuscript books of hours follow this by marking the opening of Lauds with only minimal decoration. See below, Chapter 3, p. 51, n. 14, and Chapter 4 for its more general application to English hours manuscripts.

25. This type of caption is found accompanying the pictorial sequence painted by de Brailes now in Baltimore, Walters MS 500. See Appendix 4 no.18. Other examples of captioned pictures include the Henry de

Blois Psalter, B L MS Cotton Nero C.IV, and a New Testament Picture Book in a private collection, Morgan (I), cat. 16. *The Bible Historiale* is a late thirteenth-century translation of Petrus Comestor's *Historia Scholastica*. It shows the way illustration and text were seen as a whole. Described in de Hamel, pp. 148–9. The interrelationship between words and images is discussed in Michael Camille, 'The Book of Signs: writing and visual difference in Gothic manuscript illumination', *Word and Image* 1 (1985), pp. 133–48.

26. F. 66. This shows that the designer devised his sequence before the text was written by the scribe. The designer would calculate the amount of space required for each text and mark out spaces for the large initials, which the scribe would then leave blank. In this case it seems that William also completed the captions at this early stage.

27. See for example ff. 45v, 54v and 55v, where the relationship between the characters changes. See figures 50, 58, 59.

3 The Devotional Day

1. Mark 14. 29–31; 14. 66–72

2. M. R. James, *The Apocryphal New Testament* (Oxford, 1924), pp. 38–49. Marina Warner, pp. 25–27. Few pictorial cycles survive which tell the story of the conception, birth and infancy of the Virgin. A New Testament picture book of *c.* 1200 shows seven scenes before the Annunciation, Morgan (I), cat. 16. Even earlier, four scenes occur in the prefatory pages of the Winchester Psalter, B L MS Cotton Nero C.IV. Kauffmann, cat. 78, pp. 105–106.

3. Mirella Levi d'Ancona, *The Iconography of the Immaculate Conception in the Middle Ages and the Renaissance* (1957), pp. 44–5 for images of this miraculous conception. Warner, pp. 239–42, discusses the controversy over the belief in the Immaculate Conception. The feast was already celebrated in England before the Conquest (p. 240). R. W Southern, 'The English origins of the "Miracles of the Virgin"', *Medieval and Renaissance Studies*, 4 (1958), pp. 176–216 (pp. 194, 198, and n. 1).

4. The feast of the Nativity of the Virgin had long been celebrated in England, though the event was still only rarely depicted.

5. In William's depiction there are only seven steps, but by the fourteenth century these are often carefully counted. In the Dublin Hours, Dublin, Trinity College MS F.5.21, *c.* 1340–5, this scene, with exactly 15 steps, illustrates the opening of the Gradual Psalms. Baker, cat. 25. Sandler, cat. 118. It is chiefly in

English books of hours that the sequence of Gradual Psalms occurs. Baker, p. 61. See p. 139.

6. R. W Pfaff, *New Liturgical Feasts in Later Medieval England* (Oxford, 1970), pp. 103–15, discusses the gradual acceptance of this feast between the eleventh and the fifteenth centuries. An example of the early fourteenth century is in the book of hours of Alice de Vere, Cambridge, Christ's College, MS 8, which not only marks this feast to be celebrated on 21 November, but also has a special office for it. Baker, cat. 11. See Appendix 3, no. 8, pp. 196–200.

7. This gesture may in fact be more directly related to the fear expressed by Joseph in the *Book of James* that he might become a laughing stock, *Book of James* 9.2. Warner, p. 27.

8. Te Deum laudamus 'We praise thee, O God; we acknowledge thee to be the Lord .... Thou, O Christ art the King of Glory. Thou art the everlasting son of the Father. Thou, having taken it upon thee to deliver Man, didst not abhor the Virgin's womb.'

9. Susan Groag Bell, pp. 761–4.

10. Luke 1. 26–38 gives a full account of the Annunciation. Matthew 1. 18 confines himself to the phrase: 'she was found with child, of the Holy Ghost'.

11. Celebrated on 25 March.

12. Always closely related to Matins in later French books, but it was often the Virgin and Child enthroned that took first place in English hours manuscripts. See Chapter 4.

13. Prophecies from Isaiah 7. 14, as seen to be fulfilled in gospel accounts, Matthew 1. 22–23. Warner, pp. 19–24.

14. In the Benedictine observance the Matins service was followed by Lauds without a break. It formed a complete service which would begin with the Gradual Psalms and continue through to the end of Lauds, to conclude with the individual invocations to the saints. This continuity was followed in certain English books of hours, particularly early ones, and the heading at Lauds was either smaller than usual or entirely unmarked (see Chapter 4). Sarum usage sometimes continued this through into the fifteenth century although mostly the decoration and illustration of Lauds is equal to the other Hours. Among books of hours made for England, even as late as the fifteenth century in Rouen, this may still be evident, either in a complete lack of illustration or small size illumination at Lauds. Making the same point in such Sarum-influenced manuscripts, the initial at Prime may be promoted in size, see Delaissé, pp. 203–25 (p. 217).

15. Luke 1. 39–56. The Magnificat itself, verses 46–56. In the de Brailes Hours this canticle occurs on f. 59. See p. 95.

16. The Visitation is the chosen illustration for Lauds in most 15th-century books of hours. Harthan, p. 28.

17. Psalm 99, verses 1–4.

18. Luke 2. 22–39.

19. Luke 2. 24.

20. Luke 2. 29–32. This is the canticle at Compline of the Virgin, f. 64. See p. 103.

21. Matthew 2. 1–12.

22. Matthew 2. 2.

23. Matthew 2. 5, which quotes from the prophecy of Micheas: 'And thou Bethlehem Ephrata, art a little one among the thousands of Juda: out of thee shall he come forth unto me that is to be the ruler in Israel.' Micheas 5. 2. The identifying dress of the Jews in the twelfth and thirteenth centuries in England included the wearing of the round cap, as seen here, though the pointed hat too was characteristic. In de Brailes's depictions, Jews almost always wear the round cap. R. Mellinkoff, 'The round cap-shaped hats on Jews in B M Cotton Claudius B.iv', *Anglo-Saxon England*, 2 (1973), pp. 155–65. Suzanne Lewis, '*Tractatus adversus Judaeos* in the Gulbenkian Apocalypse', *Art Bulletin* (1986), pp. 543–66 (p. 547, n. 21).

24. Matthew 2. 12.

25. Matthew 2. 16.

26. Matthew 2. 13–14 tells of Joseph's Dream, and the journey to Egypt.

27. Luke 1. 68–79.

28. Some further account of Christ's infancy occurs in the Gospels. Matthew 2. 19–23 tells of the angel appearing again after the death of Herod, and the Holy Family settling in Nazareth. In Matthew's account (3. 13) Jesus next appears as an adult, and ready to be baptised by John. Luke 2. 42–52 tells of the visit to Jerusalem and his preaching in the temple. Other stories of his infancy are told in the Apocryphal Gospel of St Thomas, James, pp. 49–70.

29. Wieck, p. 111.

30. Not an uncommon iconography throughout the Middle Ages, its symbolism relates it specifically to the adoration of the Cross itself, as is the case here. See Psalter of Robert de Lindsey, London, Society of Antiquaries, MS 59, f. 35v, Morgan (I), cat. 47, plate 157.

31. Chapter 2, p. 29, n. 12. Other suffrages too have this form of words in the captions, but they are written informally in the margin, as are all the other captions.

32. There is a church dedicated to St Laurence at North Hinksey. See discussion pp. 129–31.

33. The imagery of saints is relatively unusual so early in the century. But see the Huntingfield Psalter, New York, Pierpont Morgan Library, MS M.43, Morgan (I), cat. 30, p. 77–8. The martyrdom of St Katherine is depicted in the Salvin Hours, f. 117v and the Harley Hours f. 10. Appendix 3, nos. 4 and 6. In the Walters Hours is an image of St Katherine before King Maxentius, f. 13v. Appendix 3, no. 7.

34. Rarely depicted at this early date St Margaret becomes a familiar image in later English manuscripts. In the Huth Psalter, B L MS Add. 38116, f. 13, she strikes at the devil with a club as she emerges from the dragon. Morgan (I), cat. 67, pl. 338. In the Salvin Hours she illustrates Terce of the Trinity. Appendix 3, no. 4. David Hugh Farmer, *The Oxford Dictionary of Saints* (Oxford, 1978), p. 260.

35. The Lauds text ends half-way down f. 31, leaving empty text lines. The new full-page emphasises the division here, particularly in comparison with the beginning of Lauds, f. 13v.

36. The judgements of Christ are frequently conflated into a single image – usually the final judgement of Pilate. Christ before Caiaphas is included as a second judgement in the Munich Psalter, f. 25v, and a related psalter, B L MS Royal 1.D.X, f. 5v. Both these manuscripts derive from Oxford. See Appendix 4, nos. 1 and 3. The Salvin Hours, following the de Brailes Hours, illustrates three judgements. See Appendix 3, no. 4.

37. Luke 23. 7–14 describes his judgement by Herod.

38. See above, Chapter 1, p. 18, notes 32 and 33. St Edmund, *Speculum Ecclesiae*, edited by M. de la Bigne, *Bibliotheca Patrum et Veterum Auctorum Ecclesiasticorum*, (1610), 5. 983–1004. H. P. Forshaw, *Edmund of Abingdon*. M. M. Philomena, pp. 33–57. M. D. Legge, 'St Edmund on the "Hours" ', *Modern Language Review*, 29, (1934) pp. 72–4.

39. See above p. 19, note 33. Jennifer Sherwood and Nikolaus Pevsner, *Oxfordshire: The Buildings of England* (London, 1974) p. 192.

40. M. M. Philomena, pp. 54–7. The sequence of the judgements of Christ are set out there, just as they are in de Brailes's images.

41. See Chapter 4, p. 139 for discussion of the later development of the Passion devotions.

42. The story of Theophilus is well documented. Emile Mâle, *L'Art Religieux du Troisieme Siecle en France*, Paris, 1903 (translated by Dora Nussey, as *The Gothic Image: Religious Art in France of the Thirteenth Century* (London, 1958), pp. 258–61). Warner, pp. 323–4. Alfred C. Fryer, 'Theophilus the Penitent, as represented in art', *Archaeological Journal*, 92, (1935) pp. 287–333.

43. H. L. D. Ward, *Catalogue of the Romances in the Department of Manuscripts in the British Museum*, II (London, 1893), pp. 595–600, includes an analysis of the various stories, and catalogues their appearance in manuscripts in the British Library. Some examples are fragmentary. R. W. Southern, p. 177 deliberately excludes Theophilus on the grounds that the origins of this story antedate the main collections of Miracles of the Virgin.

44. Fryer lists 21 separate illustrated examples, in sculpture, illuminated manuscripts and stained glass. Some are single scenes, but mostly these consist of a series of scenes. He also lists manuscripts in the British Library containing the text, following Ward.

45. Fitzwilliam Museum, MS 330. see Appendix 4, no.19.

46. Michael Clanchy, p. 64, describes the types of charter and the goods conveyed through them. Close to the concept of signing away one's soul, is the recorded signing away of a wife. Wife to John de Camoys she was conveyed, as Clanchy describes, with her goods and chattels, to Sir William Paynel. Michael Camille 'Seeing and Reading: some visual implications of medieval literacy and illiteracy, *Art History*, (1985) 8, pp. 26–49 (p. 40) and note 65.

47. The caption which would (by analogy with Prime) have made this link has been trimmed from the top of the page.

48. Luke 23. 11.

49. Luke 23. 14.

50. Matthew 27. 24.

51. The self-confidence displayed by the appearance of the blessing hand of God echoes the confidence he shows in his security of being saved in his self-portait in the Last Judgement miniature in the Fitzwilliam Museum, MS 330. See p. 10 fig 2.

52. Giselbertus of Autun carved his signature 'Giselbertus hoc fecit' prominently below the feet of Christ in the tympanum over the west door of the Cathedral at Autun in c.1130. Inscribed on Wren's tomb in the crypt of St Paul's: 'Si monumentum requiris, circumspice'.

53. The caption is incomplete, cut off at the beginning. It is likely that each of these captions would have begun with that critical phrase, *A prime/terce . . .*, linking the episode with the canonical hour.

54. A. S Rappaport, *Medieval Legends of Christ* (London, 1934), p. 235. Joseph Gaer, *The Legend of the Wandering Jew* (New York, 1961). G. K. Anderson, *The Legend of the Wandering Jew* (Providence, 1965).

55. *Chronica Maiora*, Cambridge, Corpus Christi College, MS 16, Part II of the Chronicle, f. 74v. Morgan, (I), p. 137. Suzanne Lewis, p. 544 fig. 1. Suzanne Lewis, *The Illustrations of the Chronicles of Matthew Paris* (London and California, 1987).

56. The three synoptic Gospels provide this episode, with St Luke adding the colour of the crowds and the mourning women to his account. Only St John excludes this reference, 'And bearing his own cross, he went forth to that place which is called Calvary, but in Hebrew, Golgotha.' John 19. 17.

57. Simon of Cyrene does not feature in the St Edmund of Abingdon meditations at Sext. Strangely, the Way of the Cross is excluded altogether. He is important in the later devotion to the Passion, the Stations of the Cross, where Christ falls three times beneath the weight of the Cross, and each fall is venerated as one of the Stations.

58. Gradual Psalms are at ff. 90–102v, psalms nos. 119–133 and 150.

59. This is an early example of the story of the Priest who could say only the Mass of the Virgin, T. Borenius, *St. Thomas Becket in Art* (London, 1932), p. 42. This story also occurs in the large bible made in Oxford, c.1260, B L MS Royal 1.D.I, though inaccurately and in only three episodes, Morgan (II), no. 159, pp. 152–3. It later became popular, though not normally associated with St Thomas himself. It appears in Queen Mary's Psalter, B L MS Royal 2.B.VII, ff. 212v–213. Sandler, no. 56. Ward, ii. 610.

60. Moorman, pp. 90–109, 229–32.

61. Moorman. For the duties of the priesthood as set out at the end of the century by Archbishop John Pecham, Colin Platt, *The Parish Churches of Medieval England*, (London, 1981), pp. 48–9. Closer in date, Bishop Grosseteste of Lincoln ran a tight and well-ordered diocese, *Robert Grosseteste, Scholar and Bishop: essays in commemoration of the seventh century of his death*, edited by D. A. Callus (Oxford, 1955).

62. Borenius, *St Thomas Becket*. T. Borenius, 'Some further aspects of the iconography of St Thomas of Canterbury', *Archeologia* 87 (1934), pp. 1–86.

63. M. M. Philomena, p. 48, 'At this hour Christ cried out with a loud voice and gave up his spirit.' The caption of the de Brailes Hours is much trimmed, but what remains could suggest that originally it opened with *A None*.

64. Luke 23. 42.

65. John 19. 22.

66. Luke 23. 47.

67. John 19. 26–7.

68. John 19. 34. The name of the soldier was given as 'Longinus' in the Golden Legend: spear-carrier.

69. Vespers was always an important liturgical hour,

around which many different devotions gathered in the monastic community, and for the anchoress, Ackerman, p. 739. Evidence also comes from illustration where the Hour of Vespers may be illustrated with scenes of people at prayer. Baker, p. 72. See Chapter 4, pp. 140–2. The Office of the Dead was commonly included later, see Chapter 4.

70. Luke 23. 54; Mark 15. 42

71. M. M. Philomena, p. 48.

72. The celebration of the Mass of the Virgin did not include the elevation of the Host, so the image here conflicts with the message of the caption. C. Wordsworth and H. Littlehales, *The Old Service Books of the English Church* (1904).

73. The hymn *Ave Maris Stella* originated as an anthem written for the feast of the Annunciation in the seventh century, and was frequently sung in processions in later years. Warner, pp. 60, 262.

74. This image is repeated in the Salvin Hours, where it illustrates the Cantate at Lauds, f. 10v. See Appendix 3, no. 4.

75. Clanchy, pp. 178–9.

76. Clanchy, p. 179. *Matthaei Parisiensis Chronica Majora*, edited by H. R. Luard, Rolls Series 57 (1872–84), v, p. 242.

77. Luke 1. 46–56. See above, p. 51, note 15.

78. The caption, *quant nr dame deveit deuier le aungle deu lui nuncia* does not name the angel. In the apocryphal Pseudo-Melito text the angel is unnamed also, James, p. 210. In Cockerell's description he gives the angel the name Gabriel, the name given in one version of a text attributed to Joseph of Arimathea, James, p. 216. In the Coptic texts it is Christ himself who brings the news of her impending death, James, p. 195.

79. See above, p. 88, note 69. See Chapter 4.

80. Evidence of Compline as prayer at bed-time comes from the illustration of Compline for both the Hours of the Virgin and of the Holy Spirit in the Egerton Hours which shows the beds turned down and pillows straightened. Appendix 3, no. 3. As the *Ancrene Riwle* was interpreted by Ackerman, Compline was said at 5 p. m. and was followed by further prayers at bedtime at 7 p.m., p. 739. See fig. 89.

81. M. M. Philomena, p. 49.

82. According to Ackerman's timing for the anchoress's day, Compline must have followed almost immediately on the completion of the various rites of Vespers. (4 p. m. Vespers, 5 p. m. Compline), p. 739.

83. St Paul's presence is specifically mentioned in a number of the narratives. James, pp. 205–9 and 211–2; Warner, pp. 82–7. The image of the seated Ecclesia is usually crowned. Examples in Oxford-made psalters of the early thirteenth century illustrate Psalm 101 or 109 with the crowned Ecclesia. In a related psalter, BL Lansdowne 431, a similar image illustrates Psalm 109. Morgan (I), cat. 39, pp. 87–8, Plate 134. The Inter-relationship of Ecclesia and the Virgin is discussed in A. Katzenellenbogen, *The Sculptural Programs of Chartres Cathedral* (Baltimore, 1959), pp. 59–61.

84. Alternatively this may be the palm symbolising her death, as described in the Pseudo-Melito text. The angel announcing her death greets her: 'Behold, said he, this palm-branch. I have brought it to thee from the Paradise of the Lord and thou shalt cause it to be carried before thy bier ...', James, p. 210. It is mentioned further, 'So she called St John... and showed him... that palm of light which she had received from the angel...'. The Lily at the Death of the Virgin is associated with the purity of the body, 'And the body of the blessed Mary was like the flowers of the lily, and a great sweetness of fragrance issued from it...', James, p. 213. The branch held in St John's hand may be intended to be interpreted as both these symbols.

85. The legends of the Death of the Virgin are varied and conflicting. All however have the Apostles miraculously brought to the presence of the Virgin just before her death. The Latin text of the Pseudo-Melito represents the most complete account. James, pp. 209–16. St John, the protector of the Virgin, precedes the others. St Paul is specifically mentioned in one version of that text, and in most others. James discusses and edits all these texts, pp. 194–227. Warner, pp. 81–102.

86. John 19. 26–7.

87. Acts 1. 3.

88. Acts 1. 14.

89. James, pp. 209–16. Warner, pp. 81–102. It was the Pseudo-Melito version that was the basis for most depictions of these stories including, in the thirteenth century, many sculptural versions on the portals of the French cathedrals. Mâle, *The Gothic Image*, pp. 246–58.

90. James, p. 213.

91. Images of her role as intercessor are common. Fitzwilliam MS 330, leaf 3, in the roundel to Christ's right, shows the Virgin kneeling before the Christ of Judgement in intercession. St Peter's gesture indicates the Virgin as the way to salvation (St Paul, in contrast, raises an accusing forefinger and a sword). Fig. 2, Appendix 4, no. 19. In the Huth Psalter, B L MS Add. 38116, Last Judgement, f. 13v, the Virgin kneels before Christ of Judgement exposing her breast on behalf of the saved souls led to heaven by the angel.

First in the queue of the saved is a woman. Morgan (II), cat. 167, plate 339.

92. This question remained a theological hornet's nest as late as 1950, when the assumption was declared an Article of Faith. It had long been celebrated as a major feast of the Virgin. Warner, pp. 88, 252. Katzanellenbogen, pp. 57–9.

93. It is in this guise that the legend appears in the central tympanum of the north portal at Chartres. Mâle, p. 251. Katzanellenbogen, pp. 56–9. In the series of miniatures before the psalter text of Glasgow, U. L. MS Hunter U.3.2 she is borne up to heaven in her shroud by a guard of honour of angels. Kauffmann, cat. 95, plate 267.

94. By the time of the Crusaders, it was 'beautified and decorated with golden lamps'. Mâle, p. 247.

95. So established as a legend that before the end of the thirteenth century it was written in detail into the hugely popular Golden Legend by Jacobus de Voragine. *The Golden Legend*, translated by Granger Ryan and Helmut Rippenberger (New York, 1941), pp. 261–8. As Jacobus is known to have died c. 1298, the legend itself is usually dated in the 1280s.

96. Luke 2. 29–32.

97. The tradition of little white lions among foliage dates back to the latter part of the twelfth century, e.g. B L MS Cotton Claudius B.II, c. 1180, Kauffmann, cat. 93, plate 259. Also seen in many Oxford-made manuscripts of the early thirteenth century, e.g. B L MS Royal I.D.X, see Appendix 4, no.3. Morgan (I) cat. 28, plate 105. These little white lions are not a normal part of the de Brailes decorative repertoire. His decorative foliage is fleshier than for the earlier manuscripts, and even in the Tree of Jesse of the New College Psalter, the animals that appear are dragons, not lions, see Appendx 4, no.21. Morgan (I), cat. 74, plate 239. In the initial on f. 64 of the Hours they are larger in scale than in earlier examples, see fig. 68.

98. Moorman, particularly Chapters 16–17.

99. Platt, *Parish Churches*, pp. 90, 98–113.

100. J. Sumption, *Pilgrimage: An Image of Medieval Religion* (London, 1975). R. Finucane, *Miracles and Pilgrims: Popular Beliefs in Medieval England* (London, 1977).

101. *The Benedictines in Britain*, edited by D. H. Turner (London and New York, 1980), p. 41.

102. Told in 2 Kings 12, it is a parable of a rich man who stole a poor man's 'ewe lamb' to make a feast for a stranger. David's anger is recounted: 'the man that hath done this is a child of death. He shall restore the ewe fourfold: because he did this thing and had no pity'.

103. 2 Kings 12.7: 'And Nathan said to David: "Thou art the man"'.

104. 2 Kings 11. 2–27.

105. 2 Kings 12. 13: 'And David said to Nathan, "I have sinned against the Lord." And Nathan said to David, "The Lord also hath taken away thy sin. Thou shalt not die"'.

106. 2 Kings 12. 16–21.

107. Psalm 101 is the third of the tripartite division of the psalter, not always marked in later psalters. It derives from an Anglo-Saxon tradition of psalter division. The selection of this subject to accompany Psalm 101 illustrates its penitential theme, and in making this connection de Brailes is most unusual. In an earlier psalter, Oxford, Bodleian Library MS Ashmole 1525, David gazing at Bathsheba illustrates Psalm 50, the fourth Penitential Psalm. Every psalm was illustrated in this manuscript. Morgan, (I), cat. 33. In two bibles, connected to the de Brailes manuscripts, David is shown in bed with Bathsheba, illustrating 2. Kings II.4 Cambridge, University Library MS EE.2.23 and Peterborough, Cathedral Library MS 10. Morgan (I), cats. 65 and 66. Appendix 4, nos.13,14. In the latter half of the fifteenth-century the image of David and Bathsheba became very common to illustrate the Penitential Psalms. Harthan, p. 29. Wieck, p. 98.

108. See above, f. 11, where the angel Gabriel is separated from Mary by the vertical of the 'T', or f. 59 where the same effect is achieved with the 'M'. See figs.21 and 62.

109. 2 Kings 12. 25.

110. Gabriel is named in St Luke as the angel of the Annunciation, here on f. 11. The many visitations to Joachim and Anna, to Joseph and to the three Kings are simply ascribed to the 'angel of the Lord' in the apocrypha. James, pp. 40, 43, 44, 47, and elsewhere. It was Michael who, as guardian of heaven, raised the soul of the Virgin to heaven, although he is not named on f. 61. Depending on the source, either of these announced her death, on f. 59. See above, p. 95, n. 78. It is surely St Michael who fights for the soul of the burgess, f. 98v.

111. See above, pp.63–5, plate 7.

112. Called upon in this role in the hymn, Ave maris stella the hymn at Vespers, f. 58: Ave maris stella, Dei mater alma, atque semper Virgo, felix coeli porta.

113. St Matthew, 2. 16. Illustrated on f. 23v. The Feast of the Holy Innocents was celebrated throughout the Church on 28 December.

114. The popularity of St George in England is shown by a considerable number of church dedications to him. Early stained glass at Jarrow is said to have represented him. His appearance at the siege of Antioch

in 1098 assisted the victory of the Crusaders and an increase in his cult. An early twelfth-century wall painting depicts this St Botulph's Church, Hardham, West Sussex. In 1222 at the synod of Oxford his feast was made a lesser holiday. The story of St George and the Dragon became immensely popular after its inclusion in the Golden Legend. He was not made patron of England until the fifteenth century however, proclaimed England's patron by Henry V on the field of Agincourt in 1415, Farmer, p.166. He appears in almost all English litanies in the thirteenth century.

115. Despite this, St Gregory rarely heads the list in English litanies at this time. More often an English litany begins with Silvester and Leo.

116. Called the 'Hospitaller', St Julian was patron of innkeepers and travellers, but particularly the patron of ferrymen. His legend tells of an episode in his life as a guide for travellers across a river-crossing, next to which he had built a hospital for the poor and for travellers. Farmer, pp.226–7.

117. This separate invocation becomes popular in later manuscripts but is rare at this date. In the litanies of manuscripts of the Use of Rome, used by the orders of friars or those connected with them, it is the final invocation of a separate section dedicated to monks and hermits. In two early manuscripts of the Use of the Austin Friars (in which the texts are Use of Rome) this section consists of Benedict, Francis, Dominic and Anthony. The Walters Hours was identified as Austin Friars Use in Baker, pp.212–9. See Appendix 3, no.7. The Escorial Psalter was identified by Lucy Sandler as of the Austin Friars, L. F. Sandler, 'An early fourteenth-century English psalter in the Escorial', *Journal of the Warburg and Courtauld Institutes*, 41 (1979), pp.65–80 (p.68). Baker, p.219. Sandler, cat.80.

118. She is not described as 'seint' anna in the captions which describe the historiated initials in which she appears. The development of interest in the apocryphal stories encouraged her cult, particularly after the Golden Legend was written in the late thirteenth century. Her feast, on 26 July, is celebrated in the New College Psalter. She is in both the calendar and the litany of the Egerton Hours, of *c.*1260 (Appendix 3, no.3), but it is not until the fourteenth century that she is regularly celebrated. Images of St Anne teaching the Virgin to read became known in that century. Oxford, Bodleian MS Douce 231, a book of hours of *c.*1325–30, has a full page miniature of this scene. Sandler, cat.87. A similar woman and daughter are depicted in the Marciana Psalter, *c.*1270–80 (Venice, Biblioteca Marciana, MS lat.I.77(2397)), but this is interpreted as the patron and her daughter. Morgan (II) cat.166. See below, Chapter 4, pp.152, 155.

119. See Appendix 4.

120. A new shrine had been built for Frideswide's relics in the east end of the twelfth-century priory church, and her relics were translated in 1180. Her cult developed as a result of this, and the feast of the translation was celebrated on 12 February. As witness to its importance, yet another new shrine was constructed for her in 1289, and fragments of this remain in Christ Church Cathedral, also the college chapel of Christ Church. Finucane, p.128.

121. Martyred in 1170. The great Cathedral burnt down in 1174 and a new eastern end was constructed, set about with huge stained glass lancets. The relics of St Thomas were translated to a new shrine in 1220, celebrated on 7 July. It became the greatest focus of pilgrimage in England. The windows of the Trinity Chapel include images of miraculous cures at the new shrine, so datable shortly after 1220. The story of St Thomas in the de Brailes Hours suggests a specific devotion to him.

122. St Mildred was a Kentish abbess, died *c.* 700. Her relics were translated to St Augustine's Abbey, Canterbury. Archbishop Lanfranc gave a second set of relics to the hospital of St Gregory. By the thirteenth century, two rival shrines existed. Farmer, pp.279–80.

123. A new group of contemporary English saints is commonly found in the litanies of manuscripts just later than this. St Edmund of Abingdon, died 1240, canonised 1246, is just too late for inclusion in this manuscript, but became very popular before the end of the century. Bishop Robert Grosseteste, died 1253, is included among the Salvin Hours suffrages but was never canonised, despite reported miracles and vigorous campaigns. E. W. Kemp, 'The attempted canonisation of Robert Grosseteste' in *Robert Grosseteste*, edited by D. A. Callus, pp.241–6. St Richard Wych, died 1253, was canonised in 1262, and very quickly gained general acceptance throughout England. The new friar saints, St Francis and St Dominic are not recorded here, but by this time friaries of both orders had been established in Oxford.

124. The Church of St Laurence at North Hinksey, which is identified with the church of St Laurence in the story on ff.97v–101v, stands next to a main river crossing to Oxford from Abingdon. While it was a ford in summer, it would have needed the services of a ferryman throughout the winter. It would have been to St Julian that prayers would have been offered to ease and safeguard the crossing. For the importance of the Hinksey crossing, Salter, *Medieval Oxford*, pp.1–3.

125. The Gradual Psalms were also often called the Psalms of Degrees, representing the fifteen steps that the Virgin climbed on her way to the temple. A psalm was allocated for each step. See pp.47–8, notes 5 and 6, fig.18.

126. Gradual Psalms became unusual towards the latter part of the fourteenth century, when continental practice influenced the arrangement of the English book of hours. Conversely, they may still be found in some continental-made books for English use. Leroquais considered the Gradual Psalms as an occasional addition to monastic books of hours, V. Leroquais, p. xxxvii.

127. Originally prescribed to be said in procession by Benedict of Aniane, who was the source for these and other specific devotional practices set out in the *Regularis Concordia*. E. Bishop, 'The origin of the prymer', *Liturgica Historica* (1918), pp. 211–37. Turner, p. 41.

128. This is the point in the manuscript where they would be found in later books of hours whenever included. In the *Ancrene Riwle* the Gradual Psalms are prescribed to be said after Terce, together with the Litany of the Saints and the Penitential Psalms. Ackerman, p. 739.

129. Daniel 13. 4. The subsequent quotations also come from Daniel 13.

130. The identity of the tree in the Douay translation of the Bible is a 'mastick tree', Daniel 13.54. Following the idea of the orchard, a *prunier*, as Cockerell suggested, seems the likely completion of this caption.

131. A decorative initial only.

132. This psalm is also one of the sequence of Penitential Psalms.

133. For the role of the burgess in the medieval town, Platt, *Medieval Town*, pp. 22, 96–8.

134. Platt, *Parish Churches*, pp. 98–113.

135. See p. 130 below, note 146.

136. De Hamel considered the illuminated manuscript from the point of view of their owners. He introduced many more categories of owners than are mentioned here, but all treasured their books. Their immediate practical importance was equalled by the value which was placed on them. Marks of ownership, family records made on flyleaves or in liturgical calendars, private prayers, and tales of books passing from owner to owner as treasured possessions, can hardly reveal this more than the threat written into a fifteenth-century English book of hours owned by an ordinary lay-person: 'He that stelles thes boke he shal be hanked upon on hoke behend the kechen dor'. De Hamel, p. 185.

137. Taking evidence of ownership from portraits such as are found in the de Brailes Hours, and interpreting from them is not to work with certainties. Very few portraits of women before the thirteenth century depict laywomen, but Susanna's youth is evident, her unmarried status signalled by her free-flowing hair. A suppliant depicted five times in Oxford, Bodleian Library, MS Auct.D.2.6 of *c.* 1150, has been identified as Mathilda, Countess of Tuscany. Kauffmann, p. 103. The text had been written for her, and this later copy recorded her in its illustration. Like Susanna's hours, it was special, but Mathilda was hardly an ordinary laywoman. In the Berlin psalter-hours a crowned woman with a crowned man in the historiated initial to Psalm 101, it is suggested, are King John and Queen Isabella, who kneel before Christ with their son, Henry. But Isabella was hardly an ordinary laywoman either, and she is not alone. See Appendix 4, no.5. Morgan (I) cat. 35. In Cambridge, St John's College MS D.6, it may be Isabella again, this time alone, who kneels with an attendant before Christ, in the initial to Psalm 101. Appendix 4, no.6. Morgan (I) cat. 36. In the Huntingfield Psalter, New York, Pierpont Morgan Library, MS M.43, a woman kneels with a girl in the historiated initial to Psalm 50, and this family recorded its existence in the calendar, through an obit recording just the man of the family. See Appendix 4, no.8. Morgan (I) cat. 30. At any rate, the repeated image of the kneeling independent ordinary laywoman, as she appears in the de Brailes Hours, is certainly unexpected before this date. Evidently it was to become expected in books of hours. See Chapter 4.

138. St Ethelwold's Benedictional, B L MS Add. 49598, F. Wormald, *The Benedictional of St. Ethelwold* (London 1959). E. Temple, *Anglo-Saxon Manuscripts 900–1066* (London, 1976), cat. 23. The Psalter of Bishop Henry of Blois, B L MS Cotton Nero C.IV, Kauffmann, cat. 78. St Hugh of Lincoln, it is recorded, acquired a grand bible for Witham where he was Prior, through the efforts of King Henry II. W. Oakeshott, *The Two Winchester Bibles* (Oxford, 1981), p. 33. Robert de Lindesey had two psalters, London, Society of Antiquaries MS 59, perhaps originally owned by Queen Isabella (see n. 137), Morgan (I) cat. 47, and Cambridge, St John's College MS D.6 which also contained a gloss. Giles de Bridport, Bishop of Salisbury, gave his Apocalypse to Abingdon Abbey, Suzanne Lewis, 'Giles de Bridport and the Abingdon Apocalypse', in *England in the Thirteenth Century. Proceedings of the Harlaxton Symposium* (1985), pp. 107–19, (p. 107). Bury Bible, Cambridge, Corpus Christi College, MS 2. Kauffmann, cat. 56. Winchester Bible, Winchester Cathedral Library. Kauffmann, cat. 83. *Chronica Maiora*, Cambridge, Corpus Christi College, MSS 26,16. Morgan (I), cat. 88. See also cat. 92.

139. This unfavourable view is reflected in the images of the Jews. Suzanne Lewis, *Art Bulletin* (1986), pp. 543–66, discusses this in relation to the illustration of two Apocalypses. The Jews at the Passion of Christ were often shown in caricature, with grotesque faces. A notable example from the twelfth century is the

Henry de Blois Psalter, see note 138. A later example is the Salvin Hours, see Appendix 3 no. 4. B. Blumenkranz, *Le juif medieval au miroir de l'art chretien* (Paris, 1966), p. 94.

140. In the *Chronica Maiora*, f. 74v (see note 138). Gaer notes many later examples.

141. The conversion of the Jews was also much debated. Their role as the Chosen People was accepted by Christians, and tolerance, even respect, had been the pattern. They had represented little threat to the Church in the early Middle Ages, but the position of the unconverted Jew was less secure by the later twelfth century. S. Grayzel, *The Church and the Jews in the Thirteenth Century* (New York, 1966). C. Roth, *The Jews of Medieval Oxford* (Oxford Historical Society, 1951).

142. In 1217 and again in 1222, and later.

143. See pp. 32–3. fig. 9.

144. While assuming the male here, there is no reason why this anchorite should not have been a woman. Indeed the caption mentions *une recluse*. The woman anchorite at this time is well-documented. Moorman, p. 207. F. M. Powicke, 'Loretta, Countess of Leicester', in *Historical Essays in Honour of James Tait* (Manchester, 1933). A recluse called Annora had a cell at Iffley Church in the mid-thirteenth century, just the other side of Oxford from Hinksey. Sherwood and Pevsner, *Buildings of England, Oxfordshire*, p. 660. There is evidence for an anchorite at Hinksey. Among the many bequests in a will of June 1271 made by Nicholas de Weston are bequests to anchorites, including 'item anacorite de Henkeseye xii denarios'. Salter, *Cartulary of Oseney Abbey*, ii, (O. H. S. 1929), p. 563. A small round-headed window opens low on the south wall of the chancel of St Laurence, North Hinksey. The inner wall is cut away towards the east, and it would have made an ideal squint opening for an anchorite walled in a cell on the south.

145. *Encyclopaedia of Oxford* (London, 1988), p. 408. N. Pevsner, *Buildings of England, Berkshire*, (London, 1966) p. 186.

146. Bartholomew of Grimston is known to have been a Dominican, who on his deathbed recalled that he had been a scholar in Cambridge at the time of the arrival of the Dominicans. S. Forte, 'A Cambridge Dominican collector of exempla in the thirteenth century', *Archivum Fratrum Praedicatorum* 28 (Rome, 1958), pp. 115–48 (pp. 138–9). R. Ombres O. P. 'The Cambridge Dominicans' in *The Dominicans in Cambridge 1238–1538* (Cambridge, 1988) pp. 1–17.

147. See Appendix 2, for details of Use and the de Brailes Hours. Baker, pp. 26–38 deals specifically with English Hours of the Virgin before 1350. See Table Ib there for comparison of texts. See pp. 8–9 for discussion of the literature on the Use of the Hours of the Virgin. F. Madan, 'Hours of the Virgin Mary: tests for localisation', *Bodleian Quarterly Record*, 3, 1920, pp. 40–44. Janet Backhouse, *The Madresfield Hours*, (Roxburghe Club, 1976) discusses the Use of York, with an appendix in which she lists English hours and their usages, up to the mid-fourteenth century .

148. John Plummer in '"Use" and "Beyond Use"' in Wieck, pp. 149–52 discusses the question for books of hours as a whole. M. R. James, *Descriptive Catalogue of the Manuscripts in the Fitzwilliam Museum* (1895) discusses the use of antiphons and capitulae in 'Points to be observed in the description and collation of manuscripts, particularly Books of Hours', pp. xxiii-xxxviii.

149. See pp. 19–20, n. 39 and Appendix 4.

4. The Book of Hours in thirteenth-century England

1. N. J. Rogers, *Books of Hours produced in the Low Countries for the English Market in the Fifteenth Century*, unpublished MPhil dissertation, (Cambridge, 1982).

2. Following Edward VI's injunction, the Act of 1550 ensured that all books were to be delivered up, and included: 'all books called antiphoners, missals, scrails, processionals, manuals, legends, pies, portuises, primers in Latin or English, couchers, journals, ordinals or other books or writings whatsoever . .'. Though directed via the churches, these orders were to forbid such books anywhere in the 'king's dominions'. Platt, *Parish churches*, p. 153. Hoskins, *Primers*, enumerates the many printed editions from the end of the fifteenth century through to the Reformation.

3. B L MS Egerton 1151. See Appendix 3, no. 3.

4. Vienna, Museum für angewandte Kunst. MS S5 Cod. lat. XIV. See Appendix 3, no. 2.

5. Preached by Bishop John Sheppey of Rochester, W. A. Pantin, *The English Church in the Fourteenth Century* (Oxford, 1955), p. 255.

6. *The English Text of the Ancrene Riwle*, edited by E. J. Dobson, Early English Text Society, 267 (1972). R. W. Ackerman and R. Dahood, *Ancrene Riwle*, (Binghampton, 1984), R. W. Ackerman, 'The Liturgical Day in *Ancrene Riwle*', *Speculum*, 1978, pp. 734–44.

7. B L MS 48985, Appendix 3, no. 4; Baltimore, Walters Art Gallery MS 102, Appendix 3, no. 7. The large-scale psalters include many of those made in Oxford, see Appendix 4. Two psalter-hours are included in this number. The psalter-hours never became very common. Of the latter part of the century, the Carrow Psalter-Hours, Baltimore, Walters Art Gallery MS 34,

dates to *c.* 1275 and opens with a series of full-page images of the saints accompanied by suffrage prayers. Morgan (II), cat. 118. An important and finely illuminated example (in private hands) is discussed in Adelaide Bennett, 'A late thirteenth-century Psalter-Hours from London', *England in the Thirteenth Century: Proceedings of the 1984 Harlaxton Symposium* (1985), pp. 15–30. Sandler, cat. 5. A psalter-hours fragment, consisting now of only the Office of the Dead and an illuminated Hours of the Virgin, of *c.* 1300–10 is of this large format too. Cambridge, University Library, MS Dd. 8. 2. Sandler, cat. 29.

8. Paris, B M MS Lat. 919. M. Meiss, *The Limbourgs and their Contemporaries* (New York, 1974), pp. 8–41. References in this and the same patron's 'Tres Riches Heures' went far beyond heraldic motifs and devotional images of the patron. They include the famous feast of Jean de Berri with his court and his household illuminators gathered about him, and views of his castles at the different seasons of the year. J. Longnon and R. Cazelles, *Les Tres Riches Heures du Duc de Berry* (London, 1969). These books of hours are grand and showy, but intensely personal too. Harthan catalogues many more examples of such elaborate books of hours, made for individuals.

9. See Appendix 3.

10. Yale, MS Marston 22. Appendix 3, no. 1. This series of initials encourages the hourly meditation on the Passion, as in the de Brailes Hours.

11. Ackerman, 'Liturgical day' (1978), pp. 738–9, 740–41.

12. B L MS Harley 928, Appendix 3, no. 6.

13. Appendix 3, no. 4. The infancy cycle in the branches of the Tree of Jesse of the Salvin Hours, related entirely to its purpose as a book of hours, is unique. The combination of a narrative cycle and a symbolic image in this way is most unusual. See note 28 below.

14. Of this early date, two books of hours made for English owners, with English textual characteristics, were made abroad. The historiated initials of the Murthly Hours, now Edinburgh, National Library of Scotland, MS 21000, were evidently the work of a sophisticated French illuminator, but the miniatures come from a very different hand, North-French or Flemish. The text was designed for an English owner. *Angels, Nobles and Unicorns: Art and Patronage in Medieval Scotland*, edited by D. H. Caldwell (Edinburgh, 1982), cat. 26. A monograph on this manuscript is in preparation by John Higgit. The Nürnberg Hours, Nürnberg, Staatsbib. Solger 4.40, was illuminated for an English patron by the best recorded illuminator of the early fourteenth century in Paris, Maître Honoré. D. H. Turner, 'Maître Honoré', *British Museum Quarterly* (1968), p. 53.

15. For Passion variants see entries in Appendix 3. For evidence of Beatrice see Appendix 3, no. 5.

16. The Hours of St John the Baptist is not found in any other English hours manuscript at this early date. And it was evidently an addition to this manuscript though designed for it from the outset. The rubrics show that it was written after the other texts were assembled, though probably before it was bound, as they instruct the reader to turn to other places in the manuscript.

17. Appendix 3, nos. 3 and 7. For a description of the various Passion texts found in these thirteenth-century books of hours, see Baker, pp. 43–8.

18. The opening rubric in the Egerton Hours begins: *Ici comence les hures del nun Jesu pur nus crucifie lesqueles ki ke die chescun jur en le honor de la passiun. par la grace de deu il ne murra mie de male mort . . .*, 'the hours of our Jesus, crucified for us, which if you say them each day in honour of the passion will protect you from a bad death'. (There has been dispute over the precise meaning of the word 'nun', but it clearly does not mean the 'name' of Jesus. A devotion to the Name of Jesus is a later development.) This text in the Egerton Hours opens with couplets in French, describing the events of Christ's Passion moment by moment. Similar texts occur in the Beatrice Hours and the Walters Hours, and become common in an abbreviated form after about 1317, when specific indulgences were attached to them by Pope John XXII.

19. This placement follows their usage in the clerical and monastic Office. This is not the case for fifteenth-century manuscripts made in France or Flanders; their suffrages are almost always at the very beginning of the manuscript or the end. They are always written as a separate sequence. Wieck, pp. 111–23. Harthan, p. 18.

20. Ackerman, p. 743.

21. The requirement of the Office of the Dead was a small part of this. Towards the end of the century the foundation of chantries became increasingly popular for the saying of the Mass and the Office of the Dead. Later, into the fifteenth century, the numbers of Masses prescribed in the wills of the faithful to be said for the salvation of their souls increased hugely.

22. Cambridge, Christ's College MS 8, Appendix 3, no. 8.

23. The Psalter of Henry de Blois has captions to its full page pictures, some of which are narrative, but some more clearly devotional or iconic. See Chapter 3, note 138. William de Brailes produced a series of full-page miniatures with French captions, see Appendix 4, no. 8. These full-page miniatures can be compared with the purpose of a wall-painting such as the Christ in Majesty in the vault of the Holy

Sepulchre chapel of Winchester Cathedral, which dates to *c*. 1220. Even more, the roundel of the Virgin and Child in the bishop's private chapel at Chichester was similar in purpose. Painted *c*. 1250, during the bishopric of St Richard of Chichester, it would have been a devotional image for the bishop's private prayer, which would have included the recitation of the Hours of the Virgin. See Chapter 1, note 32.

24. It persisted in a number of manuscripts into the fourteenth century, many of which were based on the illuminated psalter tradition – notably the Vienna Hours, the Harley Hours (Appendix 3, nos.2 and 6) and later, amongst others in the fourteenth century, the Alice de Reydon Hours. Cambridge University Library, MS Dd. 4. 17. Baker, cat. 13. L. F. Sandler, cat. 67.

25. Vienna Hours, Appendix 3, no. 2.

26. The only text that may intervene is the calendar. Only the Walters Hours begins with a collection of misbound texts. Appendix 3, no. 7.

27. The similarities between the de Brailes and the Salvin Hours are wide-ranging. Unmistakeable links in the iconography of the Passion sequence are the image of St Peter weeping in the margin after his third betrayal of Christ, and the image of Pilate washing his hands. See Appendix 3, no. 4 and figs. 14, 42, 93.

28. The Virgin, as an important link in the ancestry of Christ, is always, or almost always, present. Variations in the iconography are discussed in A. Watson, *The Early Iconography of the Tree of Jesse* (Oxford, 1934). The Salvin Hours is not included in that study.

29. The remarkable marginalia are discussed in Florence McCulloch, 'The Funeral of Renart the Fox in a Walters Book of Hours', *Journal of the Walters Art Gallery*, 25–6 (1962–3), pp. 8–27. The omission of a verse happens twice in fact, and in both cases the omitted verse is written in the margin of the page, while the chastised scribe himself passes the end of the rope up to the corrector of the text who points to its place.

30. Harthan, p. 26.

31. T. A. Heslop, 'English seals in the thirteenth and fourteenth century', in *Age of Chivalry: Art in Plantagenet England, 1200–1400*, edited by J. J. G. Alexander and Paul Binski (London, 1987) pp. 114–7, and cats. 141–2, pp. 251–2.

32. See above, Chapter 3, note 137.

33. Marston Hours, Egerton Hours, Vienna Hours, Harley Hours, Walters Hours. See Appendix 3.

34. Venice, Biblioteca Marciana MS Lat. I. 77 (2397). Morgan (II), cat. 166. The pose of the woman with her daughter, on f. 13 (Morgan, pl.329) resembles the image of the Virgin being taught to read by her mother, St Anne. See f. 3 of Bodleian Library MS Douce 231, for comparison. Baker, cat. 19. Sandler, cat. 87.

35. Now the Burrell Collection, Glasgow Museums and Art Galleries, 45/2. *Age of Chivalry* no. 226, p. 290.

36. Ian Nairn and Nikolaus Pevsner, *The Buildings of England: Sussex* (London, 1965), p. 356. *Age of Chivalry*, cat. 138.

37. Veronica Sekules, 'Women and art in England in the thirteenth and fourteenth centuries', in *Age of Chivalry*, pp. 41–8.

38. F.153, Penitential Psalms, f.173v, Gradual Psalms. Appendix 3, no.2.

Appendix 1 *Table of Iconography: the de Brailes Hours*

Note: Size of illustration in the manuscript is expressed as the number of text lines occupied. Horizontal dotted lines define each quire.

Quire	Folio	Text	Size	Illustration	Plate, fig.
· 1 ·					
1–8	1–65	HOURS OF THE VIRGIN			
	1–13	*Matins of the Virgin*			
	1	Versicle: Domine labia mea	10	HISTORIATED INITIAL, 4 Medallions: Betrayal; Scourging of Christ, with Peter's first denial; Mocking of Christ, second denial; Spitting at Christ, and Peter's third denial. Peter weeping.	pl.4 fig.13 fig.14
	1ᵛ	Versicle: Deus in adiutorium	3	Joachim's expulsion from the temple	fig.15
		Invitatory Psalm 94: Venite exultemus	3	Anna abused for her infertility	fig.15
	3ᵛ	Hymn: Quem terra ponthus	3	Angel tells Joachim to return	fig.10
	4	Psalm 8: Domine Dominus noster	3	Angel tells Anna that she will conceive	fig.10
	5ᵛ	Psalm 18: Celi enarrant	3	Joachim and Anna embrace	fig.16
	7ᵛ	Psalm 23: Domini est terra	3	Birth of the Virgin	fig.17
· 2 ·					
9–16	9	Lesson: Sancta Maria virgo	3	Presentation of the Virgin in the temple	fig.18
	9ᵛ	Lesson: Sancta Maria piarum	3	Virgin's suitors, Joseph holds flowering rod	fig.19
	10ᵛ	Lesson: Sancta Dei genetrix	3	Marriage of Mary and Joseph	fig.20
	11	Canticle: Te Deum	3	Annunciation	fig.21
	13ᵛ–31	*Lauds of the Virgin*			
	13ᵛ	Versicle: Deus in adiutorium	3	Visitation of Mary to Elizabeth	fig.22
		Psalm 92: Dominus regnavit	3	Angel reassures Joseph	fig.22
	14ᵛ	Psalm 99: Jubilate Deo	3	3 medallions: Nativity; annunciation to shepherds	fig.23
	15	Psalm 62: Deus Deus meus	3	Presentation of Christ	fig.24
	16ᵛ	Psalm 66: Deus misereatur	3	Magi ask Herod about Christ	fig.25

Quire	Folio	Text	Size	Illustration	Plate, fig.

Quire	Folio	Text	Size	Illustration	Plate, fig.
	39–43	*Terce of the Virgin*			
	39		Full-page	MINIATURE 4 medallions: Seated Pilate with Christ before him; Pilate washes his hands; Jews lead Christ away	fig.42
	39	Versicle: Deus in adiutorium		(beneath miniature)	
	39ᵛ	Hymn: Veni Creator	2	–decorative–	fig.43
	39ᵛ	Psalm 119: Ad dominum	3	Virgin appears to Theophilus	fig.43
·6·					
40–47	40ᵛ	Psalm 120: Levavi oculos	3	Virgin wins back charter	fig.44
	41ᵛ	Psalm 121: Letatus sum	3	Virgin returns charter	fig.45
	42ᵛ	Capitulum: Ab initio	3	Theophilus burns charter	fig.46
	43	Prayer: Concede nos	3	William de Brailes in prayer	pl.1 figs.1, 46
	43ᵛ–47	*Sext of the Virgin*			
	43ᵛ		Full-page	MINIATURE 4 medallions: Story of the Wandering Jew; Way of the Cross; Christ's garments removed; Christ before cross	pl.8 fig.11 fig.47 fig.48
	43ᵛ	Versicle: Deus in adiutorium		(beneath miniature)	fig.11
	44	Hymn: Veni creator	2	– decorative –	fig.11
	44	Psalm 122: Ad te levavi	3	Theophilus dead, Virgin lifts soul to God	pl.9 fig.11
	44ᵛ	Psalm 123: Nisi quia	3	Priest chanting Mass of Virgin	fig.49
	45ᵛ	Psalm 124: Qui confidunt	3	Thomas Becket suspends priest	fig.50
	46ᵛ	Capitulum: Et sic in Syon	3	Priest appeals to Becket	fig.51
	47	Prayer: Concede nos	3	William de Brailes in prayer	fig.51
	47ᵛ–52	*None of the Virgin*			
	47ᵛ		Full-page	MINIATURE Scene above: Crucifixion with thieves; Medallions: Crucifixion with Mary and John; Crucifixion with two witnesses	pl.10 fig.52
	47ᵛ	Versicle: Deus in adiutorium		(beneath miniature)	
·7·					
48–56	48	Hymn: Veni creator	2	– decorative –	pl.11
	48	Psalm 125: In convertendo	3	Priest in supplication	pl.11

Quire	Folio	Text	Size	Illustration	Plate, fig.
	49	Psalm 126: Nisi dominus	3	The Virgin gives Thomas a hair shirt	fig.53
	49ᵛ	Psalm 127: Beati omnes	3	Priest travels across the sea	fig.54
	50ᵛ	Capitulum: Et radicavi	3	Priest appeals to Thomas	fig.55
	53–59	*Vespers of the Virgin*		– full-page illustration excised –	
	53	Psalm 121: Letatus sum	3	Virgin tells Thomas's secret	fig.56
	54	Psalm 122: Ad te levavi	3	Priest crosses the sea	fig.57
	54ᵛ	Psalm 123: Nisi quia	3	Priest tells Thomas his revelation	fig.58
	55ᵛ	Psalm 124: Qui confidunt	3	Thomas reinstates priest	fig.59
	56	Psalm 125: In convertendo	3	Priest elevates Host at Mass	fig.59

·8· . . . .

Quire	Folio	Text	Size	Illustration	Plate, fig.
58–65	58	Capitulum: Beata es Maria	3	Priest dead, Virgin lifts soul to God	fig.60
	58	Hymn: Ave maris stella	3	Three singing clerks	figs.60, 61
	59	Canticle: Magnificat	3	Angel tells Virgin of her death	fig.62
	60–64	*Compline of the Virgin*		– full page illustration excised –	
	60	Psalm 12: Usquequo domine	3	Apostles honour the Virgin	fig.63
	61	Psalm 42: Judica me deus		5 medallions: Death of Virgin; Angel lifts soul to Heaven; Virgin crowned; Burial procession, with disbelieving Jews; her body entombed and venerated	pl.5 fig.64
	61ᵛ	Psalm 128: Sepe expugnaverunt	3	Jews blinded for mocking Virgin	fig.65
	62ᵛ	Psalm 130: Domine non est	3	Believing Jew's sight restored	fig.66
	63	Capitulum: Sicut cynamomum	3	Converted Jew cures believer	
	63ᵛ	Hymn: Virgo singularis	3	Convert fails to cure unbeliever	fig.67
	64	Canticle: Nunc dimittis	3	– decorative – foliage with white lions	fig.67 fig.68
	64ᵛ	Prayer: Graciam tuam	3	The patron, Susanna, in prayer	pl.2, fig.6
	65	Prayer (added): Salve regina			

·9· . . . .

Quire	Folio	Text	Size	Illustration	Plate, fig.
66–73	66–81	PENITENTIAL PSALMS		HISTORIATED INITIALS	
	66	Psalm 6: Domine ne in furore	4	David accused by Nathan	pl.12 fig.12
	67ᵛ	Psalm 31: Beati quorum	3	David buried in ground	pl.13 fig.69

Quire	Folio	Text	Size	Illustration	Plate, fig.
	69	Psalm 37: Domine ne in furore	3	David composes seven psalms	fig.70
	72	Psalm 50: Miserere mei	3	David scourged	fig.71
·10·					
74–81	75	Psalm 101: Domine exaudi	3	Susanna in penitence	pl.15
	78	Psalm 129: De profundis	3	David in penitence	fig.72
	79	Psalm 142: Domine exaudi	3	David requests mercy	fig.73
	81–89ᵛ	LITANY AND COLLECTS		HISTORIATED INITIALS	
	81	Kyrie eleison	4	Christ enthroned – as judge	pl.14
·11·					
82–89	87ᵛ	Collect: Deus cui proprium	3	Susanna in supplication	fig.74
	88	Collect: Pretende domine	3	Susanna prostrate, blessed by God	fig.74
	88ᵛ	Collect: Deus qui es	3	William de Brailes praying	fig.75
·12·					
90–97	90–102	GRADUAL PSALMS		HISTORIATED INITIALS	
	90	Psalm 119: Ad Dominum	3	Susanna in tribulation	pl.16a
	90ᵛ	Psalm 120: Levavi oculos	3	Susanna accused	fig.76
	91ᵛ	Psalm 121: Letatus sum	3	Elder identifies tree	fig.77
	92ᵛ	Psalm 122: Ad te levavi	3	Second elder identifies tree	fig.78
	93	Psalm 123: Nisi quia Dominus	3	Elders before judge	fig.78
	94	Psalm 124: Qui confidunt	3	Elders burnt in fire	fig.79
	94ᵛ	Psalm 125: In convertendo	3	– decorative –	
	95	Psalm 126: Nisi Dominus	3	Susanna gives praise	fig.80
	96	Psalm 127: Beati omnes	3	Susanna lies dead, soul raised	fig.81
	97	Psalm 128: Sepe expugnaverunt	3	– decorative –	
	97ᵛ	Psalm 129: De profundis	3	Burgess donates chalice	pl.16c fig.82
·13·					
98–105	98	Psalm 130: Domine non est	3	Burgess lies dead	pl.16c fig.82
	98ᵛ	Psalm 131: Memento Domine	3	Angel and Devil dispute over soul	fig.83
	100ᵛ	Psalm 132: Ecce quam bonum	3	Recluse alerts St Laurence	fig.84
	101	Psalm 133: Ecce nunc benedicere	3	St Laurence adds chalice	pl.16b
	101ᵛ	Psalm 150: Laudate Dominum	3	Soul of burgess to Heaven	fig.85
	102ᵛ–105ᵛ	Added prayers		No illustration or decoration	fig.86

Appendix 2 Text of the de Brailes Hours

1. Use of the Hours of the Virgin

INTRODUCTION

Evidence for the Use of a text of the Hours of the Virgin comes from the details of the various services. Broadly, the structure and format of the Hours of the Virgin is much the same from Use to Use, but the details differ. These variations have been much studied, and simplified 'tests' have been devised to enable the Use to be determined. The obvious importance of the determination of the Use of a book of hours lies in the localisation of its origins, and thereby the determination of its place in the history of art-historical style and iconography. As a tool for determining the history of manuscript illumination, many scholars have attempted to refine the understanding of Use. Employing evidence from both manuscripts and the printed editions of books of hours in France, which usually identify the Use on the title page, the first step was to determine the critical indicators within the text which show differences in the Use.

In the works of James, Madan, Leroquais and, most recently, Plummer, this question has been considered.* As a result of his extensive recording of many and varied Uses of the Hours of the Virgin, Plummer has suggested that the simplified tests devised by Madan will give only broad indications. Plummer himself has recorded a greater number of textual indicators as essential in order to draw firm conclusions. Plummer has defined the specific part of the text that he records in ' "Use" and "Beyond Use" ' (in Wieck, pp. 149–52).

Madans' tests certainly were minimal: recording only the antiphon and capitulum at Prime and None. In addition to the very large number of French diocesan usages, he also identified a wide range of English variations, though many of these were followed with a doubting question mark. These identified uses are impossible to verify, as Madan did not cite the manuscripts (or printed editions) that he had used in collat-

ing these indicators. Therefore the proposed Use of '? St Frideswide Oxford' (Prime: Ant. *Salve sponsa patris*; Cap. *Ab initio*; None: Ant. *Gaude virtutem/Ecce Maria genuit*; Cap. *Tota est speciosa*) may have depended on these forms in the text of B L MS Arundel 157 (see Appendix 4), which uses the *Ecce Maria* antiphon at None. The evident importance of St Frideswide in the Calendar and the suffrage to her in the Hours section indicates an origin in Oxford, and together with St Augustine's importance in the Litany suggests that it was made for the Augustinian Priory of St Frideswide in Oxford. References to other sources used would have provided the basis for comparison, and the possibility of establishing the Use.

Similarly, his 'Augustinian (English)' conforms to the first version of the Hours of the Virgin, to be said during Advent, of a book of hours in the Bodleian, MS Laud misc. 188. Later in the manuscript a rubric defines the Office of the Dead as following the Use of the Austin Friars. The third text of the Hours of the Virgin in this manuscript, that used for most of the year and therefore the text that would be used in an Hours with only a single unvariable version, is of the Use of Rome, according to Madan's test. As the Austin Friars used the Use of Rome, this manuscript is clearly following the Use of the Austin Friars. It may be that it was this manuscript that suggested these variants for Madan's identification, and hence the confusion between variants for the times of the year and true variants in Use. (See my *Books of Hours in England*, pp. 34–7.)

Despite the difficulties, Madan remains a major source of textual tests for the study of Use in English Hours. Madan's tests consider a wide range of English usages, where most other commentators have concentrated on the more easily verifiable, and more numerous, French variants. The materials for the determination of variable usage in English Hours texts before 1300 are few and difficult to verify. Moreover, English standardisation to the Use of Sarum was all but complete by the beginning of the fourteenth century, at just the time when the book of hours began to be made in greater numbers. This is borne out by the comparison of the texts of early Hours of the Virgin and those of the fourteenth century and later. (See Table 1b in my *Books of Hours in England*. Also discussion there on pp. 26–38.)

Because of the complications of Use in the early

---

*M. R. James, see Chapter 3, note 148; Madan, see Chapter 3, note 147; Leroquais, see Chapter 3, note 4; Plummer, in Roger S. Wieck, see Chapter 2, note 2 and Chapter 3, note 148.

examples of the Hours of the Virgin in England, it has been decided to record the whole text of the Hours of the Virgin as it has been established for the Use of Sarum, and to record the significant variations from this text, as they occur in the de Brailes Hours. The significant indicators as recorded by Plummer are marked in italics. In all of these the de Brailes Hours conforms with the Use of Sarum. The recorded variants therefore may not be significant in determining its origins, but they do indicate that, by this date, the Use of the Hours of the Virgin had not yet been firmly established.

HOURS OF THE VIRGIN

Use of Sarum		Variations in de Brailes
MATINS		
V.	Domine labia mea aperies	
R.	Et os meum annunciabit	
V.	Deus in adiutorium	
R.	Domine ad adiuvandum me festina	
Ps.94	Venite exultemus	
Hymn	Quem terra ponthus	
Ps.8	Domine Dominus noster	
Ps.18	Celi enarrant	
Ps.23	Domini est terra	
Ant.	Benedicta tu in mulieribus	
V.	Sancta Dei genetrix	
R.	Intercede pro nobis	
Ben.	Jube Domine benedicere	
Rec.	Alma virgo virginum	Sancta Dei genetrix
Lc.1	*S M virgo virginum*	
R.	*Sancta et immaculata/Quia quem*	
V.	Benedicta tu in mulieribus/Quia quem	
Ben.	Jube Domine benedicere	
Rec.	Ora mente pia	Christe filius Marie
Lc.2	Sancta Maria piarum	
R.	Beata es Maria/Genuisti	
V.	Ave Maria/Genuisti	
Ben.	Jube Domine benedicere	
Rec.	Sancta Dei genetrix	Sancta Maria intercessio fiat
Lc.3	Sancta Dei genetrix	
R.	Felix namque/Quia ex te orto	
V.	Ora pro populo/Quia ex te orto	
Cant.	Te Deum	
V.	Ora pro nobis	Aduivabit eam
R.	Ut digni et efficiamur	Deus in medio
LAUDS		
V.	Deus in adiutorium	
R.	Domine ad adiuvandum me festina	
Ps.92	Dominus regnavit	

Use of Sarum		Variations in de Brailes
LAUDS *continued*		
Ps.99	Jubilate deo	
Ps.62	Deus Deus meus	
Ps.66	Deus misereatur	
Cant.	Benedicite omnia opera	
Ps.148	Laudate Dominum	
Ps.149	Cantate Domino	
Ps.150	Laudate Dominum	
Ant.	*O admirabile*	
Cap.	*Maria virgo semper*	
Hymn	O gloriosa domina	
V.	Elegit eam/Et pre-elegit	
R.	Et habitare/Et pre-elegit	Habitare eam facit
Cant.	Benedictus Dominus	
Ant.	*O gloriosa*	
V.	Domine exaudi orationem	
R.	Et clamor meus ad te veniat	
PRIME		
V.	Deus in adiutorium	
R.	Domine ad adiuvandum me festina	
Hymn	Veni creator	
Ps.53	Deus in nomine	Ps.1 Beatus vir
Ps.116	Laudate Dominum	Ps.2 Quare fremuerunt
Ps.117	Confitemini Domino	Ps.5 Verba mea auribus
Ant.	*O admirabile*	
Cap.	*In omnibus requiem*	
V.	Ave Maria/Dominus tecum	
R.	Benedicta tu/Dominus tecum	
V.	Sancta Dei genetrix	
R.	Intercede pro nobis	
V.	Domine exaudi orationem	
R.	Et clamor meus ad te veniat	
Or.	Concede nos	
TERCE		
V.	Deus in adiutorium	
R.	Domine ad adiuvandum me festina	
Hymn	Veni creator	
Ps.119	Ad Dominum	
Ps.120	Levavi oculos	
Ps.121	Letatus sum	
Ant.	*Quando natus*	

Use of Sarum		Variations in de Brailes
TERCE *continued*		
Cap.	*Ab initio*	
V.	Sancta Dei genetrix/Virgo virginum	
R.	Intercede pro nobis/Virgo virginum	
V.	Post partum virgo	
R.	Dei genetrix intercede	
V.	Domine exaudi orationem	
R.	Et clamor meus ad te veniat	
Or.	Concede nos	
SEXT		
V.	Deus in adiutorium	
R.	Domine ad adiuvandum me festina	
Hymn	Veni creator	
Ps.122	Ad te levavi	
Ps.123	Nisi quia	
Ps.124	Qui confidunt	
Ant.	*Rubum quem*	
Cap.	*Et sic in Syon*	
V.	Post partum/Inviolatum	
R.	Dei genetrix/Inviolatum	
V.	Speciosa facta es	
R.	In deliciis tuis	
V.	Domine exaudi orationem	
R.	Et clamor meus ad te veniat	
Or.	Concede nos	
NONE		
V.	Deus in adiutorium	
R.	Domine ad adiuvandum me festina	
Hymn	Veni creator	
Ps.125	In convertendo	
Ps.126	Nisi dominus	
Ps.127	Beati omnes	
Ant.	*Germinavit radix*	
Cap.	*Et radicavi*	
V.	Speciosa facta es/Et suavis	
R.	In deliciis tuis/Et suavis	
V.	Dignare me	– excised –
R.	Da in virtute	– excised –
V.	Domine Dominus virtutem	– excised –
R.	Et ostende	– excised –
Or.	Concede nos	– excised –

Use of Sarum		Variations in de Brailes
VESPERS		
V.	Deus in adiutorium	– excised –
R.	Domine ad adiuvandum me festina	
		Ps. Dixit dominus (added)
		Ps. Laudate pueri (added)
Ps.121	Letatus sum	
Ps.122	Ad te levavi	
Ps.123	Nisi quia	
Ps.124	Qui confidunt	
Ps.125	In convertendo	
		Ps. Lauda verbum (added)
Ant.	*Post partum*	
Cap.	*Beata es Maria*	
Hymn	Ave maris stella	
V.	Diffusa est	
R.	Propterea benedixit	
Cant.	Magnificat	
Ant.	*Santa Maria succure*	– excised –
V.	Domine exaudi orationem	– excised –
R.	Et clamor meus ad te veniat	– excised –
Or.	Concede nos	– excised –
COMPLINE		
V.	Converte nos Deus	– excised –
R.	Et averte iram tuam	– excised –
V.	Deus in adiutorium	
R.	Domine ad adiuvandum	
Ps.12	Usquequo Domine	
Ps.42	Judica me Deus	
Ps.128	Sepe expugnaverunt	
Ps.130	Domine non est	
Ant.	*Cum iocunditate*	
Cap.	*Sicut cynamomum*	
Hymn	Virgo singularis	
V.	Ecce ancilla	Elegit eam deus et preelegit
R.	Fiat michi	Habitare eam facit
Cant.	Nunc dimittis	
Ant.	*Glorificamus te*	
V.	Domine exaudi orationem	
R.	Et clamor meus ad te veniat	
V.	Benedicamus	
R.	Deo gracias	
Or.	Graciam tuam	
		Salve regina –
		added on inserted folio

2. Penitential Psalms

This is the usual sequence, as found in nearly all books of hours.

Ps.6	Domine ne in furore
Ps.31	Beati quorum
Ps.37	Domine ne in furore
Ps.50	Miserere mei
Ps.101	Domine exaudi
Ps.129	De profundis
Ps.142	Domine exaudi

3. The Saints

3a SUFFRAGES

Blesed Virgin Mary
Holy Spirit
Holy Cross
St Laurence (added – contemporary)
St Katherine
St Margaret
All Saints
For Peace

3b LITANY

Kyrie eleison	
Christe eleison	
Christe	audi nos
Pater de celis	Deus miserere nobis
Fili redemptor mundi	Deus miserere nobis
Spirito sancte deus	Deus miserere nobis
Sancta trinitas	Deus miserere nobis
Sancta Maria	ora pro nobis
Sancta Dei genetrix	ora pro nobis
Sancta virgo virginum	ora pro nobis
St Michael	ora pro nobis
St Gabriel	ora pro nobis
St Raphael	ora pro nobis
Omnes sancti angeli et archangeli	orate pro nobis
Omnes sancti beatum spiritum ordines	orate pro nobis
St Iohannes Baptista	ora pro nobis
Omnes sancte patriarche et prophete	orate pro nobis
St Petre	ora pro nobis
St Paule	ora pro nobis
St Andrea	ora pro nobis
St Iacobe	ora pro nobis
St Iohannes	ora pro nobis
St Thoma	ora pro nobis
St Iacobe	ora pro nobis
St Philipe	ora pro nobis
St Bartholomee	ora pro nobis
St Thadee	ora pro nobis
St Symon	ora pro nobis
St Mathia	ora pro nobis
St Barnaba	ora pro nobis
St Marce	ora pro nobis
St Luca	ora pro nobis
Omnes sancti apostli et evangelisti	orate pro nobis
Omnes sancti discipuli Domine	orate pro nobis
Omnes sancti innocenti	orate pro nobis
St Stephane	ora pro nobis
St Clemens	ora pro nobis
St Laurenti	ora pro nobis
St Vincenti	ora pro nobis
St Eustachi cum soqiis eius	ora pro nobis
St Dionisi cum soqiis eius	ora pro nobis
St Ipolite cum soqiis eius	ora pro nobis
St Fabiane	ora pro nobis
St Sebastiane	ora pro nobis
St Columbane	ora pro nobis
St Albane	ora pro nobis
St Oswald	ora pro nobis
St Eadmunde	ora pro nobis
St Edwarde	ora pro nobis
St Thoma	ora pro nobis
St Geruasi	ora pro nobis
St Prothasi	ora pro nobis
St Leodegari	ora pro nobis
St Blasii	ora pro nobis
St Georgi	ora pro nobis
Omnes sancti martyres	orate pro nobis
St Gregori	ora pro nobis
St Martine	ora pro nobis
St Nicholae	ora pro nobis
St Augustine	ora pro nobis
St Ieronime	ora pro nobis
St Dunstane	ora pro nobis
St Benedicte	ora pro nobis
St Egidii	ora pro nobis
St Leonarde	ora pro nobis
St Botulfe	ora pro nobis

St Juliane	ora pro nobis
Omnes sancti confessores	orate pro nobis
Omnes sancti monachi et heremite	orate pro nobis
St Maria magdalene	ora pro nobis
St Maria egyptiaca	ora pro nobis
St Agatha	ora pro nobis
St Agnes	ora pro nobis
St Lucia	ora pro nobis
St Katerina	ora pro nobis
St Margareta	ora pro nobis
St Cecilia	ora pro nobis
St Frideswida	ora pro nobis
St Mildrida	ora pro nobis
St Radegundis	ora pro nobis
St Helena	ora pro nobis
Omnes sancti virgines	orate pro nobis
Omnes sancti vidue et continentes	orate pro nobis
Omnes sancti	orate pro nobis
Propitius esto parce nobis domine	
Ab omni malo	libera nos Domine
Ab dampnatione perpetua	libera nos Domine
Ab immentibus peccatorum	libera nos Domine
Ab insidiis diaboli	libera nos Domine
Ab infestationibus demonitas	libera nos Domine
Per invocationis	

(*continues*)

COLLECTS:

Deus cui proprium

Pretende Domine famulus et famulabis tuis

Deus qui es sanctorum tuorum splendo mirabilis

4. *Gradual Psalms*

The Gradual Psalms number 16, the usual fifteen Gradual Psalms, numbers 119–133, together with Psalm 150.

Ps.119	Ad Dominum
Ps.120	Levavi oculos
Ps.121	Letatus sum
Ps.122	Ad te levavi
Ps.123	Nisi quia Dominus
Ps.124	Qui confidunt
Ps.125	In convertendo
Ps.126	Nisi Dominus
Ps.127	Beati omnes
Ps.128	Sepe expugnaverunt
Ps.129	De profundis
Ps.130	Domine non est
Ps.131	Memento Domine
Ps.132	Ecce quam bonum
Ps.133	Ecce nunc benedicite
Ps.150	Laudate Dominum

The Beatrice Hours (B L MS Add. 33385) has fifteen Gradual Psalms but replaces Psalm 133 with Psalm 150. Two early fourteenth-century hours (Christ's College MS 8, the de Vere Hours, and Cambridge University Library MS Dd. 4. 17, the Alice de Reydon Hours *c*.1320) have the same sequence of 16 as found in the de Brailes Hours.

Appendix 3   Thirteenth-century Books of Hours in England

Contents

1. THE MARSTON HOURS
Yale University Library, Marston MS 22
*c.*1250 – East Anglia/Norwich

2. THE VIENNA HOURS
Vienna, Museum für angewandte Kunst.
Cod. lat XIV (S5)
*c.*1250–5 – Oxford

3. THE EGERTON HOURS
British Library, MS Egerton 1151
*c.*1260 – Oxford

4. THE SALVIN HOURS
British Library, MS Add. 48985
*c.*1270 – Oxford

5. THE BEATRICE HOURS
British Library, MS Add. 33385
*c.*1260–70

6. THE HARLEY HOURS
British Library, MS Harley 928
*c.*1280–90

7. THE WALTERS HOURS
Baltimore, Walters Art Gallery, MS 102
*c.*1290–1300

8. THE DE VERE HOURS
Cambridge, Christ's College MS 8
*c.*1300–05 – Fenlands

1. *The Marston Hours*
Yale University Library, Marston MS 22
*c.*1250 – East Anglia/Norwich

A. CONTENTS
The original section of the manuscript consists of the Hours of the Virgin troped (intermingled) with the Hours of the Holy Spirit, (ff.2–90). Written in a hand of the later thirteenth century is a section containing the Penitential Psalms, (ff.93–102) and Litany (ff.102ᵛ–106ᵛ).

B. PHYSICAL FEATURES
Page size: 14.7 cm × 10.2 cm. 115 ff. 1 column of 13 lines. Large gothic script. Extensively repaired, rebound and trimmed. Single line initials occur in left hand column. Verses do not begin on a new line, so there are no line endings. Small initials occur in the middle of the line. The ruling structure is simple.

C. LITURGY
The Hours of the Virgin are Use of Sarum, with no significant variations. The suffrages after Lauds are: Holy Spirit, Saints Peter and Paul, St John the Evangelist, St Andrew, All Apostles and Evangelists, St Stephen, St Laurence, St Edmund King and Martyr, St Thomas of Canterbury, All Martyrs, St Nicholas, St Edmund of Abingdon, St Benedict, All Confessors, St Susanna, All Virgins, Relics, All Saints, Peace, Annunciation of the Virgin.

Each of the troped Hours of the Holy Spirit opens with the *Deus in adiutorium*. It seems that this is the earliest example of an Hours of the Holy Spirit text, and this is the only example of these Hours troped, in the thirteenth century, or among English fourteenth-century examples. This same text is found in the de Vere Hours (no.8).

D. COMMENTARY
The liturgical evidence for the East Anglian origin of the Marston Hours is slight, based on the inclusion in the suffrages of St Edmund, King and Martyr and on the added Litany of Saints Osith, Radegund and Etheldreda. Stylistically, with small figures overlapping the initials, clothed in curling, flowing drapery and defined with strong outlines, this manuscript is related to a small-scale bible which has later Norwich connections (Oxford, Bodleian Library MS Auct D.4.8. Morgan (I) no. 75).

Folio	Text	Illustration
1	Prayer	. . .
2–90	Hours of Holy Spirit troped with Hours of the Virgin	HISTORIATED INITIALS
2–5	Matins of Holy Spirit	– excised –
6–17	Matins of the Virgin	– excised –
17ᵛ	Lauds of the Virgin	Annunciation
31ᵛ	Suffrages	SOME HISTORIATED INITIALS
32	St Peter and St Paul	Head of St Peter with Key
37	St Nicholas	Head of St Nicholas
43ᵛ	Prime of Holy Spirit	Flagellation of Christ
46	Prime of the Virgin	Visitation
54ᵛ	Terce of Holy Spirit	Carrying of the Cross
57	Terce of the Virgin	Annunciation to Shepherds
61	Sext of Holy Spirit	– excised –
63ᵛ	Sext of the Virgin	Nativity
	(None of Holy Spirit excised completely)	
68	None of the Virgin	– excised –
73	Vespers of Holy Spirit	– excised –
74	Vespers of the Virgin	– excised –
81ᵛ	Compline of Holy Spirit	Three Maries at the Tomb
84	Compline of the Virgin	Flight into Egypt
	(late thirteenth-century section)	
91ᵛ	added Prayer (XVc.)	. . .
93–102	Penitential Psalms	– excised –
102ᵛ	Litany	. . .
108	Collects	. . .
112	Prayers in French	. . .
115	'*In principio . . .*'	. . .

2. *The Vienna Hours*

Vienna, Museum für angewandte Kunst. Cod. lat XIV (S5)

*c.*1250–5 – Oxford

A. CONTENTS

The manuscript consists of: three fifteenth-century drawings of saints, (ff.1ᵛ, 2, 3ᵛ); Calendar, (ff.4–9ᵛ); series of full page illustrations, (ff.11ᵛ–24); Hours of the Virgin, (ff.25–151); drawing, (f.152ᵛ); Penitential Psalms, (ff.153–173); Gradual Psalms, (ff.173ᵛ–190); Litany, (ff.190ᵛ–201).

B. PHYSICAL FEATURES

Page size: 16 cm × 11 cm, 201 ff. Single column of 12 lines, with a number of folios having a considerable amount of plain-song music, on a stave of four lines. Small initials are set in a separate column to the left, with a ruling scheme including a narrow vertical column either side of the text area, and both top and bottom lines ruled across the whole page. No border ruling. Good even script, black ink. No rubrics. The calendar is in a different, near-contemporary hand. The preface of miniatures is by a different artist from the text illustration.

C. LITURGY

The calendar is based on a Sarum model, but it also has many non-Sarum saints. A number are North-country in origin, including St Gilbert of Sempringham (4 February), St John of Beverley (7 May), St William of York (8 June), St Helen (18 August), St Paulinus (22 June). The Hours of the Virgin is Use of Sarum but with variants. It has a Matins service with nine lessons. Musical notation occurs, notably at the opening of each Hour and the blessings before lessons. Suffrages include St Frideswide, which is notated. The litany includes no saints suggesting a specific locality.

D. COMMENTARY

A small-format hours with large script, seemingly assembled in sections – calendar, pictorial preface, text, and other additions. Musical notation is not otherwise found in contemporary English books of hours. The text and illustration suggest an origin in Oxford, linked with the de Brailes workshop through the decorative style, but with a figure style linked more closely with the Rutland Psalter (B L MS Add.62925), which also has affinities with the de Brailes type of ornament. The emphasis on the variety of praying figures in the illustration is shared by other mid-century books of hours. Particular importance is given to the laywoman who, large in scale, occupies the historiated initials to the Penitential and Gradual Psalms.

E. TABLE OF ICONOGRAPHY

Folio	Text	Illustration
1^v–3^v	...	FIFTEENTH CENTURY DRAWINGS
1^v	...	St George and the Dragon
2	...	St Etheldreda (?) and St Katherine
3^v	...	Bearded Bishop saint, with two female donors
4–9^v	Calendar	...
11^v–24	...	PREFACE OF FULL PAGE MINIATURES
11^v	...	Annunciation
12	...	Nativity
13^v	...	Annunciation to shepherds
14	...	Adoration of Magi
15^v	...	Massacre of Innocents
16	...	Baptism
17^v	...	Presentation in temple
18	...	Entry into Jerusalem
19^v	...	Washing feet of apostles
20	...	Betrayal
21^v	...	Flagellation
22	...	Way of the Cross
23^v	...	Crucifixion
24	...	Entombment
25–151	Hours of the Virgin	HISTORIATED INITIALS
25	Matins (*Domine labia*)	Woman in prayer, Christ with host above
25^v	. (*Deus in ad..*)	Woman praying from book
36	. (lesson 1)	Man kneels before crowned Virgin
37	. (lesson 2)	Visitation

Folio	Text	Illustration
38ᵛ	. (lesson 3)	Crowned woman before seated Virgin and Child
47ᵛ	. (lesson 4)	Crowned man before seated Virgin
49	. (lesson 5)	Nativity
51	. (lesson 6)	Standing Christ and Virgin with book
60ᵛ	. (lesson 7)	Tonsured man kneels before seated Virgin and Child
62	. (lesson 8)	Angel with censer before crowned standing Virgin
64	. (lesson 9)	Man kneeling before seated Virgin and Child
68ᵛ	Lauds	Seated Virgin and Child
	Suffrages	. . .
102ᵛ	Prime	Tonsured cleric in blue and white talks to four in black and white
112	Terce	Nun in black kneels before enthroned Virgin
119	Sext	Priest with deacon before altar
125ᵛ	None	Tonsured man in blue kneels before seated Virgin
133	Vespers	Seated Virgin and Child with 2 censing angels
144	Compline	Christ as Judge shows wounds, Virgin and St John
152ᵛ	. . .	(Fifteenth century) St Laurence with male donor
153–173	Penitential Psalms	Woman holding prayer roll
173ᵛ–190	Gradual Psalms	Woman kneels before lectern
190ᵛ–201	Litany	. . .

3. *The Egerton Hours*

British Library, MS Egerton 1151
*c.*1260 – Oxford

A. CONTENTS

Calendar, (ff.1–6); Hours of the Virgin (ff.7–63); Penitential Psalms (ff.64–74ᵛ); Litany (ff.75–83); Hours of the Holy Spirit (ff.84–94ᵛ); Hours of Christ crucified (ff.95ᵛ–118); Office of the Dead (ff.118–158).

B. PHYSICAL FEATURES

Page size: 16.4 cm × 10.8 cm. Text area. 8.8 × 6 cm. 159 ff, with paper flyleaves. 1 column of 14 lines. Thin, fine, rather white parchment. Some pricking remains. Ruled in black or brown ink. Small, even and clear gothic script in black ink. Rubrics in red, some long and descriptive, mainly in French. The devotional couplets of the Hours of Christ crucified text are also written in red.

C. LITURGY

The Calendar is basically Sarum, though with saints from the Worcester region: St Egwin of Evesham (10 September and 30 December), St Wulfstan of Worcester (19 January and 7 June). St Frideswide's Translation (12 February) is celebrated, though her November feast is not.

The Hours of the Virgin is not Use of Sarum, and the variants of Use of Arras.

Suffrages to: Virgin, Holy Spirit, Holy Trinity, Holy Cross, St Michael, St John the Baptist, Saints Peter and Paul, St Andrew, St John the Evangelist, St James, All Apostles, St Stephen, St Laurence, St Edmund the King, St Thomas of Canterbury (defaced), St George, St Blaise, All Martyrs, St Martin, St Nicholas, St Swithun, St Leonard, All Confessors, St Mary Magdalen, St Katherine, St Margaret, All Virgins, All Saints, Peace.

The Litany includes St Hugh, St Wulfstan and St Swithun among the Confessors, St Brigid and St Frideswide among the Virgins. The high grading of St Victor, together with the invocation of both St Marcellus and St Opportuna, has suggested a Victorine importance.

The Hours of the Holy Spirit is included, but None is omitted. A number of variations which appear in the text are similar to those found in the Beatrice Hours, BL MS Add.33385 (no.5).

The Hours of Christ crucified is the first example of this text in a book of hours.

The Office of the Dead follows the Use of Sarum, with minor variants.

D. COMMENTARY

Literal illustration is adopted for the hours texts, illustrating the time of day to which the hour refers. This book of hours shows evidence of French influence in both style and iconography, and derives from a group of manuscripts which includes the William of Devon Bible (B L MS Royal 1.D.I), the Cuerdon Psalter (New York, Pierpont Morgan Library MS 756), the Blackburn Psalter (Blackburn Museum, Hart MS 21001), together with other bibles. Stylistic and iconographic similarities are evident. The Egerton Hours is the smallest and most delicate of this group. The centre where this group was made was obviously sophisticated, making high-quality manuscripts and, with the occurence of St Frideswide and saints important in the diocese of Lincoln and from the Worcester region, Oxford is the most likely location for this workshop.

E. TABLE OF ICONOGRAPHY

Folio	Text	Illustration
1–6	Calendar	. . .
7–63	Hours of Virgin	HISTORIATED INITIALS
7	Matins	Virgin and Child enthroned, donor in niche
17	Lauds	. . . (no initial, division not marked)
27	Suffrages	. . .
38	Prime	Sunrise
43	Terce	– excised –
45	Sext	– excised –
47	None	Afternoon entertainment, dance and music
50	Vespers	Evening prayer; two monks sing, woman kneels
57^v	Compline	Bed-time, lamp over figures arranging beds
62	*Salve regina*	. . .
64–74^v	Penitential Psalms	– excised –
75–83	Litany	. . .
84–94^v	Hours of Holy Spirit	HISTORIATED INITIALS
84	Matins	– excised –
85	Lauds	. . . (no initial, division not marked)
88^v	Prime	Getting up with the Holy Spirit
90	Terce	Morning prayer with the Holy Spirit
91	Sext	– excised –
92	Vespers	Evening prayer with the Holy Spirit
93^v	Compline	Bed-time with the Holy Spirit
95^v–117^v	Hours of Christ crucified	TWO HISTORIATED INITIALS ONLY
95^v	Matins	Betrayal
99^v	Lauds	. . .
104	Prime	. . .
106	Terce	. . .
108	Sext	. . .

Folio	Text	Illustration
109	None	. . .
111	Vespers	. . .
114	Compline	Resurrection
118–158	Office of Dead	Service over coffin, with clerics, a man and a woman

4. *The Salvin Hours*

British Library, MS Add. 48985

*c.*1270 – Oxford

A. CONTENTS

Hours of the Virgin, (ff.2–46) including a list of 69 suffrages after Lauds; Hours of the Holy Spirit (ff.46ᵛ–92); Hours of the Trinity (ff.92ᵛ–116).

B. PHYSICAL FEATURES

Page size: 32 cm × 21.8 cm. Text area: 21 cm × 12 cm. 128 ff of fine even parchment, with 40 additional folios of heavy unused parchment at the end of the volume. Single column of 22 lines. Single line initials in a separate margin to left of the text area. Large even script, in black ink, with Latin rubrics in red. Dark blue tooled skin binding. Full page historiated initials face major openings (excised at f.92, Trinity), historiated initials for each Hour.

C. LITURGY

The Hours of the Virgin is Use of Sarum, with certain variants. The suffrages after Lauds are exceptionally numerous. Written in litany order: the Virgin, Holy Spirit, Trinity, Holy Cross, St Michael, St John the Baptist, Saints Peter and Paul, St John the Evangelist, St Andrew, St James, St Thomas, Saints Philip and James, St Bartholomew, St Matthew, Saints Simon and Jude, St Mathias, St Barnabas, St Mark, St Luke, St Stephen, Holy Innocents, St Laurence, St Thomas of Canterbury (defaced), St George, St Nicholas, St Martin, St Leonard, St Giles, St Gregory, St Edmund, St Adrian, St Edmund the King, St Francis, St Benedict, Robert a Bishop (probably Robert Grosseteste), St Richard of Chichester, St Vincent, St Christopher, St Eustace, St Bernard, St Dominic, St Blaise, St Pantaleon, St Lupus, St Leodegarius, St Mary Magdalen, St Anne, St Katherine, St Margaret, St Agnes, St Agatha, St Potentia, St Cecilia, St Lucy, St Juliana, St Christina, St Fidis, St Felicitas, St Eufemia, St Anastasia, the Holy Virgins, St Cuthburga, St Etheldrede, St Scolastica, St Radegund, St Petronilla, St Edith, All Angels, All Saints.

The Hours of the Holy Spirit is complex, and unlike other contemporary versions. It opens with a first Vespers and Compline (to be said on the eve, suggesting occasional use only), followed by the full eight Hours. Matins has three lessons, and each Hour has five psalms.

The Hours of the Trinity also opens with Vespers and Compline, but the text is incomplete and final quires are misbound. Lauds now follows None, and no second Vespers and Compline survive. Matins has nine lessons.

D. COMMENTARY

A grand and stately book of hours, built on the lines of a psalter. It combines contemporary psalter iconography (the opening Tree of Jesse, the images of saints opening Hours of Holy Spirit and Trinity) with iconography derived from the de Brailes Hours (the Infancy cycle imagery of the Jesse Tree and the Passion cycle opening Hours of the Virgin). The overall design relates closely to the Huth Psalter, B L MS Add.38116. Two main styles of illumination also derive from these two sources, reflecting the de Brailes manuscripts and the Huth and Grandisson Psalters (B L MS Add.21926). As the Oxford tradition is evident for both these styles, the Salvin Hours was surely made in Oxford by artists who had contact with the de Brailes circle. Post-dating the canonisation of St Richard of Chichester in 1262, its style suggests a date around 1270.

E. TABLE OF ICONOGRAPHY

Folio	Text	Illustration
1^v–46	Hours of the Virgin	HISTORIATED INITIALS
1^v	Matins *Domine labia mea*	Tree of Jesse: ancestors of Christ lead to Christ enthroned, with Evangelists; Infancy cycle in side branches: Marriage of Virgin; Annunciation; Nativity; Annunciation to Shepherds; Adoration of Magi; Dream of Magi; Presentation; Flight into Egypt
2	*Deus in adiutorium* Ps. *Venite*	Betrayal Birching of penitent by monk
7	Lauds	Christ before Annas
10^v	Ps. *Cantate*	Three monks singing, woman pulling bells
29	Prime Hymn: *Veni creator*	Christ before Caiaphas Pentecost
32^v	Terce	Christ before Pilate, Pilate washing hands
35	Sext	Christ being mocked and denied by Peter, with cock crowing
37^v	None	Flagellation
40	Vespers	Crucifixion
43^v	Compline	Resurrection
46^v–92	Hours of the Holy Spirit	HISTORIATED INITIALS
47	Vespers	FULL PAGE INITIAL: Ascension; Noli me tangere; Doubting Thomas; Pentecost
52	Compline	– decorative –
54	Matins	Martyrdom of St Andrew
62	Lauds	– no major initial –
66^v	Prime	Decollation of St Paul
74	Terce	St John Evangelist survives draught of poison
77^v	Sext	Decollation of St John Baptist, with Salome
80^v	None	Flaying of St Bartholomew
84	Vespers	St Edward Confessor, legend of the ring
88^v	Compline	Martyrdom of St Laurence
92^v–116	Hours of the Trinity	HISTORIATED INITIALS
92^v	Vespers	– paged excised – (offset of initial)
95^v	Compline	Martyrdom of St Edmund the King
99	Matins	Martyrdom of St Thomas of Canterbury
117^v	Prime	Martyrdom of St Katherine
124^v	Terce	St Margaret emerging from dragon
128	None	– decorative –
*111	Lauds	St Nicholas sending cakes to sick man

* final folios misbound.

5. *The Beatrice Hours*

British Library, MS Add.33385

*c.*1260–70

A. CONTENTS

Hours of the Trinity (ff.2–26); Hours of the Passion of Christ (ff.27–40); Hours of the Holy Spirit (ff.41–53); Hours of the Virgin (ff.54–106); Hours of St John the Baptist (ff.107–124); Hours of St Katherine (ff.125–139); Penitential Psalms (ff.141–150); Litany (ff.151–158ᵛ); Gradual Psalms, (ff.159–168); prayer to St Roger (ff.168ᵛ–169ᵛ); Office of the Dead (ff.171–196), additional prayers.

B. PHYSICAL FEATURES

Page size: 15.8 cm × 9.8 cm. Text area: 10.2 cm × 6.5 cm. 196 ff. + 3 paper flyleaves. Yellow/brown parchment of even quality, trimmed. Single column of mostly 15 lines. Small initials set in a separate column. The ruling layout is complex including bas-de-page ruling. Variable script in black ink. Frequent, informative red rubrics, mostly French.

C. LITURGY

The Hours of the Trinity is short, only a single psalm at each Hour.

The Hours of the Passion of Christ opens with rubric *del nun iesu*, as in the Egerton Hours (no.3), but with different text. Similar to that in de Vere Hours (no.8), there entitled *ures dela pasiun le duz ihesu crist*, both these lack the devotional couplets of the Egerton Hours text. Followed by an added prayer for Beatrice.

The Hours of the Holy Spirit is slightly abbreviated, with a single lesson Matins. Most Hours lack the capitulum, versicle and response. Vespers lacks the *Magnificat*; the *Nunc dimittis* at Compline replaced by the Psalm, *Domine exaudi*.

The Hours of the Virgin is Use of Sarum, stated in rubrics, as at the end of Prime: *Sulun l'us de Sales-birii*.

Matins has three nocturnes, each marked by a rubric. Each includes three psalms and three lessons, with a special antiphon for each psalm. No suffrages after Lauds.

The Hours of St John the Baptist, not otherwise recorded, forms a separate section evident from different type of parchment, different number of lines (20 for this text only), distinct script. However rubric instructions confirm that it was written for this manuscript, and for this particular place in the text: *E tuz les autres saumes suivez si cum es laudes es houres nre dame devant.* Matins has three psalms, and lessons of the life of St John. Prime has only a single psalm.

The Hours of St Katherine differs from the text in the Walters Hours (no.7). Matins has three psalms and lessons. Rubrics refer the reader to the Hours of the Virgin for the *Te Deum*, and certain psalms. All antiphons and capitulae refer to St Katherine by name.

The Penitential Psalms are standard.

The Litany includes St Patrick among the confessors and St Frideswide among the virgins.

The Gradual Psalms are nos. 119–132 and 150.

The Office of the Dead is Use of Sarum.

D. COMMENTARY

Without illumination but with script and penwork decoration typical of *c.*1260–70, the manuscript must have been most valued for its function – and it was evidently much used. Its greatest importance remains its complex text, and the variety of Hours texts it includes (some unique survivals at this date), suggesting the growing popularity of such devotional routines, particularly, it seems, for women. A number of prayers were added for the soul of a lady called Beatrice, with royal connections (particularly f.124). Beatrice, daughter of Henry III, wife of John, Earl of Richmond (Duke of Brittany in 1286) died in 1272 or 3. These prayers are witness to her family's care, and the continuity of use of such manuscripts.

E. TABLE OF ICONOGRAPHY

Folio	Text	Illustration
2–26	Hours of the Trinity	– DECORATIVE INITIALS –
2	Matins	– excised –
9	Lauds	
13	Prime	
15	Terce	
17	Sext	

Folio	Text	Illustration
19	None	
21	Vespers	
24	Compline	
27–40	Hours of the Passion of Christ	– DECORATIVE INITIALS –
27	Matins	– excised –
27	Lauds	
30	Prime	
32	Terce	
33	Sext	
35	None	
36^{v}	Vespers	
38^{v}	Compline	
41–53	Hours of the Holy Spirit	– DECORATIVE INITITALS –
41	Matins	– excised –
	? Lauds –f excised	
45	Prime	
46^{v}	Terce	
48	Sext	
49^{v}	None	
50^{v}	Vespers	
52	Compline	
54–106	Hours of the Virgin	– DECORATIVE INITIALS –
54	Matins	– excised –
73^{v}	Lauds	
84	Prime	
88^{v}	Terce	
91	Sext	
93^{v}	None	
97	Psalms to be said before Vespers	
99	Vespers	
101^{v}	Compline	
	Salve Regina	
107–124	Hours of St John the Baptist	– DECORATIVE INITIALS –
107	Matins	
111	Lauds	
112	Prime	
114	Terce	
116	Sext	
119	None	

Folio	Text	Illustration
121	Vespers	
122ᵛ	Compline	
125–139	Hours of St Katherine	– DECORATIVE INITIALS –
125	Matins	
129	Lauds	
130ᵛ	Prime	
132	Terce	
133	Sext	
134ᵛ	None	
135ᵛ	Vespers	
138	Compline	
140	Added Prayers	
141	Penitential Psalms	– DECORATIVE INITIAL –
151	Litany	– DECORATIVE INITIAL –
159	Gradual Psalms	– DECORATIVE INITIAL –
168ᵛ	Prayer to St Roger	
170	Private prayers	
171–196	Office of the Dead	– DECORATIVE INITIAL –

6. *The Harley Hours*

British Library, MS Harley 928
*c.*1280–90

A. CONTENTS

Prayers and full page miniatures alternating (ff.3–9ᵛ); Hours of the Virgin (ff.10–107); Penitential Psalms (ff.107–128); additions of the fifteenth century, including the Office of the Dead (ff.128–257).

B. PHYSICAL FEATURES

Page size: 11.3 cm × 7.5 cm. Text area: 7 cm × 4.8 cm. 257 ff, but later additions following f.128. Folded parchment deed pasted in front. Stiff yellowish parchment, trimmed, quires resewn with catchwords remaining. Faint ruling, with 10 lines of text. Large-scale gothic script in black, with rubrics in red, many in French. Decorative initials and line-fillers. Bas-de-page features on each page, with border stems from larger initials.

C. LITURGY

Prayers accompanying full-page miniatures concentrate on image depicted. Not otherwise recorded.

Hours of the Virgin is Use of Sarum, with minimal variants. Suffrages after Lauds to: Holy Spirit, Trinity, Holy Cross, St Michael, Saints Peter and Paul, St John the Baptist, St Thomas, St Stephen, St Laurence, St Edmund of Abingdon, St Nicholas, St Mary Magdalen, St Katherine, St Margaret, All Saints, Peace.

Penitential Psalms are standard.

Remaining texts of the fifteenth century, according to seventeenth-century note, written in 1428 at Glastonbury, and belonged to Abbot Ambrose de la Peerie.

D. COMMENTARY

Not a luxury product, but with high-quality illumination, richly coloured, and of two distinct styles, one graceful and modelled, the other with more stocky figures, using black lines to define faces and drapery. The decorative features of the manuscript include border stems and sprays, and an amazing range of animals, grotesques and scenes (as f.97ᵛ, a monkey riding a dog with another attacking a castle). These are consistent with a date in the 1280s, as is the figure style. The pictorial preface clearly links the image with a prayer – a short meditative type of routine – on the Life of Christ. The historiated initials to the Hours of the Virgin are a remarkably inconsistent series, including further episodes of the life of Christ intermixed with images of saints. Throughout, the illustration seems haphazard – even the prefatory miniatures are not strictly chronological. Its lady owner is depicted in prayer before the enthroned and blessing Christ. Minimal in text, this manuscript has a personal quality to it – guide to the lady's own devotional routine in honour of the Virgin. The fifteenth-century additions are evidence of continued use, adapting it for more general use as a devotional book, but respecting its original text.

E. TABLE OF ICONOGRAPHY

Folio	Text	Illustration
1–2	17th-century Deed	. . .
3–9	Prayers . . .	MINIATURES
3	– prayer –	. . .
3ᵛ	. . .	Nativity
4	. . .	Visitation
4ᵛ–5	– prayer –	. . .
5ᵛ	. . .	Adoration of Magi
6–7	– prayers –	. . .
7	. . .	Presentation of Christ
8	. . .	Betrayal
8ᵛ	– prayers –	. . .
9	. . .	Resurrection
9ᵛ	– prayers –	. . .
10–107	Hours of Virgin	HISTORIATED INITIALS
10	Matins	St Katherine
30	Lauds	St Margaret
49ᵛ	Suffrages	. . .
63	Prime	Coronation of the Virgin
72	Terce	– excised –
77ᵛ	Sext	St Laurence
83	None	St John the Baptist
89	Vespers	Ascension
99	Compline	Pentecost
107–128	Penitential Psalms	HISTORIATED INITIAL Praying lady blessed by enthroned Christ
128–257	– added texts –	

7. *The Walters Hours*

Baltimore, Walters Art Gallery, MS 102
*c.*1290–1300

A. CONTENTS

Rebound (nineteenth century) with the loss and dis-arrangement of text. Texts included: Hours of the Virgin, with a variant text for both Advent and the period from Christmas to Candlemas; Hours of Christ crucified, Hours of the Holy Spirit, prayers to the crucified Christ, Hours of St Katherine, Penitential Psalms, Gradual Psalms, Litany, Office of the Dead.

B. PHYSICAL FEATURES

Page size: 26.8 cm × 14.3 cm. Text area: 17.4 cm × 11.6 cm. 105 ff. Soft, beige parchment of even quality. Trimmed and resewn. Catchwords. 19 lines in a single column. Pricking remains on vertical ruling. Text space and border defined by ruling, border by double lines. Large, even, gothic script in black ink. Rubrics in red; Latin and French descriptive and instructional rubrics. Much page decoration, including profusion of line endings, particularly in the litany. High-quality penwork throughout.

C. LITURGY

Hours of the Virgin is substantially incomplete. Three variant forms existed, as defined by rubrics. Use of Rome variable parts, although no complete text remains.

Hours of Christ crucified is similar to text of the Egerton Hours (also Norwich Hours, Castle Museum, MS 158. 926 4f). Sequence of French and Latin couplets relate events of the Passion to canonical hour, concentrating on human suffering of Christ, at each hour followed by short version of Hours of the Cross.

Hours of Holy Spirit has no Matins lesson, and no Lauds service.

Prayers to crucified Christ is not otherwise recorded. Including seven parts, each has an introduction, responsory and prayer.

Hours of St Katherine opens with first Vespers. Matins has three psalms and nine lessons, which tell the life of the saint. Hymns to St Katherine, and prayers at each of the Hours. This text is not other-wide recorded.

Penitential Psalms standard, Gradual Psalms nos.119–133.

Litany has a special category, invoking All Monks and Hermits, which includes four, Saints Benedict, Francis, Anthony and Dominic. Following Use of Rome, this was used particularly by the Austin Friars, (L. F. Sandler, 'An early fourteenth-century English Psalter in the Escorial', *Journal of Warburg and Courtauld Institutes*, 42 (1979). pp.64–80).

Office of the Dead is non-Sarum, but identical to the Office in Oxford, Bodleian Library MS Laud misc. 188, of *c.*1380, which is described in the rubric as Use of the Austin Friars.

D. COMMENTARY

Although mutilated, this remains a most remarkable manuscript, in contents, iconography and style. Large in scale, and full of illustration all related to its text, although, as in the Funeral of Renart the Fox in the border of the Office of the Dead, or the large scale line-fillers in the litany, not always solemnly religious. Its texts suggest it is Use of the Austin Friars (the first recorded example) and it contains a rich variety of texts, defining a complex devotional routine. The Hours of St Katherine suggests a special devotion to her, and there may have been further illustration of her life. The images of praying figures show lay and clerical figures, men and women. Both decorative and figure style is sophisticated and high quality, to create a stately manuscript. It is stylistically related to a bible in Oxford, Bodleian Library MS Auct. D.3.2, the Windmill Psalter, New York, Pierpont Morgan MS 102, and group. This group dates to the 1290s, but its location is not certain.

E. TABLE OF ICONOGRAPHY

Folio	Text	Illustration
2–3	Compline of Hours of Christ crucified	Tree of Jesse
4–11	Prayers to Christ crucified	HISTORIATED INITIALS
4	Preface	Crucifixion
5	Part 1	Carrying of Cross
6	Part 2	Crucifixion, thieves in mandorla

Folio	Text	Illustration
6ᵛ	Part 3	Trinity with crucified Christ
7ᵛ	Part 4	Three Maries at the Tomb
8	Part 5	Harrowing of Hell
9	Conclusion	Christ child blessing man and woman
10ᵛ	Prayer and Psalm Dixi custodiam	Christ blesses king who kneels pointing to mouth
11ᵛ	Prayer before Mass	Noli me tangere
12ᵛ–15ᵛ	Hours of St Katherine Vespers	. . .
13ᵛ	Matins	King Maxentius, doctors of Alexandria
16	Sext of Hours of Virgin	Woman prays before altar
17–21ᵛ	Hours of Virgin for Advent	– NO ILLUSTRATION –
17ᵛ	Matins	. . .
17ᵛ	Lauds	. . .
18	Prime	. . .
19ᵛ	Terce	. . .
20	Sext, None, Vespers	. . .
22–35ᵛ	Hours of Holy Spirit	HISTORIATED INITIALS
22	Matins	Priest singing, with acolyte
24ᵛ	Prime	Woman in prayer
25ᵛ	Terce	Man in prayer
26ᵛ	Sext	Woman in prayer
27	end Penitential Psalms	. . .
28	Litany	– MARGINAL ILLUSTRATIONS –
31	Gradual Psalms	. . .
35	Sext of Holy Spirit ends	. . .
35ᵛ	None of Holy Spirit	Woman in prayer
36	end Litany	. . .
36ᵛ	Collects	. . .
39	Gradual Psalms	Man kneels before executioner
41	Vespers of Holy Spirit	. . .
42	Compline of Holy Spirit	. . .
43	Penitential Psalms	Christ reads, book held by cleric
51–74	Office of Dead	HISTORIATED INITIALS
51	Matins	Two clerics in white sing from book.
55	Lesson 1	Funeral service, two clerics, layman
70	Vespers	Man and woman kneel, hand of God
74ᵛ–85ᵛ	Hours of Christ crucified	HISTORIATED INITIALS
74ᵛ	Matins	Betrayal
75	Lauds	Scourging of Christ
76	Prime	Carrying of Cross
77ᵛ	Terce	Crucifixion
79ᵛ	Sext	Descent from Cross
81ᵛ	None	Anointing of Christ

Folio	Text	Illustration
83	Vespers	Resurrection
84^v	Compline, incipit	– see f.2–
85	end None of Holy Spirit	
	Vespers	
86	Terce of Virgin cont.	
87	Lauds of Virgin cont.	
88^v	Prime of Virgin	Woman in prayer
91	Sext cont. from f.16	
92^v	Terce of Virgin begins	Woman in prayer
94	Hours of St Katherine cont.	. . .
99^v	Lauds	. . .
100	Prime	. . .
102	Terce	. . .
102^v	Sext	. . .
102^v	None	. . .
102^v	Vespers (second)	. . .
103	Compline	. . .
103^v	Prayer on journey	. . .
104	Prayer to St Julian	. . .
104	Prayer	. . .
104	Prayer to be said on rising in morning	. . .

8. *The de Vere Hours*

Cambridge, Christ's College MS 8
c.1300–05 – Fenlands

A. CONTENTS

Calendar (ff.1–6); Hours of the Trinity (ff.1–12); Hours of the Virgin for the whole year, divided into three main sections, with variations (ff.12–57^v); Hours of the Conception of the Virgin (ff.57^v–64^v); Hours of the Purification (ff.65–72^v); Hours of the Annunciation (ff.73–78^v); Hours of the Assumption (ff.79–157^v); Hours of the Nativity of the Virgin (ff.158–175); Hours of the Passion (ff.176–188); Hours of the Holy Spirit (ff.188^v–199); the Penitential Psalms (ff.200^v–209^v); Litany (ff.209^v–219); Gradual Psalms (ff.219–226); the Seven Joys of the Virgin (ff.227^v–229); Office of the Dead (ff.230–257); single misbound folio of the beginning of Matins of the Nativity of the Virgin.

B. PHYSICAL FEATURES

Page size: 27.4 cm × 18 cm. Text area: 17.2 cm × 10.3 cm. 258 ff. Single column of 18 lines. Heavy white parchment. Large regular liturgical script, in black ink. Long French rubrics in red ink describing texts and the times and manner in which they should be said. Many decorative initials and line fillers, few historiated.

C. LITURGY

The liturgy of the manuscript is remarkable in its complexity and variety, and is unique among surviving English books of hours.

Calendar contains Sarum saints, but also includes St Hugh of Lincoln (17 November), St Etheldreda (23 June, 17 October), St Peter Martyr (29 April) in red. Presentation of the Virgin (21 November) is an exceptionally early occurrence of this feast.

Hours of the Trinity has lost portions of text, but is closest to certain fourteenth-century examples. Three lessons at Matins.

Hours of the Virgin has a full series of Offices, with variations, for the three periods of the Church's year, and different ferie of the week. Each Matins has three nocturnes or, at least, nine psalms. Only minor variants from the unchanging Use of Sarum. Suffrages prescribed after each Hour, the full list follows Lauds for Purification until Advent. Suffrages: Holy Spirit,

Holy Cross, All Angels, St John the Baptist, Saints Peter and Paul, St Andrew, St John the Evangelist, St Stephen, All Apostles, St Laurence, St Edmund King and Martyr, St Thomas Becket (defaced), St Martin, St Nicholas, St Edmund, St Francis, All Confessors, St Etheldreda, St Mary Magdalen, St Katherine, All Saints, Peace.

Hours of the Conception of the Virgin opens with Vespers and Compline of the Vigil. Matins has nine lessons, with variations for the antiphon Te Deum.

Hours of the Annunciation has lost its first Vespers and Compline. Matins has three nocturnes.

Hours of the Assumption is preceded by vigils, has a nine psalm Matins, prayers and suffrages at Prime. Service for the second day (nine psalm, three lesson Matins) has suffrages after Lauds, Vespers, and Compline. Rubric prescribes this for the rest of the week with variations. Matins for the octave has nine lessons.

The Hours of the Nativity of the Virgin opens with a vigil, services for the octave, with three nocturne Matins on Sunday. Suffrages for each day.

Hours of the Passion (rubric: *Ici comence les ures de la pasiun le duz ihesu crist*), as found in the Beatrice Hours. Only a single lesson at Matins, minor Hours one psalm, with hymn, responsory and prayers.

Hours of the Holy Spirit are the usual form.

Penitential Psalms are standard.

Litany is remarkably long, indicates devotion to saints of the diocese of Lincoln, towards Ely. Saints invoked include: St Edmund the King, St Ethelberte,

St Alban, martyrs; St Francis, St Dominic, St Guthlac (twice), St Wulfstan, St Anthony, St Wandregesile, St Neot, St William, St Hugh, confessors; St Etheldreda, St Wythburga, St Sexburga, St Ermenilda, St Brigid, St Frideswide, St Radegund, St Osith, St Eufemia, virgins.

Gradual Psalms lacks psalm 119 and opening of psalm 120 (excised), but includes both psalm 133 and psalm 150.

Prayers to the Virgin celebrate the joys of the Virgin.

Office of the Dead is Use of Sarum, with few variations, but ends imperfectly.

D. COMMENTARY

Liturgically most unusual, including texts expected only in a breviary. It was presumably made for Alice de Vere, Countess of Oxford, whose obit (1312) was added to the calendar, together with obits of other members of the de Vere family. It seems she had a special devotion to the Virgin (separate offices for each of the feasts of the Virgin are otherwise unknown in books of hours), and a wide-ranging devotion to the saints. The illustration of the manuscript was sparse, though much is now lost, but with the fine penwork and decorative initials and the interesting range of line-fillers, of foliate and animal designs, both painted and reserve work, it remains a fine manuscript. Stylistically it must date from the earliest years of the fourteenth century, *c*.1300–05, conforming with Alice's ownership. One of the few remaining historiated initials, at the Penitential Psalms, may well show Alice at prayer, blessed by the enthroned Christ.

E. TABLE OF ICONOGRAPHY

Folio	Text	Illustration
a–c	– added –	
1–6	Calendar	– decorative –
(foliation changes, begins here at f. 1)		
1–12	Hours of the Trinity	HISTORIATED INITIAL
1	Matins	Trinity,
5–11ᵛ	Lauds – Compline (Prime, Terce, Vespers excised)	– decorative –
12–29	Office of the Virgin, Advent	– no illustration remains –
14	Memorie at end of Vespers	. . .
15	Compline	. . .
18	Matins	. . .
19ᵛ–29	Lauds-None	. . .

Folio	Text	Illustration
29	Incipits to variations for the 6 ferie Vespers and Compline as before	
29ᵛ–33ᵛ	Service for Saturdays in Advent	. . .
29ᵛ	Matins (9 psalms, 3 lessons)	. . .
32ᵛ	Lauds (includes suffrages)	. . .
32ᵛ	Prime (plus prayers for Assumption)	. . .
32ᵛ–33	Terce-Compline	. . .
33ᵛ–37ᵛ	Hours of the Virgin, after Christmas	. . .
33ᵛ	Vespers	. . .
34	Compline	. . .
34ᵛ–37ᵛ	Matins – Compline	. . .
38–42	Matins – None	. . .
42–50	Hours of the Virgin, after Purification	. . .
42	Vespers	. . .
42ᵛ	Compline	. . .
42ᵛ	Service for Saturday, (variations at Vespers)	. . .
43ᵛ	Matins (2 sets of 6 lessons)	. . .
49–50	Lauds – Compline	. . .
50	Second feria Matins	. . .
50–57	Lauds – Compline	. . .
57ᵛ–64ᵛ	Hours of the Conception	. . .
57ᵛ	Vespers	. . .
58ᵛ	Compline	. . .
58ᵛ	Matins (9 lessons)	. . .
63ᵛ–64	Lauds – None	. . .
65–72ᵛ	Hours of the Purification	– no illustration remains –
65	Vespers (beginning gone)	– excised –
66	Compline	. . .
66ᵛ	Matins (9 lessons)	. . .
71ᵛ–72	Lauds – None	. . .
73–78ᵛ	Hours of the Annunciation	– no illustration remains –
73–76ᵛ	Matins	. . .
77–78ᵛ	Lauds – None	. . .
79–89	Vigil of the Assumption	– no illustration remains –
79	Vespers	. . .
84ᵛ	Compline	. . .

Folio	Text	Illustration
90–157	Hours of the Feast of the Assumption	LARGE HISTORIATED INITIALS
90	Matins (3 nocturnes)	– excised –
107	Lauds (beginning gone)	. . .
114	Prime	Death of the Virgin
124ᵛ	Terce	Burial with disbelieving Jews
129	Sext	St Peter preaching
133	None (beginning gone)	. . .
136ᵛ	Vespers	Apostles mourning over coffin
141	Compline (as before)	. . .
141–145ᵛ	Hours for the Second Day	
141	Matins (9 psalms, 3 lessons)	
143–144	Lauds – Vespers	. . .
144ᵛ	Suffrage – St Laurence, All Saints	. . .
145ᵛ	Compline (as before)	. . .
145ᵛ	Matins for the Third Day	
146ᵛ	Matins for the Fourth Day	. . .
148ᵛ	Matins for the Fifth Day	. . .
150ᵛ	Matins for Saturday	. . .
151ᵛ	Matins for Sunday	. . .
152ᵛ	Octave of the Assumption	
142ᵛ	Matins (9 lessons)	. . .
157ᵛ	Vespers	. . .
158–175	Hours of the Nativity of the Virgin	– no illustration remaining –
158	Vespers (folio missing)	. . .
159–164ᵛ	Matins – Vespers	. . .
164ᵛ–166	Hours for the Second Day	. . .
164ᵛ	Matins	. . .
166	Lauds	. . .
166	Prime	. . .
166	Vespers (other Hours as for First Day)	
166ᵛ	Matins for the Third Day	. . .
166ᵛ	Matins for the Fourth Day	. . .
168	Matins for the Fifth Day	. . .
169	Matins for the Sixth Day	. . .
170	Matins for the Sunday (3 nocturnes, 9 lessons)	. . .
172ᵛ	Vespers for the Octave	. . .
173	Compline (as above)	. . .
173	Matins as above (9 lessons)	. . .
176–188	Hours of the Passion of Christ	HISTORIATED INITIAL
176	Matins	Betrayal of Christ
177ᵛ–188	Lauds – Compline	. . .

Folio	Text	Illustration
188ᵛ–199	Hours of the Holy Spirit	HISTORIATED INITIAL
188ᵛ	Matins	Pentecost
191ᵛ–199ᵛ	Lauds – Compline	. . .
200–209ᵛ	Seven Penitential Psalms	Christ blessing kneeling woman
209ᵛ–219	Litany	. . .
219–226	Gradual Psalms (beginning gone)	– no illustration remaining –
226	Collects	. . .
227ᵛ	Seven Joys of the Virgin	. . .
230–257	Office of the Dead	– no illustration remaining –
258	Hours of the Nativity of the Virgin – end Compline	
258ᵛ	Matins of Nativity of the Virgin	HISTORIATED INITIAL
		Birth of the Virgin

Appendix 4 Handlist of Illuminated Manuscripts made in Oxford: 1200–1270

The history of illuminated manuscripts made in Oxford during the thirteenth century has yet to be written. It will be a major task. The list of manuscripts which, on reliable grounds, can be identified as 'Made in Oxford' is immensely varied. It includes many different types of text, and manuscripts of diverse sizes, quantity of illustration and decoration. The liturgical/devotional manuscripts are in the majority, though the illustration of the glossed psalters suggests a dual function of devotion and study, with the illustration picking out the liturgical divisions. Books for study contain a number of highly illuminated and illustrated texts of Aristotle and others, like the bibles, illustrated with a quantity of small images.

Characteristically these manuscripts were painted and decorated by collaborative groups of artists working together. Various individual hands can be identified working in different groupings, and William de Brailes is just one of these hands, though notably of consistently high quality. To identify and trace more of the individual hands may not lead to the identification by name of more artists from the lists of illuminators of Oxford, but it would lead to a much more thorough knowledge of the 'workshop' arrangements in Oxford, the ways in which artists collaborated and took decisions on the 'luxury' or 'economy' nature of the different manuscripts.

The work of Graham Pollard on the existence of the book trade in thirteenth-century Oxford was developed through an investigation of certain manuscripts, particularly those around 1200–1220, a study which has remained unpublished. The source for so much of the information given here comes from the identification of Oxford-made manuscripts which is just one element of Nigel Morgan's catalogue of thirteenth-century illuminated manuscripts. He rightly points to the further work needed to identify the different artists and their collaboration.

The handlist that follows is far from comprehensive. It does not set out to do more than bring these Oxford-made manuscripts together, adding a few, notably the Rutland Psalter which, despite observing close links with Oxford manuscripts, Dr Morgan ascribes to London. As discussed in Chapter 1, the fact that they are made in Oxford by no means requires them to be made *for* Oxford – indeed their far-flung destinations are often part of the evidence that they were Oxford-made. More will surely emerge in time.

Less elaborate manuscripts have not always been included, and these have not always received the attention that would lead to their localisation. Furthermore this list may well omit certain much-studied manuscripts that will, in the light of the accumulated evidence for Oxford makers-of-books, also come to be recognised as Oxford products.

1. Munich, Bayerische Staatsbibliothek Clm. 835
Psalter (Munich Psalter)
(277 × 195 mm) *c.*1200–1210
Extensive pictorial cycle of the Old and New Testaments, as a preface to the whole text and as inserts, supplemented by a programme of historiated initials at the major liturgical breaks between psalms. Perhaps owned by a woman (prayers with female pronouns) as biblical women are celebrated, including Susanna and the Elders. Linked to books with Oxford evidence, the Arundel Psalter (no.2) and the Royal Psalter (no.3).

2. London, British Library, MS Arundel 157
Psalter and Hours of the Virgin.
(Arundel Psalter)
(294 × 195 mm) *c.*1200–1210
Pictorial cycle, iconographically and stylistically related to the Munich Psalter, with historiated initials at liturgical divisions. With evident Augustinian influence on the Litany, and three feasts of St Frideswide in the Calendar and a suffrage, its Oxford origin is confirmed. Contains an early example of the Hours of the Virgin attached to a psalter, and with distinct and different script and decoration for this section (beginning with the Office of the Dead) suggesting the compilation in stages as seen so regularly in books of hours (see pp. 135–6).

3. London, British Library MS Royal I.D.X.
Psalter
(345 × 235 mm) *c.*1210
Pictorial cycle, close to the Arundel and the Munich Psalters. A different hand but similar style of figures to these two. Two feasts of St Frideswide in the Calendar, together with an invocation to her suggest that the manuscript was made in Oxford, despite Winchester features in the Calendar.

4. Edinburgh, National Library MS 10000
Psalter (Iona Psalter)

(289 × 195 mm) *c.*1210

Contains little illustration (only two historiated initials) it is of fine quality design and decoration. Evidence from the Calendar and Litany show conflicting loyalties – to a Scottish Augustinian from Iona, and to Oxford through the recurrence of St Frideswide. Stylistically it clearly belongs to the Oxford group.

5. Berlin, Kupferstichkabinett MS 78.A.8
Psalter and Hours of the Virgin
(Margrete Skulesdatter's Psalter)

(286 × 195 mm) *c.*1210–20

Extensively illuminated, illustrated Calendar and pictorial preface, Virgin and Child initial at Hours of Virgin. Provenance of Norwegian royal family. Iconographic and stylistic links with Oxford. (Not considered Oxford-made by Morgan).

6. Cambridge, St John's College MS D.6
Psalter with gloss and Hours of the Virgin

(275 × 183 mm) *c.*1210–20

Extensively illuminated, illustrated Calendar, pictorial preface and historiated initials. Owned by Robert de Lindesey, Abbot of Peterborough (d.1222). Same artist as Berlin Psalter-Hours. (Not considered Oxford-made by Morgan).

7. Oxford, Bodleian Library MS Bodley 284
Glossed Psalter (gloss of Alexander of Neckham)

(410 × 300 mm) *c.*1210–20

Historiated initials (liturgical divisions) and fine borders. Stylistically linked to Oxford group, particularly Huntingfield Psalter group, no.9. Used in the Augustinian Abbey of Cirencester *c.*1400.

8. New York, Pierpont Morgan Library MS M.43
Psalter (Huntingfield Psalter)

(315 × 230 mm) *c.*1210–20

An elaborate extensive pictorial cycle, with 40 full-page miniatures, and a further group of images of saints, four to a page. A lavish *Beatus* initial is designed with much stringy foliage, and individual vesica-shaped medallions containing scenes, similar to the de Brailes Hours. Provenance of the Huntingfield family in the thirteenth century, through obits in the Calendar. The lady kneeling at Psalm 50 may represent the original owner.

9. New York, Pierpont Morgan Library MS M.791
Bible (Lothian Bible)

(470 × 320 mm) *c.*1220

Large-scale and richly decorated, with full page frontispiece and historiated initials. Complex decorative initial frames and borders. Text links with St Albans, stylistic links with Oxford, and the early de Brailes style.

10. London, B L MS Cotton Claudius B. VI
Chronicle of Abingdon Abbey

(315 × 216 mm) *c.*1220

Illustrated, miniatures of Kings and Queens of England. Stylistic links with Oxford, particularly Huntingfield Psalter group.

11. London, B L MS Royal 12. F. XIII
Bestiary and Lapidary

(298 × 214 mm) *c.*1230

Illustrated with framed miniatures. A group of illuminated books linked through artists shared with de Brailes group.

12. London, Lincoln's Inn MS Hale 123
Bible

(240 × 158 mm) *c.*1230–40

Elaborately illustrated with historiated initials, though mutilated. Links with the style of de Brailes group. (Not considered Oxford-made by Morgan).

13. Cambridge, University Library MS Ee.2.23
Bible

(335 × 212 mm) *c.*1230–40

Extensively illustrated, historiated initials throughout. Linked to de Brailes through shared artists. (Not considered Oxford-made by Morgan).

14. Peterborough, Cathedral Library MS 10
Bible

(128 × 90 mm) *c.*1230–40

Extensively illustrated, and linked through artists shared with de Brailes group. (Not considered Oxford-made by Morgan).

15. Stockholm, National Museum B. 2010
Psalter (Stockholm Psalter)

(180 × 134 mm) *c.*1230–40

A small-scale, but extensively illustrated psalter, with Calendar illustration and historiated initials. Despite evidence of an origin in London, its decorative style is closely linked to Oxford, and shows collaboration with at least one Oxford artist, William de Brailes. (Not considered Oxford-made by Morgan).

16. Oxford, Bodleian Library MS lat. bibl. e.7
Bible, with some masses (de Brailes Bible)

(167 × 116 mm) *c*.1234 (or earlier)-40

Probably the earliest of the bibles chiefly illuminated by William de Brailes, and extensively illustrated. Mass of St Dominic, together with Oxford provenance (on liturgical and stylistic grounds together with the evidence of de Brailes) suggests an origin connected with the early Dominican community in Oxford. See figure 4.

17. Cambridge, Gonville and Caius College MS 350/567
Bible

(245 × 157 mm) *c*.1230–40

Larger scale but with an equally compressed script, extensively illustrated and decorated with characteristic ornamental foliage blocks. Most elaborate of bibles from the de Brailes group.

18. Baltimore, Walters Art Gallery MS 106;
Paris, Wildenstein Collection, Musée Marmottan

Pictorial leaves (variable, but about 135 × 100 mm) (24 in Baltimore, 7 in Paris) *c*.1235–40

Old Testament scenes, some derived from extensive cycle evidently drawn on in some of earlier Oxford books, e.g. Munich Psalter. May have been designed as part of a preface to a psalter or a bible.

19. Cambridge, Fitzwilliam Museum, MS 330;
Pierpont Morgan Library MS M.913

Leaves – presumed from a psalter – (variable, but about 250 × 175 mm – Morgan leaf much smaller, 215 × 143 mm) *c*.1240

Pictorial leaves, divided into separate medallions by complex decorative patterns. Includes a *Beatus vir* leaf, to open the psalter text (whether within a bible or psalter). Painted by de Brailes, and includes signature on Last Judgement leaf. See figure 2.

20. London, B L MS Add. 49999
Book of hours (de Brailes Hours)

(150 × 123 mm) *c*.1240

Extensively illustrated, signature of W de Brailes.

21. Oxford, New College MS 322
Psalter

(350 × 250 mm) *c*.1240–50

Large-scale and extensively illustrated, historiated initials and borders. Calendar includes Winchester saints with additions of contemporary saints, but conflicts with Litany. Hand of de Brailes in major historiated initials (and one complete bifolium f.113 and f.122), and various other recognisable hands contribute decoration and line fillers. See Figure 5.

22. Vienna, Museum für angewandte Kunst Cod. Lat. XIV (S.5)
Book of hours (Vienna Hours)

(158 × 110 mm) *c*.1250

Small-scale but extensively illustrated, with historiated initials and separately produced preface. See Appendix 3, no. 2. See Figures 96–7.

23. New York, Pierpont Morgan Library MS M.103
Psalter

(240 × 175 mm) *c*.1250

Provenance of Cluniac Priory in Reading, but with decorative links with Oxford manuscripts, particularly the Huntingfield Psalter, New College Psalter.

24. London, B L MS Add. 62925
Psalter (Rutland Psalter)

(285 × 200 mm) *c*.1260

Most elaborately illustrated and decorated of its date, with original and highest-quality grotesques and marginalia. Links with de Brailes group, particularly with similar use of rectangular and spiked blocks in the border and pen flourishing. Links too with an artist of the Vienna Hours. No specific destination suggested by the text. (Not considered Oxford-made by Morgan.)

25. Preston, Harris Museum and Art Gallery
Psalter and hymnal

(230 × 150 mm)

London B L MS Add. 15749
Devotional texts, Anselm and Augustine

(230 × 152 mm) *c*.1250–5

Considered as originally a single volume (Morgan II, pp.124–6), he identifies a considerable group of manuscripts made by this same group of artists, probably in Oxford. Elaborately illustrated, with rare imagery to illustrate the devotions.

26. Rome, Biblioteca Apostolica Vaticana MS Urb. Lat. 206
Aristotle, *Libri Naturales*

(316 × 220 mm) *c*.1247–54

An elaborately illuminated Aristotle, possibly datable through pledge notes, the first of 22 February 1254, to an Oxford chest.

27. Paris, B N MS lat. 6323 A
Aristotle *Libri Naturales*
(340 × 225 mm) *c*.1255–60
Historiated initials with decorative extensions. Ornament clearly linked to de Brailes patterns.

28. Berlin, Deutsch Staatsbibliothek MS Phill. 1781
Averroes, *Commentary on the Metaphysics*
(275 × 192 mm) *c*.1255–60
Illuminated initial and decorative initials with penwork linked to de Brailes patterns.

29. Paris, B N MS lat. 6505
Averroes, *Commentary on the Physics*
(327 × 212 mm) *c*.1255–60
Partly illuminated, with spaces for illuminated initial in later part of book. Influence and patterns from de Brailes manuscripts.

30. Oxford, Merton College MS 269 (F. 1. 4)
Averroes, *Commentary on the metaphysics of Aristotle*
(298 × 214 mm) *c*.1255–60
Despite loss of some initials many remain with interesting, original, iconography. Fine quality, decorative extensions typical of Oxford-made manuscripts.

31. Oxford, All Souls College MS 2
Bible
(265 × 175 mm) *c*.1260
Fully illustrated bible, evidently derived from the Oxford workshop, with iconographic and stylistic links, and French influence.

32. New York, Pierpont Morgan Library MS Glazier 42
Bible
(398 × 244 mm) *c*.1265
Large-scale and elaborate bible, fully illustrated with historiated initials, of the same group but mostly the work of the best of these artists.

33. Durham, Cathedral Library MS A. II. 10
Psalter with Gloss
(394 × 255 mm) *c*.1265
Historiated initials at liturgical divisions, some the work of the best artist of the Glazier Bible.

34. Cambridge, Trinity College MS R.14.9
Bestiary (ff.89–108, bound with other texts)
(261 × 181 mm) *c*.1260–70
Small framed miniatures, by same group of artists.

35. London, B L MS Harley 3487
Aristotle, *Libri Naturales*
(377 × 245 mm) *c*.1265–70
An elaborately illustrated university text, illuminated by the same group of artists.

36. Cambridge, Jesus College MS Q.A.11
Bible
(282 × 186 mm) *c*.1265–70
Elaborately illustrated, with decorative elements from Oxford repertoire.

37. London, B L MS Add. 50000
(+ Add. 54215)
Psalter (Oscott Psalter)
(302 × 196 mm) *c*.1265–70
Most elaborate illustration, including full page miniatures (some multi-medallioned), calendar illustration and historiated initials at liturgical divisions. Ornamental work suggests Oxford origins, as does the work of a number of the illuminators.

38. London, B L MS Royal I.D.I.
Bible (Bible of William of Devon)
(314 × 200 mm) *c*.1260–70
Large-scale bible, with scribe's colophon 'Willelmus Devoniensis'. Images of various mendicants. Stylistically a distinctive type of ornament characterises this manuscript and a closely related group, with clear French influence. This group has been attributed to Oxford, and links with other French influenced manuscripts made there strengthens the argument.

39. London, B L MS Egerton 1151
Book of hours (Egerton Hours)
(162 × 107 mm) *c*.1260
Stylistically related to William of Devon Bible group, with its distinctive decorative style and precise and jewel-like illumination and figure style. See Appendix 3, no. 3. See figures 87, 89–91.

40. New York, Pierpont Morgan Library MS M 756
Psalter (Cuerdon Psalter)
(295 × 196 mm) *c*.1265
Elaborately illuminated, and full of illustration. Illustrated calendar, full-page miniatures (frequently six framed images per page), with historiated initials to open each psalm, large in scale at liturgical divisions. Elaborate border decoration, with grotesques.

41. Blackburn, Museum and Art Gallery
MS 091.21001
Psalter

(215 × 138 mm) *c.*1270

Calendar suggesting an owner in the Diocese of Lincoln, together with stylistic links of both decoration
and figure style with William of Devon manuscripts.
Full-page miniatures in preface, historiated initials
for the liturgical divisions.

42. London, B L MS Add. 48985
Book of hours (Salvin Hours)

(322 × 218 mm) *c.*1265–70

Two main styles, divided both by decoration and
figure style, one clearly linked with the de Brailes
group, the other related to the later Huth Psalter (B L
MS Add. 38116), probably also made in Oxford,
*c.*1280. See Appendix 3, no. 5. See figures 88 and 93.

43. Oxford, Bodleian Library MS Laud lat. 114
Psalter

(422 × 305 mm) *c.*1260–65

Only partly illuminated at this date, completed in the
fifteenth century. Decoration related to the de Brailes
workshop, and artist linked to the first artist of the
Salvin Hours, though softer in style.

Appendix 5 William de Brailes in the documents of Oxford

The identification of *w de brail'* with the William de Brailes who occurs in the documents of Oxford is all but certain, but cannot be confirmed. The illuminator who signed both the book of hours and the Last Judgement miniature of the group of leaves in the Fitzwilliam evidently worked in Oxford, as the style in which he worked is identifiable with earlier examples of manuscripts made there, established through textual details. The disparate destinations of these manuscripts argue for a professional, not monastic, manuscript making setting. The evidence is overwhelming for professional illuminated manuscripts being made in just the area of Oxford in which the William de Brailes of the documents is recorded. Evidently this William was a man of some substance, and he was closely associated, for the thirty years during which he was recorded, with members of the book trade.

The documents in which the name of William de Brailes have been found suggest an active member of the community, called in among others to witness deeds and grants of land. The spelling of his name varies, but taking note of the 'signatures' that survive 'de Brailes' has been taken as the standard form by most writers, although Pollard added an extra 'l'.

In addition to these mentions of William de Brailes, later occurrences of the name 'de Brailes' might refer to his descendants. It has been suggested that de Brailes came from the Warwickshire village of that name north of Oxford towards Stratford, more significant then than now. Many of the names of this community suggest that they came to Oxford from shorter distances, such as Eynsham, Thame, Sandford, Dorchester. Some suggest more distant origins, such as Winchester, Derby, and Coventry. The surnames of many of these figures identify their trades (scriptor, luminour, parchiminer, liur), and it is largely, although not exclusively, on this evidence that the book-making community can be identified here. Many of these names recur in other documents recording their lives; John Pilet, John de Curci, Walter of Eynsham, Augustine the bookbinder (Liur) are all found in other connections. Women holding property are commonplace, though they tend to be described as 'wife of', 'widow of' or 'daughter of'.

1. William de Brailes first appears as a witness to a transfer of property in *c*.1230. The property stood just off School Street, on its eastern side, and was the second house along the lane facing the north door of St Mary's. It is identified as 'Godstow tenement' (no.98 on Salter's map, NE III, see figure 3).

In *c*.1230 this was granted to Walter de 'Einesham', illuminator, by John Pilet, who also had interests in both neighbouring properties, and held all three properties at some time. This middle house he granted first to Walter of Eynsham, who passed it on to Master Martin of Winchester in 1238. He granted the rent to Oseney Abbey in 1247, and by 1267 this house was in the hands of the nuns of Godstow.

The heading: Transcriptum carte quam Iohannes Pilet fecit Walter de Haynsham illuminatori (quam) accepimus transcribendam per manum magistri Martini de Wintonia, uerbo ad uerbum.

Sciant (etc.) quod ego Iohannes Pilet de Oxonia dimisi, concessi et dedi (etc.) Waltero filio Paulini de Einesham et uxori eius Iohanne terram meam una cum muro et eius contentis in longitudine quinque ulnearum et trium quateriorum, proximam iacentem inter maximum thalamum meum in parochia sancte Marie ex una parte et terram quam Agatha filia Agnetis tenuit ex altera parte; tenedam (etc.) . . . Pro terra uero predicta et pro muro et eius contentis dederunt michi duos solidos in garsumma. Et ut (etc. sealing) hiis testibus, Radulfo le Liminur, Roberto le Luminur, Thoma Lenker, Galfrido de Sanford, Petro de Couintre, Iohannes Olim, Simone le Perchiminer, Iob le Luminur, Waltero le Liur, Augustino le Liur, Adam le Liur, Willelmo de Brailles et multis aliis.

London, B L Cotton MS Vitell. E.XV, f.110ᵛ, *c*.1230. *Cartulary of Oseney Abbey*, edited by H. E. Salter, 1 (O.H.S. 89, 1929) p.189, no.202.

2. This same property was granted to Magister Martinus de Wintonia in 1238. Again it is identified as standing between the land of Agatha and John Pilet.

Sciant presentes et futuri quod ego Walterus de Enesham Illuminator dedi et concessi et quietum clamavi pro me et heredibus meis magistro Martino de Wintonis illud mesuagium cum omnibus pertinentiis . . . inter terram Iohannes Pilet et terram Agathe filie Agnetus iuxta cimiterium beate Marie virginis in Oxonia . . . Hiis testibus Galfrido de Stocwelle tunc maiore Oxonie, Laurentio Log et Iohanne Pille tunc prepositis, Thoma le Werrur, Alano Submuro, Roberto le Rus, Iohanne Stanleya, Thoma Scriptore, Roberto de Derbi, Thoma Pasche, Willelmo de Breiles, Adam de Coventre, Iohanne Bulbanne et aliis.

Cartulary of the Hospital of St John, edited by H. E. Salter, 1 (O.H.S. 66, 1914) pp.476–7.

3. William appears again as a witness to the transfer of a property in the parish of St Peter le Bailey (in the West), near St Ebbe's. Thomas, son of Laurence, granted to Richard Marshall a rent of 4s 8d, payable from the house that once belonged to William of Waus. His fellow witnesses here do not, on the whole, appear in the records of the area around Catte Street, and none of them appear to be members of the book-trade, although the mayor, Adam Feteplace, is constantly recorded elsewhere.

'Sciant (etc.) quod ego Thomas filius Laurencii filii Radulfi de Oxonia dedi et concessi et assignaui Ricardo Marscallo dicto de Thame quartuor solidatas et octo denariatas redditus annui et perpetui percipiendias annuatim, de tenemento quod fuit aliquando Willelmi de Uaus in parochia sancti Petri occidentalis in Oxonia ... Ut igitur (etc. sealing) hiis testibus, Adam Feteplace tunc maiore Oxon', Nicholao de Kingestone, Iohanne de Coleshulle tunc preposiis Oxon', Willelmo de Breles, Willelmo de Mildecumbe, Willelmo Leudin, Rogero Noif, Ricardo Person, Iohanne Achard, Warin de Aula, Galfrido de Hencteshe, Walter Molendinario et aliis.'

Between Michaelmas 1245 and Michaelmas 1246. *Cartulary of Oseney Abbey*, edited by H. E. Salter, 2 (O.H.S. 90, 1929) pp.75–6.

4. William de Brailes and his wife Celena received $4\frac{1}{2}$ marks in recompense for yielding their share of a property in the suburb of Oxford. No further identification of the site of this has been possible, but the negotiation that was undertaken to resolve the issue of the land is clearly set out, with the role of William and Celena apparently as voices of moderation and reconciliation between neighbours. The piece of land held by William and Celena would have been considerable to justify the sum of $4\frac{1}{2}$ marks, unless Henry Perle considered that their role in the success of the negotiation was worth extra payment.

37 Hen III Oxford, the morrow of St Andrew (1 December) 1252.

John de Halywelle and Alice his wife (pet.) and Henry Perle (ten.), a moiety of a messuage in the suburb of Oxford, also the same John and Alice (pet.) and William de Breyles and Celena his wife (ten.) a moiety of a messuage exception 10 feet in length and three in breadth in the same vill; also the same John and Alice (pet.) and Henry le Arcener and Agatha his wife (ten.) land 10 feet in length and 3 in breadth; a plea. Henry Perle recognised that the moiety was the right of Alice, and William and Celena and Henry and Agatha recognised that the tenement which John

and Alice claimed against them was the right of Alice and rendered it to her; in return John and Alice at the instance of William and Celena, Henry and Agatha yielded to Henry Perle the whole tenement, to be held by him and his heirs of them and the heirs of Alice for ever; rendering to them a clove of gilliflower at Easter and doing to the chief lords the services due; Henry Perle gives to John and Alice 40 shillings and to William and Celena $4\frac{1}{2}$ marks.'

The feet of fines for Oxfordshire 1195–1291, transcribed and calendared by H. E. Salter (O.R.S. 12, 1930) p.265, no.55.

5. Taken together, the following two items identify the ownership of a tenement in Catte Street as of William de Brailes. One identifies the tenement granted to William Russel by Philip Burgeis as standing between the tenements of John Curci and William de Brailes, and the other locates the tenement of John Curci as next to that of Agnes de Trop, itself next to that of John Stanley. On Salter's map these tenements all fall into the large area identified as Charleston's Inn, numbered 164 on his NE III map, figure 3. This is given this name in 1376, when it was described as 'mesuagium cum tenementis et shopis'.

'Sciant presentes et futuri quodit conuenit inter Philippum Burgeis ex una parte et Willemmum Russel ex altera uidelicet quod dictus Philippus dedit et concessit et presenti scripto confirmauit dicto Willelmo totum illud tenementum cum omnibus ubique pertinenciis suis in uilla Oxonie in parochia beate Marie quod est prope Kattestrete inter tenementum Iohannis Curci et tenementum Willelmo de Breiles, tenendum et habendum ...'

Medieval archives of the University of Oxford, edited by H. E. Salter 1(O.H.S. 70, 1920) p.329.

This deed was among the city archives, and later transferred to the University archives.

The holding of John Curci is located with reference to Agnes de Trop: 'inter terram Iohannes de Curci et terram que fuit aliquando Iohannes de Stanleya' in 1247. This land is located on the site named in Salter's map as St Frideswide, who owned it after c.1255. (Cart. St Frideswide I. 315)

Cartulary of the Hospital of St John the Baptist 1, p.477.

6. The name of de Brailes, perhaps William and Celena's son, is connected with another property in Catte Street later in the century, when the rent from a small parcel of land, identified on Salter's map as no.132, between Eynsham and Cat Hall, passed from Walter de Brayles to John le Luminour in 1288, and again in 1291 at an increased figure. A John de Brailles is also mentioned on this site in 1307. (Salter, *Survey*, 1, pp.93–4.)

Select Bibliography

Introduction

This selection of references has been made to support the themes of this study of the de Brailes Hours, and to hint at the pursuit of other areas of interest that have not been its focus. The emphasis of this study has been on the purpose and context of this newly designed book of hours – its place in the history of the making of books in Oxford, the reasons for its design as it is, the way in which it was used by the lady for whom it was designed, and the developing role of books of hours in the later thirteenth century. Its art historical character has emerged through its context, and its style through the wealth of illustration, but its stylistic position in thirteenth-century painting has not been developed in a separate discussion – a point to be followed up in this bibliography. Whilst each chapter is documented separately, each is listed alphabetically.

Certain volumes have been consulted for each part of my book, and first of these must be Nigel Morgan's two volumes of the *Survey of Manuscripts Illuminated in the British Isles; Early Gothic Manuscripts (I) 1190–1250* (London, 1982) and *Early Gothic Manuscripts (II) 1250–1285* (London, 1988). In addition to a very full catalogue of thirteenth-century illuminated manuscripts, this includes an invaluable introduction to some of the key questions of thirteenth-century manuscript studies, about the types of manuscript made and the location of the centres of production.

Also constantly at my elbow has been Christopher de Hamel's *A History of Illuminated Manuscripts* (Oxford, 1986). Categories of owners and the way they used their manuscripts makes for an invaluable insight into their origins and context and provides the follow-up for all four chapters of my book.

Chapter 1

For the history of Oxford and the history of the University relevant to the thirteenth-century book trade and the making of books in Oxford, the works of Salter, Pantin and Pollard are invaluable. The background to William de Brailes and studies of his manuscripts may be followed up through the work of Pollard, Cockerell and Morgan. Histories of medieval church life are provided particularly by Moorman and Southern, and the medieval social context, through archaeology and buildings, by Platt.

Brown, T. J., Meredith-Owens, G. M., Turner, D. H., 'Manuscripts from the Dyson Perrins Collection', *British Museum Quarterly* 23 (1960–1) pp. 30–1. (The de Brailes Hours.)

Callus, D. A., (editor), *Robert Grosseteste, Scholar and Bishop; essays in commemoration of the seventh century of his death* (Oxford, 1950).

Cartulary of Oseney Abbey, edited by H. E. Salter, 1 (O.H.S. 89, 1929).

Cartulary of the Hospital of St John, edited by H. E. Salter, 1 (O.H.S., 66, 1914).

Clanchy, M. T., *From Memory to Written Record: England 1066–1307* (London, 1979).

Cockerell, S. C., *The Work of W. de Brailes* (Roxburghe Club, 1930).

Davis, R. H. C., 'An Oxford charter of 1191 – the beginnings of municipal freedom', *Oxoniensia*, 33 (1968).

Destrez, J., *La Pecia dans les Manuscrits Universitaires du XIIIe et du XIVe Siecle* (Paris, 1935).

de la Mare, A. C. and Gillam, S. (editors), *Duke Humfrey's Library and the Divinity School 1488–1988*, Catalogue of an exhibition held at the Bodleian Library (Oxford, 1988).

St Edmund of Abingdon, *Speculum Ecclesiae*, edited by M. de la Bigne, *Bibliotheca Patrum et Veterum Auctorum Ecclesiasticorum*, (1610), 5. 983–1004.

Emden, A. B., *An Oxford Hall in Medieval Times* (Oxford, 1968).

The feet of fines for Oxfordshire 1195–1291, transcribed and calendared by H. E. Salter (Oxfordshire Record Series, 12, 1930) p.265, no.55.

Gibbs, Marion and Lang, Jane, *Bishops and Reform 1215–1272* (Oxford, 1934).

Grayzel, S., *The Church and the Jews in the Thirteenth Century* (New York, 1966).

Hassal, Tom, *Oxford: The Buried City* (Oxford, 1987).

Henderson, G., 'Late antique influences in some English medieval illustrations of Genesis', *Journal of the Warburg and Courtauld Institute*, 25 (1962), pp.192–4.

Kemp, E. W., 'The attempted canonisation of Robert Grosseteste' in *Robert Grosseteste*, edited by Callus, pp.241–6.

Medieval archives of the University of Oxford, edited by H. E. Salter, 1 (O.H.S. 70, 1920).

Millar, E. G., 'Additional Miniatures by W. de Brailes', *Journal of the Walters Art Gallery*, 2 (1939).

Moorman, J. R. H., *Church Life in England in the Thirteenth Century* (Cambridge, 1945).

Pantin, W. A., 'Instructions for a devout and literate layman', in *Medieval learning and literature: Essays presented to Richard William Hunt*, edited by J.J.G. Alexander and M. T. Gibson (London, 1976), pp. 398–422.

Parkes, M. B., 'The Literacy of the Laity', in *Literature and Western Civilisation: The Medieval Period*, edited by D. Daiches, A. K. Thorlby (London, 1973), pp. 555–77.

Pevsner, N. and Sherwood, J., *The Buildings of England: Oxfordshire*, (London, 1974).

Platt, Colin, *The English Medieval Town* (London, 1976).

Platt, Colin, *Medieval England: A Social History and Archaeology from the Conquest to 1600 AD* (London, 1978).

Platt, Colin, *The Architecture of Medieval Britain* (London, 1990).

Pollard, G., 'The Pecia system in the Medieval Universities', *Medieval Scribes, Manuscripts and Libraries: Essays presented to N. R. Ker.* edited by M. B. Parkes, A. G. Watson (London, 1978), pp. 145–61.

Pollard, G., 'The University and the Book Trade in Medieval Oxford', *Miscellanea Medievalia*, 3 (1964), pp. 336–44.

Pollard, G., 'William de Brailles', *Bodleian Library Record*, 5, no.4 (1955), pp.202–9.

Poole, R. L., *Medieval Reckonings of Time* (London, 1935).

Powicke, F. M. and Cheney C. R. (editors), *Councils and Synods with other documents relating to the English Church II AD 1205–1313* (Oxford, 1964).

Reynolds, Susan, *An Introduction to the History of English Medieval Towns* (London, 1977).

Roth, C., *The Jews of Medieval Oxford* (Oxford Historical Society, 1951).

Salter, H. E., *Map of Medieval Oxford* (Oxford, 1934).

Salter, H. E., *Medieval Oxford* (Oxford, 1936).

Salter, H. E., *Survey of Oxford*, edited by W. R. Pantin and W. T. Mitchell (O.H.S., new series, 14, 1960; 20, 1969).

Southern, R. W., *Western Society and the Church in the Middle Ages* (London, 1970).

Swarzenski, H., 'Unknown bible pictures by W. de Brailes and some notes on early English bible illustrations' *Journal of the Walters Art Gallery*, 1 (1938).

Turner, D. H., 'The Work of God', in *The Benedictines in Britain*, (London, 1980), pp.40–52.

van Dijk, S. J. P., 'An advertisement sheet of an early fourteenth-century writing master at Oxford', *Scriptorium*, 10 (1956), pp.47–64.

Victoria County History, 3, edited by H. E. Salter and M. D. Lobel (1954): The University of Oxford.

Warner, G. F., *Descriptive Catalogue of the Illuminated Manuscripts in the Library of C. W. Dyson Perrins* (1920), no.4 (de Brailes Hours, entry written by S. C. Cockerell), no.5 (Oxford bible – Bodelian Library MS lat. bibl. e.7).

Chapter 2

The formulation of the text, the design and making of the book, the style of decoration and illumination may be followed up in a considerable literature on the illuminated manuscript. A selection is given here.

Alexander, Jonathan and Binski, Paul (editors), *Age of Chivalry: Art in Plantagenet England 1200–1400* (London, 1987).

Backhouse, J., *The Illuminated Manuscript* (Oxford, 1979).

Bishop, E., 'On the origin of the prymer', *Liturgica Historica* (Oxford, 1918) pp.211–37.

Brieger, P., *English Art 1216–1307* (Oxford, 1968).

de la Mare, A. C. and Barker-Benfield, B., *Manuscripts at Oxford: R. W. Hunt memorial exhibition* (Oxford, 1980).

Delaissé, L. M. J., 'The importance of Books of Hours for the history of the medieval book', in *Gatherings for Dorothy E. Miner* edited by Ursula E. McCracken, Lilian M. C. Randall, Richard H. Randall, Jr. (Baltimore, 1974), pp.203–25.

Dewick, E. S., *Facsimiles of Horae de Beata Maria Virgine*, Henry Bradshaw Society (London, 1901).

Hoskins, E., *Horae Beatae Mariae virginis, or Sarum and York Primers* (London, 1901).

James, M. R., 'Points to be observed in the description and collation of manuscripts, particularly Books of Hours', pp.xxiii–xxxviii, in *Descriptive Catalogue of the Manuscripts in the Fitzwilliam Museum* (1895).

Ker N. R., 'From "above top line" to "below top line"', *Celtica*, 5 (1960), pp.13–16.

Lamb, J. A., *The Psalms in Christian Worship* (London, 1962).

Leroquais, V., *Les Livres d'heures manuscrits de la Bibliotheque Nationale* (Paris, 1927).

Madan, F., 'Hours of the Virgin Mary: Tests for localisation', *Bodleian Quarterly Record*, 3, 1920. pp.40–4.

Millar, E. G., *English Illuminated Manuscripts of the Tenth to the Thirteenth Centuries* (Oxford, 1926).

Pächt, O., *Book Illumination in the Middle Ages* (London, 1986)

Pächt, O., and Alexander, J.J.G., *Illuminated Manuscripts in the Bodleian Library, Oxford* 3, British School (Oxford, 1973)

Plummer, John, in '"Use" and "Beyond Use"' in Roger S. Weick, *The Book of Hours in Medieval Art and Life* (London, 1988), pp.149–52.

Pollard, Graham, 'The Construction of English twelfth-century bindings', *The Library*, 18 (1962), pp.13–14.

Randall, R. H., 'The medieval artist and industrialized art', *Apollo* 84 (1966) pp.434–41.

Saunders, O. E., *English Illumination*, 2 vols. Florence and Paris, 1928.

Chapter 3

The use of imagery accompanying texts, the inconographic legacy, and the impact of the religious context as it is expressed through the illustration, the main themes of this chapter, may be followed up through the works listed here.

Anderson, G. K., *The Legend of the Wandering Jew* (Providence, 1965).

Blumenkranz, B., *Le juif medieval au miroir de l'art chretien* (Paris, 1966).

Borenius, T., *St Thomas Becket in Art* (London, 1932), p.42.

Borenius, T., 'Some further aspects of the iconography of St Thomas of Canterbury', *Archeologia* 87 (1934), pp.1–86.

Camille, Michael 'The Book of Signs: Writing and visual difference in Gothic manuscript illumination', *Word and Image* 1 (1985), pp.133–48.

Camille, Michael, 'Seeing and Reading: some visual implications of medieval literacy and illiteracy', *Art History* 8 (1985) pp.26–49 (p.40) and note 65.

Camille, Michael, *The Gothic Idol, Ideology and Image Making in Medieval Art* (Cambridge, 1990).

Levi d'Ancona, Mirella, *The Iconography of the Immaculate Conception in the Middle Ages and the Renaissance* (1957).

de Voragine, Jacobus, *The Golden Legend*, translated by Granger Ryan and Helmut Rippenberger (New York, 1941).

Farmer, David Hugh, *The Oxford Dictionary of Saints* (Oxford, 1978).

Finucane, R., *Miracles and Pilgrims: Popular Beliefs in Medieval England* (London, 1977).

Forshaw, H. P., *Edmund of Abingdon: Speculum Religiosorum and Speculum Ecclesiae*, (1973).

Fratris Thomae, vulgo dicti de Eccleston, tractatus de adventu fratrum minorum in Angliam, edited by A. G. Little, (1951).

Fryer, Alfred C., 'Theophilus the Penitent, as represented in art', *Archaeological Journal*, 92, (1935) pp.287–33.

Gaer, Joseph, *The Legend of the Wandering Jew* (New York, 1961).

Grayzel, S., *The Church and the Jews in the Thirteenth Century* (New York, 1966).

Henderson, G., 'Narrative illustration and theological exposition in medieval art', *Studies in Church History*, 17, (1981), pp.19–35.

James, M. R., *The Apocryphal New Testament* (Oxford, 1924).

Katzenellenbogen, A., *The Sculptural Programs of Chartres Cathedral*, (Baltimore, 1959)

Kauffmann, C. M., *Romanesque Manuscripts 1066–1190* (London, 1975).

Lawrence, C. H., *St Edmund of Abingdon: a study in hagiography and history* (1960).

Legge, M. D., 'St Edmund on the "Hours"', *Modern Language Review*, 29, (1934) pp.72–4.

Lewis, Suzanne, '*Tractatus adversus Judaeos* in the Gulbenkian Apocalypse', *Art Bulletin* (1986) pp.543–66.

Lewis, Suzanne, *The Illustrations of the Chronicles of Matthew Paris* (California and London, 1987).

Lewis, Suzanne, 'Giles de Bridport and the Abingdon Apocalypse', in *England in the Thirteenth Century, Proceedings of the Harlaxton Symposium* (1985), pp.107–19.

Matthaei Parisiensis Chronica Majora, edited by H. R. Luard, Rolls Series 57 (1872–84), v. p.242.

Mâle, Emile, *L'Art Religieux du Treisieme Siecle en France*, Paris, 1903 (translated by Dora Nussey, as *The Gothic Image: Religious Art in France of the Thirteenth-century* (London, 1958).

Morgan, N.J. and Sandler, L.F., 'Manuscript Illumination of the Thirteenth and Fourteenth Centuries', in *Age of Chivalry* (London, 1987), pp.148–56.

Nairn, Ian and Pevsner, Nikolaus, *The Buildings of England: Sussex* (London, 1965)

Oakeshott, W., *The Two Winchester Bibles* (Oxford, 1981).

Pfaff, R. W. *New Liturgical Feasts in Later Medieval England* (Oxford, 1970).

Sister Mary Philomena, 'St. Edmund of Abingdon's Meditations before the Canonical Hours', *Ephemerides Liturgicae* (1964), pp.33–57.

Platt, Colin. *The Parish Churches of Medieval England*, (London, 1981)

Powicke, F. M., 'Loretta, Countess of Leicester', in *Historical Essays in Honour of James Tait* (Manchester, 1934).

Rappaport, A. S., *Medieval Legends of Christ* (London, 1934).

Sherwood, Jennifer, and Pevsner, Nikolaus, *The Buildings of England: Oxfordshire* (London, 1974).

Southern, R. W., 'The English origins of the "Miracles of the Virgin"' *Medieval and Renaissance Studies*, 4 (1958) pp.176–216.

Temple, E., *Anglo-Saxon Manuscripts 900–1066* (London, 1976).

Warner, Marina, *Alone of All Her Sex: the myth and the cult of the Virgin Mary* (London, 1976).

Watson, A., *The Early Iconography of the Tree of Jesse* (Oxford, 1934).

Chapter 4

Books of hours made in England, their purpose and patrons, form the main themes of this chapter. The following references follow up the art history of book illumination in this period, within the liturgical and devotional context, and particularly the relevance of books of hours to medieval women.

Ackerman, R. W., Dahood, R., *Ancrene Riwle*, (Binghampton 1984).

Ackerman, R. W., 'The liturgical day in the *Ancrene Riwle*', *Speculum*, (1978) pp.734–44.

The English Text of the "Ancrene Riwle", edited by E. J. Dobson, Early English Text Society, 267 (1972).

Backhouse, Janet, *Books of Hours* (London, 1985).

Backhouse, Janet, *The Madresfield Hours*, (Roxburghe Club, 1976).

Baker, C.M., *The Early Development of the Illustrated Book of Hours in England*, PhD University of East Anglia (1981).

Bell, Susan Groag, 'Medieval Woman Book Owners: arbiters of lay piety and ambassadors of culture', *Signs: Journal of Women in Culture and Society*, VII, 4, (1987), pp.742–68.

Bennett, Adelaide, 'A late thirteenth-century Psalter-Hours from London', *England in the Thirteenth Century: Proceedings of the 1984 Harlaxton Symposium* (1985), pp.15–30.

Bennett, Adelaide, 'A book designed for a noble-woman: An illustrated *Manuel des Péchés* of the thirteenth century', *Medieval Book Production: Assessing the Evidence*, edited by L.L. Brownrigg (California, 1990), pp.163–81.

Donovan, Claire, 'The mise-en-page of early Books of Hours in England', *Medieval Book Production: Assessing the Evidence*, edited by L.L. Brownrigg (California, 1990), pp.147–62.

Harthan, John, *Books of Hours and their Owners* (London, 1977).

Heslop, T. A., 'English Seals in the thirteenth and fourteenth century', in *Age of Chivalry* pp.114–7.

McCulloch, Florence, 'The Funeral of Renart the Fox in a Walters Book of Hours' *Journal of the Walters Art Gallery*, 25–6, (1962–3), pp. 8–27.

Meiss, M., *The Limbourgs and their Contemporaries* (New York, 1974).

Power, Eileen, *Medieval Women* (London, 1975).

Rogers, N. J., *Books of Hours produced in the Low Countries for the English Market in the Fifteenth Century* M Phil (Cambridge, 1982).

Sandler, L. F., *Gothic Manuscripts 1285–1385. A survey of manuscripts illuminated in the British Isles*, 5, 2 volumes, (London, 1986).

Sandler, L. F., 'An early fourteenth-century English psalter in the Escorial', *Journal of the Warburg and Courtauld Institutes*, 41 (1979), pp.65–80.

Sekules, Veronica, 'Women and art in England in the thirteenth and fourteenth centuries', in *Age of Chivalry*, p.41–8.

Weick, Roger S., *The Book of Hours in Medieval Art and Life* (London, 1988).

Index